Hiking Trails of
SOUTHWESTERN COLORADO

Fourth Edition

John Peel and
Paul Pixler

PRUETT PUBLISHING COMPANY
BOULDER, COLORADO

FIRST EDITION 2006
09 08   5 4 3 2

ISBN: 0-87108-939-4

Library of Congress Cataloging-in-Publication Data

Pixler, Paul, 1920–
    Hiking trails of southwestern Colorado / Paul Pixler and John Peel—
    4th edition
    p. cm.
    Includes index
    ISBN: 0-87108-939-4
    1. Hiking—Colorado—San Juan National Forest—Guidebooks.
2 Hiking—Colorado—Uncompahgre National Forest—Guidebooks
3. San Juan National Forest (Colo.)—Guidebooks. 4. Uncompahgre
National Forest (Colo.)—Guidebooks. 5. Colorado Trail (Colo.)—
Guidebooks. I. Title

GV199.42.C62 S265 2006
917.88′25—dc21   00-036604

*To my wife, Bettie, and the hikers who have accompanied
me on many of these trails: Adeline Becay, John Fleming,
Charlotte Hammond, Audine Hayden, Anne Pixler,
Glenn Phillips, Ed and Winnie Sinden, Diane Skinner,
and Marianna Stanley.*

—Paul Pixler

CONTENTS

Contents

Contents

PREFACE TO FOURTH EDITION

If you've purchased one of the three previous editions of this book, you've probably noticed an addition to this edition. There are now two authors.

Paul Pixler has graciously turned the reins over to me and has gracefully allowed me to rewrite his work. Hopefully I have acquitted myself well and not stepped all over Paul's decades-long handiwork, first released by Pruett Publishing in 1980—back before hiking boots even existed. Okay, not funny.

In fact, 1980 is about the year I discovered the San Juan Mountains. My friend Jim Wadge and I climbed Mount Sneffels from Blue Lakes Pass, then camped out near the Blue Lakes. Early the next morning a near-tornado struck and demolished the tent, bending the poles even as we fought from inside the tent to hold them upright. But that experience didn't keep me away from the San Juans; a couple years later several of us, including my buddy Steve Chapman, backpacked into Navajo Basin to climb the Wilsons.

About a decade later I moved to Durango, lured by visions of the San Juans. One of my immediate goals was to become reacquainted with the mountains. I'm pretty sure the first book I purchased was—you guessed it—

Hiking Trails of Southwestern Colorado. It is the bible for day hiking the San Juans.

Still, every guidebook needs a little tweaking every few years. Here's what I've done: I've added a few trails and have rewritten many trail descriptions to bring them up-to-date and make them clearer (I have the benefit of Global Positioning System [GPS]). I've also fixed directions to trailheads where some had changed and have improved many of the maps (again, thanks to GPS). I've reorganized the format, creating four parts for each trail description: an introduction, the approach to the trailhead, directions for the hike, and options.

You'll also quickly notice a bunch of numbers (i.e., N 37 18.796, W 107 47.933) in most trail descriptions. Where possible, I've added GPS readings to give GPS-bearing hikers another tool to ascertain their location.

I've also dealt with a few issues regarding private land that continue to crop up as more people inhabit some of the areas where we hike. For more on that subject, see the notes on private land in the introduction. Some trail options have disappeared over the years, and I've deleted those. Some changes occurred to Missionary Ridge hikes after the huge fire in 2002.

Thanks to the many friends who helped, either with advice or by doing these hikes with me: my wife Judy (invaluable encouragement and support), Steve Chapman (came out from California so he could whip me at cribbage atop Wetterhorn), Eric and Karen Backer (who shivered along with me and Judy on a snowy Labor Day hike from Coal Creek to Deer Creek), Ken Hulick (for pointing out a few discrepancies), Shawna Off and Kent Ford (let me pick the route), Rich Stewart (helped keep me in shape to do this), and my parents (got me started down the right trail).

It was a lot of hard work (yeah, like hiking around the San Juans is just a horrible, horrible vocation), but how easy it was to do this without having to start from scratch. In fact, much of Paul Pixler's original text remains. Thanks, Paul, for allowing me to be a part of this book.

— John Peel
Durango, Colorado

INTRODUCTION

Man, are you going to have fun. There might be better ways to appreciate life, but hiking in southwestern Colorado ranks way up there. You get exercise, breathe fresh air, and see spectacular country. You feel alive. This part of the state offers a variety of terrain and altitude on large amounts of public land, along with an excellent and varied climate. It doesn't take long to get deep into the backcountry. This book can be your launching pad, so to speak, to get you into this great outdoors—and, hopefully, to keep you from getting lost.

Some general things to know: The lower altitudes can be hiked typically from April through November, sometimes earlier or later. Some trails you can keep using all year long with snowshoes. Altitudes up to 10,000 feet can be hiked without special snow equipment typically from late May to early November if you do not go into heavily shaded areas. Above 10,000 feet, the season is shorter—typically late June until the early fall snows, which usually are not permanent until after the middle of October or even later, depending on the particular year and the altitude.

But each year varies widely. There have been years when you could hike city trails into January, and other years when you get snowed on at 11,500 feet below Jura Knob on Labor Day (that's another story).

The area offers vast hiking opportunities; this guidebook covers much of the best of it, but it cannot cover all of it. What follows in the next few paragraphs are some of the ground rules for what is covered, and why.

The hikes selected for inclusion here use Durango and Silverton as the starting points for directions. Most hikes are near these two towns, although this book offers valuable information for anyone in Southwest Colorado. The hikes are planned for half-day and full-day trips. This is not a backpacker's book, although some of the trails cited here make excellent backpack trips or are the starting points for such trips.

A few of the hikes are best handled by driving in the day before the hike and car camping. But for all of the trips in this book, only a day pack is needed. With its lighter weight, it is a more pleasant burden.

The hikes described range from easy to difficult, from short to long, from relatively level to some long climbs. All types of hikers should be able to find something to suit their own tastes. None of the climbs require any technical gear or skills. Some places pose a degree of danger, but these only require carefulness. Cliff edges, for example, should always be approached cautiously, but they frequently furnish breathtaking views and are safe to anyone exercising due care. Of course, you should make sure that the cliff edge is not cracking away before trusting it.

Most of the hikes are exclusively on public land. A few national forest trails cross private land, and the forest service has made proper arrangements with owners. Occasionally public and private lands are so intermixed that boundaries cannot be identified. This is particularly true of small patented mining claims in mineralized areas, as, for example, in some spots of La Plata Canyon. There are also a few places in or near Durango where private property may be crossed. Where private property is identifiable, due care for private rights should be exercised as appropriate anywhere, whether in the mountains or in town.

The Headings

At the beginning of each hike description, information is listed to help you judge the difficulty of the trail. Some explanation of the list is due.

After the name of the hike comes the **distance**. This is identified as one-way, round-trip, or loop-trip. It is difficult to be exact on distances, but they should be very close and help in estimating the time involved; however, this will vary from person to person, from steep uphill to flat or downhill, and from smooth to rough. The average hiker takes nearly twice as long to go up steep terrain as to descend. The higher the altitude, the greater will be the differential.

Elevations are given for the starting and highest points; total **elevation gain** is also listed. This gives some clue as to difficulty and steepness when compared to distance. Usually, altitude gain is the simple difference between the starting point and the high point, but in some cases, where an intervening loss must be regained, total gain will be more. The level of difficulty depends on the altitude to be climbed and on the steepness and roughness of the trail.

The rating system takes all of these into consideration. Also, a 1,000-foot climb that begins at 6,000 feet is much easier than a 1,000-foot climb that starts at 13,000 feet.

Animas Canyon and the Grenadier Range from the Molas Trail.

Higher altitudes are in themselves a hazard to some people. To those who live in Durango or Silverton or at similar elevations and who are in good health and are used to some exercise, any altitude in Colorado should pose no special problem. People coming into this area from low altitudes may experience some difficulty. Some visitors are breathless even in town.

Altitude affects you in several ways, most of which are dependent on the lowered atmospheric pressure and a resulting lower oxygen content per breath. If you find yourself panting at or below 10,000 feet with very little effort expended, you are not ready for any long hikes described here. Also, people with a history of heart problems or high blood pressure should probably consider only the easier and lower hikes.

Acclimatization to high altitude seems to be basically an increase in red blood cell count, which makes for a more efficient use of the available oxygen in the thinner air. People from lower altitudes who have done some sustained (aerobic) exercise may have a higher red blood cell count and may have fewer altitude problems in Colorado; others may help the situation by staying a couple of days or more at altitudes of 5,000 to 8,000 feet before climbing above 11,000 feet.

Some people even in apparently good health may have some problems. Besides shortness of breath, headaches can come on. Some may experience lightheadedness or an upset digestive system. If any of these symptoms become severe, it is a good idea to get down to a lower altitude quickly to recover from "altitude sickness." Often these symptoms will subside with a good rest and a slower pace so that the hike can be continued satisfactorily. Remember to stay hydrated; sometimes headaches are simply caused by not drinking enough water.

On the Cascade Trail, looking toward Engineer Mountain.

The percentage of people who have severe problems is small, so this word of caution should not deter most people in good health from taking any of these hikes. For most people, high-altitude hiking can be an exhilarating experience, especially when they top their first peak and look down with awe on the other side. It is a moment of achievement and beauty that puts a new dimension into living!

Each of the hikes is rated for level of difficulty. The *ratings* used are easy, moderate, difficult, and very difficult. Any usage of terms like these is, of course, relative to the condition and experience of each hiker. The goal is for the ratings to at least be consistent, so that once you've done a couple of hikes, you'll be able to use the rating to judge your ability to do the hike.

The ratings are based on someone being in reasonably good health and having at least a minimum level of experience hiking a few miles.

Several factors are included in arriving at the ratings; these are length of the hike, altitude gain, difficulty in following the route, and difficulty in getting over the route. Of these, two are the most important. First is altitude gain. Practically all of these hikes include some climbing. This makes the hike much more interesting, especially if a summit with good views is attained and if the trail takes you through changing climatic zones. Altitude gain can bring more difficulty than just increased effort, however. It can bring "altitude sickness," which will require you to slow down a bit.

Mostly, climbing should be fun and a way to get good exercise. The fun comes by observing interesting vegetation, animals, rocks, waterfalls, babbling brooks, and mountains; by gaining a sense of accomplishment; and by enjoying your hiking companions. But those who are in good physical condition are likely to enjoy it more than others.

Rock scrambling.

The most important problem in the ratings has to do with the actual surface to be traversed. There is a great deal of difference between a smooth trail and a rocky one. None of the hikes described here are technical climbs involving ropes or other special equipment, but some involve negotiating talus areas and some rock scrambling.

Talus, or loose rock that varies roughly from eight inches to two feet in size, is typical at altitudes above timberline and often slightly below it. Talus areas may vary from being nearly flat to being so steep that they are ready to slide with any loosening. The slide point is called the angle of repose. When the talus is this steep, great care is necessary to avoid starting a slide or even the fall of a single rock. This can endanger yourself, but it is especially hazardous for any companions below you.

The most common problem with talus is not from falling rocks, but just that it is more difficult to walk on. With some experience, you can walk on it almost as fast as on smooth ground; it takes concentration on each step to see that the rock about to be stepped on is firmly placed. Without this, you are likely to turn an ankle or jab a shin or ankle with a sharp-edged rock.

Rock scrambling means using your hands as well as your feet to climb over rocks. Many climbs have some rock scrambling, especially near the top. It can be fun and offer variety to a hike. It can get you over near-vertical obstacles and on to higher glory.

Time allowed is estimated for an average hiker, but, of course, there is no average hiker. Therefore, the times must be treated as guidelines, not fixed truths. The times given do not allow for time used in driving to or from trailheads. Also, times given are for actual hiking and short breath-catching stops. If you want to take long stops for pictures, lunch, a nap on a sunny hillside, or just to drink in the beauty or to talk with a companion, these should be added to the estimates.

A word about rest stops is appropriate. At higher altitudes in steep areas, almost everyone has to rest occasionally. When you are working hard, short rests of thirty seconds to a minute and a half are best. These can be frequent if necessary. Long rests of five to twenty minutes can be devastating. In the first place, they increase the total hiking time an amazing amount, but more importantly, they make you lose your "second wind." This makes it difficult to get going again and to get up to the same pace that you were maintaining earlier with relative ease. It slows down the whole cardiovascular system and slows the efficiency that you have previously attained in your climbing muscles. You have to get your second wind all over again.

Maps can be a big help. People who are used to hiking in the eastern United States, such as along the Appalachian Trail, may not need maps there due to the heavy traffic and the well-defined trails marked with frequent cairns. Hiking in Colorado, where altitudes are higher, where terrain and climate change more, where trails may be sketchy or nonexistent, and where the whole area is so much more vast, is a much different experience.

The maps given in this book are for describing the hike, but on longer hikes, other maps are useful for showing more of the surrounding territory. Two kinds of maps are typically listed in the headings. The U.S. Forest Service maps show roughly where the trails go. They are limited, however, due to their small scale and their lack of altitude gradations.

The U.S. Geological Survey maps give much more detail. The 7.5-minute series of quad maps show topographical gradations of forty feet from one line to the next, with 200-foot lines heavier to delineate the larger gradations. Even these maps cannot show small cliffs that can cause significant detours from straight-line hiking. While many of the hikes are over established trails, some are not, and some of the trails have breaks in them due to inadequate maintenance; hiking at this point becomes "bushwhacking," i.e., finding your own way. This may literally be through the bushes, or it may be over rocks or through trees. This can add its own challenge. The hike descriptions attempt to lead you through these areas without difficulty.

You can obtain U.S. Forest Service maps at forest service headquarters offices and ranger stations and at many sporting-goods stores. The topo maps are carried by several sporting-goods stores, especially those that carry hiking and climbing gear.

New technology can help, too. Maps are available on CD-ROM and can be used in conjunction with GPS units to determine where you're going or where you've been.

Of course, no map helps if you don't know how to read it. Experience and a good teacher will help most people learn the basics of reading topo maps fairly quickly. It's all about thinking three-dimensionally!

The Weather

Hikers in higher altitudes in the Rockies must always be aware of the weather. It can change from beautiful to dangerous very quickly. This is especially true from June to early September, when afternoon thunderstorms are frequent. During this period, it is better to plan to reach the highest altitude in your hike by noon if possible. These storms can be severe, even though short-lived. They can bring wind, cold, rain, and small hail, depending on the particular storm. The greatest hazard, however, is lightning. It is high-voltage static electricity and can kill or maim in a split second. High points where the charged cloud is closest are the strike points. This makes high or isolated peaks especially vulnerable. Tall trees below the peak are also common targets.

Any dark cloud nearby in the summer should be suspect, even if it is small. There are additional signs of an imminent lightning flash. If you are on or near a high point above surrounding territory and you hear a buzzing in the rocks, or if the hair on your arms or legs or even your head begins to stand up, you're in prime territory. Get down to a lower level as fast as possible—not so fast, how-

Snowshoeing.

ever, that you trip and fall, which is a much more likely way to get hurt. Also, if you seek shelter from rain under a tree, make it a tree that is lower than others nearby.

Lightning is the worst danger from storms, but not the only one. Rocks that call for scrambling can be very slick when they get wet. Lichens on them increase this problem. Once on El Diente, it began drizzling just after our party started down from the top; the rocks were near-vertical and are very irregular in this area. I slipped on one that would have held easily when dry. Although I fell only three feet, that led to an edge where there was another drop followed by another and another. Fortunately, two companions were at the edge of the first one and stopped me before I could go to the next drop. It was embarrassing, but it served as a reminder to me to become more cautious, because the fall could have been disastrous.

In the high country, it can snow any month of the year, although significant amounts are rare in the summer. Only a light coating, however, slickens up the footholds and handholds.

Another danger from rainstorms is hypothermia. This is a condition in which the core body temperature begins to drop below normal. Cold fingers and toes are uncomfortable, but a cold body core is highly dangerous. Soaked clothes and some wind can bring this on quickly at high altitudes, even in July. When you begin to shiver violently, hypothermia is starting. Companions must come to the rescue and furnish heat immediately, because the victim soon becomes disoriented and does not recognize the danger. Fires are usually out of the question because of the rain. Extra clothing will help if the situation is not too bad; also, a faster pace can help when possible. However, in more severe cases, skin-to-skin transfer of body heat is likely to be the only answer.

Emergencies

It is best when hiking in hazardous backcountry to go in parties of not fewer than three. If one falls and is hurt to the point of not being able to go on, another can stay with that person while the third goes for help. The one who stays should administer first aid and keep the injured person as warm and comfortable as possible. This will call for a fire if it becomes cold or dark. The patient should also be given plenty of fluids, for dehydration occurs rapidly at high altitudes. Dehydration of an injured person adds to the danger as well as to the discomfort.

One of the most common hazards is the possibility of getting lost. While this guide was written with a great deal of care to prevent this from happening, there is no guarantee against it. A slightly different interpretation of the text than intended can sometimes cause trouble. Also, it is possible (doubtful, of course, but possible) that the text has errors.

The best approach is to not get lost. Several things help. Keep the hiking group fairly close together. Each person should take note of prominent features in the area as guideposts, just in case. Also, a compass is a good idea; learn how to read and use it. It can be used in connection with the trail map, which you should also learn to read and use.

Suppose you do get lost? Think through where you were just before getting lost, and take your bearings from this. Usually, the trail map will show you enough to keep drainages sorted out to the point where you can get back to the one you came up. Study any prominent peaks, trees, or rocks that you remember seeing before, and reorient yourself by using them. Check your compass. Check the sky for direction. The sun and the moon are great guides when available. On a starry night with no moon, the Big Dipper is your clue. The North Star is straight out from the lip of the Big Dipper. It is a faint star; if you can't find it, the lip star of the Big Dipper itself will approximate north, but its position varies during the night. The position of the North Star does not.

Any drainage will always eventually lead to civilization, so you can follow down the nearest one if all else fails. This, however, has its drawbacks. First, it may be a long way out. Second, drainages have their own difficulties: Cliffs or waterfalls must be skirted; cliff walls next to the stream may cause you to walk in the water or cross the stream frequently; brush and mud near the creek don't help. If you know that you are a considerable distance from a road, house, or camp, and if you are hopelessly lost, the best answer is to build a fire and make yourself as comfortable as possible while awaiting rescue. If you can't build a fire, keep warm by stomping your feet or walking in circles. People have done this all night to survive, even when temperatures hovered near 0 degrees.

Both La Plata and San Juan counties have excellent search-and-rescue organizations, and if you are alive and capable of yelling, it's hard to imagine they would not find you fairly quickly once daylight comes.

A cellular phone in a hiking group can be a big help in an emergency, although some of us purists don't like carrying them or having them around. GPS units, as long as the batteries work, can get you out of most situations if you've plotted in your starting point. If you have a cell phone and a working GPS unit, a search-and-rescue group will find you so fast it will embarrass you.

Equipment

A part of preparation is having the proper equipment. There are a number of good manuals about this subject, so it will be treated only briefly here.

Any hiker's equipment starts with appropriate shoes. They should be comfortable and large enough, both in length and width, especially across the toes. The size should allow for fairly thick socks, or even two pair—one thin pair and a second thicker pair. Two pair, if one is thin and a bit slick, can reduce friction and blisters. Also, the risk of blisters, if you are prone to them, can be reduced by lubricating the skin at wear points with petroleum jelly or even margarine.

The best insurance against blisters is wearing the proper shoes. Many people think that you need a heavy and expensive hiking boot. The only real requirements are comfort and adequate protection. Lighter-weight boots with rugged treaded soles are usually adequate and will not tire you as much as heavier boots. Actually, tennis or jogging shoes are fine for easy, well-worn trails where the surface is not very rocky or rough.

A day pack will be necessary for carrying food, extra clothing, a first-aid kit, water, maps, and a camera. Any day pack should be waterproof to protect its contents. Or, put your clothing and other contents you don't want getting wet inside a garbage or thick plastic bag.

Coats, jackets, sweaters, and T-shirts are all appropriate to consider for the upper body. Even in hot weather, be sure to have enough layers along if you are going to go up to any significant altitude. Eighty-five-degree weather can quickly change to fifty degrees or lower with a cold wind when you climb. For the upper body, layers for varying temperatures and windchill factors are best. At least one layer should be wool, for it is warm and can insulate even when it is wet. Down will not do any good when it is wet, although it is lightweight and very good when dry. There should always be a windbreaker jacket in your supply; even just a thin plastic one can be a major help. Wind seeping through sweaty or rain-soaked clothes can turn them into a deep-freeze quickly. Actually, wind is not typical in southwestern Colorado even on high peaks, but it can come up strongly without much warning. You should also have rain gear. This can be a lightweight poncho or a rain suit; even a large garbage bag will do in an emergency.

Long pants are nice for those of us who sunburn easily and for anyone who's likely to be on a trail that demands some bushwhacking. Oak brush, for instance, can scratch exposed legs unmercifully.

Usually, you should also take along a warm cap that is capable of covering the ears, because nearly half any body heat that is lost can escape through the head. A pair of gloves should be included, too—they are needed at times for warmth but are often useful in rock scrambling as protection against abrasion of the skin.

There should be at least one first-aid kit in any hiking group. It should include Band-Aids, moleskin (for foot blisters), water purifier, aspirin, an Ace bandage, gauze, a sunscreen lotion, some dry matches, a compass, and a flashlight. Persons who cannot whistle naturally should carry a whistle to use as a signal if they become lost.

Some of us like to carry a piece of one-eighth-inch nylon rope. It can be used for repairs on equipment, for shoelaces, for a makeshift arm sling, and for untold other things. Others carry a twenty-foot-long 7-mm rope, or something similar, to help people and packs up extremely steep pitches.

On trips of any significant length, be sure to take a quart or two of water and food.

Finally, if you are a photographer, by all means have your camera along and handy. A pair of lightweight binoculars is often useful, too.

Trail Users

There are three primary recreational groups that use the trails in this book: hikers, horseback riders, and mountain bikers. There are also some people who occasionally use machines such as trail motorcycles, all-terrain vehicles

(ATVs), and snowmobiles. Traffic can therefore get a bit congested at times. All users have the right to enjoy the trails, but there is a rule about the right-of-way.

Horses are easily spooked in tight, steep places. Safety demands that they have first right-of-way priority. All others must stand aside and let them pass. Hikers are next, followed by bikers, and then the machines. In tight situations, uphill travelers always have priority over downhill travelers. (The immediate tight situation may allow for some variation of these rules.)

The main overall rule is courtesy and goodwill. I have found most people on trails to be courteous; in fact, there is often a brief stop to socialize a bit and to exchange good wishes.

Bon voyage!

EXPLORING WITH GPS

A tool, or a crutch?

This fourth edition of *Hiking Trails of Southwestern Colorado* adds a new wrinkle—Global Positioning System (GPS) coordinates. First off, I would like to state that GPS points were added after the fourth edition was written. In other words, you're fine without your GPS. The trail descriptions and distances alone are designed to help you find your way.

But let's face it: GPS is fun. With the proper computer program and a functioning GPS, you can wander around all day, come home, and see on a computer topographical map exactly where you've been, how far you've gone, and the elevation you've gained. It's just . . . neat.

And it works in reverse. You can input a route or a few coordinates (latitudes and longitudes) into the GPS unit before your hike, then go out into the wilds and find your way there.

It adds a layer of safety, too. As long as your GPS continues to function during a hike (extra batteries are essential here), you can always keep from getting lost by simply retracing your route. Basically, that's the reason why GPS was added to this edition. It is another tool that can help reassure you that you are where you think you are. Say you're at a trail junction and the book says to turn left. But maybe the trail to the left appears overgrown or brand new, or maybe going to the left leads you west and the book says to go north. Pull out the GPS and see if it matches where you think you are.

True, not every trail junction in this book has assigned GPS coordinates yet. That will take another edition or two.

GPS came in handy in other ways during the rewriting of this guidebook. It helped me refine some of the maps used in this book and helped determine trail distances and elevations.

I won't cover the ins and outs of using GPS. But those who utilize the coordinates in this book should know a couple of things. First off, the coordinates use typical latitude and longitude, with the equator at 0 degrees latitude and Greenwich, England, at 0 degrees longitude. This book's coordinates are broken down into degrees, minutes, and fractions of minutes (degrees, minutes.minutes), all the way down to thousandths of minutes. In other words, N 37 16.025 is 37 degrees, 16.025 minutes north latitude.

Being able to use GPS, however, is *not* a replacement for map and compass skills. At some point, your GPS *will* fail, and you'll have to rely on basic skills. Never rely on anything with batteries—that includes your cell phone. Be self-reliant.

I did my best to double-check all the coordinates, but it's possible there's a mistake in here somewhere. Or maybe my GPS wasn't reading from the same satellites as yours, and there's a discrepancy. I relied on a computer program to help locate some of the coordinates.

And please don't drive your hiking partners crazy. ("Hey, Stanley—we've gone 0.05 miles since that green rock back there, and we've gained 13 feet elevation!" "Who invited this guy?")

All right, enough disclaimers.

Have fun with your GPS. It's a neat tool.

HIKES IN AND NEAR DURANGO

❖ City Trails ❖

It's obvious that the city of Durango is enthusiastic about trails. That enthusiasm started long ago, but the formation in 1990 of Trails 2000, the local trails advocacy group, really got things cooking. Thanks to the foresight of Trails 2000, the Durango Parks and Recreation Department, La Plata County, the San Juan Mountains Association, the Colorado Division of Wildlife, the San Juan National Forest, and the Bureau of Land Management, there are miles of trails inside and just outside city limits.

The **Telegraph Trail System** is one popular option. It's covered later in this chapter in the Raider Ridge hike, and in the Meadow Loop and Telegraph Trail hike. Plenty of other trails exist, and the maps that accompany those hikes show many of the various trails.

Also, the approximately ten-acre **Durango Dog Park** lies under the north shadow of Smelter Mountain, just west of the Animas River where U.S. Highway 160 crosses it. There is no legal parking at the entrance to the dog park, so the official way to get there is to park at Schneider Park at Ninth Street and Roosa Avenue, or along Roosa Avenue where legal. A path crosses under the highway bridge on

1

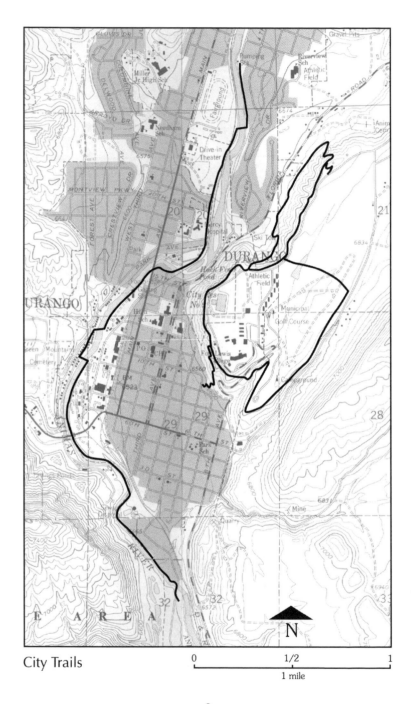

City Trails

the west side of the river and connects you to the entrance to the dog park (N 37 16.086, W 107 53.210).

Five trails, or trail systems, appear on the map titled "City Trails." Following is a description of each.

Centennial Nature Trail is used by many Fort Lewis College students because it connects the lower town areas with the college campus and with the Rim Trail. The nature trail can be found near the junction of East Sixth Avenue and Tenth Street. Through a series of switchbacks, the trail moves up some 300 feet to the campus mesa, coming out on the west side of the campus just south of the little chapel on the rim. Here, among other places, you can catch the Rim Trail.

The **Rim Trail** takes a little sleuth work to follow, particularly on the southern end, but you can make a complete 2.7-mile loop around campus. If you go counterclockwise from where the nature trail meets it, you'll cross Eighth Avenue (N 37 16.385, W 107 52.181), go south, and then go northeast, paralleling Goeglein Gulch Road for a while. You pass by the eleventh hole at Hillcrest Golf Club, cross Rim Drive near a three-way intersection (N 37 16.877, W 107 51.943), then walk by the top of the city's Chapman Hill Ski Area. (Another good way to access the Rim Trail is to come up the Lions Den Trail from Chapman Hill.)

The west and northwest parts of the Rim Trail offer excellent views over the town and across the valley to the La Plata Mountains.

The Chapman Hill–Lions Den trails can be reached by going northeast 0.5 miles on Florida Road from the intersection of East Third Avenue and Fifteenth Street. Park in the lot for the Chapman Hill Recreation Area. Look for a trail just north of the skating rink—that's the Lions Den Trail (N 37 17.050, W 107 52.040). Take it about a mile uphill, then veer right at an intersection that contours the hillside (a left takes you to the actual lions' den, and you meet Rim Drive at the golf course clubhouse).

It's another quarter mile south, paralleling Rim Drive just west of the golf course, to the intersection with the Rim Trail. If you take the Rim Trail west from here a couple hundred yards, you can return back down to the Chapman Hill parking area via a steep, closed road.

The **Animas River Trail** is an asphalt and concrete route that follows the river closely all the way from the north end of town to the south end. There was one big, obvious gap in the middle, but in the fall of 2005, with the required pomp and circumstance, city officials celebrated the opening of a tunnel under Main Avenue to close the gap. Planning and construction took twenty or thirty years, depending on who's counting.

The river trail is approximately four and a half miles long. On the north end, it starts at the intersection of Twenty-Ninth Street and East Third Avenue (N 37 17.702, W 107 52.203) with the Opie Reams Trail on the east side of the river in Memorial Park. A restroom (open during warm-weather months) and parking are available at the trailhead. In less than a half mile, the trail crosses the river over a good footbridge. It continues south along the river around the east side of the high-school grounds, crosses a bridge over Junction Creek, and goes behind the old Mercy Medical Center (the hospital moved in June 2006). Then it crosses another footbridge, goes past a gazebo at Rotary Park, and heads under Main Avenue (N 37 16.838, W 107 52.701).

The trail continues behind Burger King on the east side of the river to Vietnam Memorial Park. There, a nice bridge takes you across to the west side of the Animas River at the north end of Schneider Park. After a couple of blocks, you cross the Animas again at the Ninth Street Bridge, then loop around and under the bridge.

After passing the DoubleTree Hotel, the trail goes under the U.S. Highway 160 bridge (N 37 16.125, W 107 53.150). It proceeds south along the highway about a mile to Santa Rita Park, goes under another highway bridge, and crosses the river to the west side over a rickety, wooden-planked bridge. It moves along a nice riparian area without any development for a half mile until coming to a BMX track. (A bridge from the BMX track links to the Rivergate townhomes and Animas Surgical Hospital.) The river trail continues uphill another half mile, and (as of late 2005) ends abruptly behind a Harley-Davidson dealer just a hundred yards short of the Durango Mall (N 37 14.623, W 107 52.234). Plans exist for the trail to continue, crossing the Animas near the highway and extending to Escalante Middle School and beyond. Some of these links may be made as early as 2006.

Parts of a trail already connect the school to Sawmill Road, a frontage road (some of it rough dirt) along Colorado Highway 3.

Keep in mind that there are numerous access points to the Animas River Trail along its route.

Durango Mountain Park encompasses a series of hills and valleys in nearly 300 acres of wild land on Durango's western boundary. This land was acquired by the city in the 1990s. The lowest point of the park is about 6,600 feet at the city boundary; the highest point is the Hogsback (discussed later in this section) at 7,484 feet, giving a net relief of 884 feet.

There is a network of several miles of trails (the city claims thirteen), providing some good short exploratory hikes. Some trails are steep and some are gentle. Winter also can be good for snowshoeing and ski touring, although most times snow just makes a mucky mess of things, particularly in the spring. You could get lost in the maze of trails, but not badly, because Durango is always to the east of you and is visible from various high points.

The area is composed of Mancos shale—a gray, flaky soil that is usually soft at the surface. Some places are bare, while others have piñon pines and junipers along with some large ponderosa pines.

There are several access points. A primary one is at the west end of Leyden Street in the Crestview area (N 37 17.054, W 107 53.264). A map is posted on a sign at the trailhead. One trail sticks to the main gulch, known locally as Slime Gulch, but side trails begin branching off, one immediately to the right. Other options soon branch off to the left uphill.

There is also access off the west end of Montview Parkway and at Arroyo Drive at its intersection with North Glenisle Avenue. South of Leyden, you can cross the drainage ditch at the intersection of Kearney Street and Glenisle Avenue. This route goes up steeply at first. Another access route goes north off Avenida de Sol just east of the Falcon Heights development. If you explore, you'll find other trails, as well as unofficial trails. Please honor private-property signs.

Durango Mountain Park is very popular with mountain bikers, and hikers need to be on the lookout for sudden biker appearances around sharp corners. Bikers owe the right-of-way to hikers, but hikers must be alert to the presence of the bikers.

The rule for dogs is that they must be on a leash.

One of the newest trails, located northeast of town off Florida Road, is the 1.2-mile-long **Pioneer Trail**. The hope is that someday this will connect with the Missionary Ridge Trail, but for now it connects only with a subdivision road. Following the road higher could eventually lead you to the Missionary Ridge Trail near the top of Haflin Creek Trail. But until that link is made, the Pioneer Trail is probably best for a quick out-and-back.

From the intersection of County Roads 250 (East Animas Road) and 240 (Florida Road), go 3.0 miles up Florida Road. About 150 yards before the big sign for Edgemont Ranch (a subdivision), look for a gravel road on the left. Drive up that 100 yards to a small parking area (N 37 18.796, W 107 47.933), and find the trailhead at a 7,360-foot elevation. The trail begins by heading south, going right up to the Edgemont sign, then switches back northward, winding its way uphill through a ponderosa-dominated forest. At 1.2 miles it ends abruptly at Nusbaum Road (N 37 19.423, W 107 47.743) at an elevation of 7,900 feet. You've climbed 540 feet.

If you hike up Nusbaum Road, which turns into Silver Mesa Drive, it's about a mile to the national forest, at which point a barrier prevents cars from getting through. From the barrier it's approximately 2.5 miles to the Missionary Ridge Trail, which you hit about a mile or so north of the top of Haflin Creek.

❖ Hogsback ❖

Distance: 2.0 miles (round trip)
Starting elevation: 6,660 feet
Elevation gain: 824 feet
High point: 7,484 feet
Rating: Moderate, due to steep finish
Time allowed: 75 minutes
Maps: 7.5′ Durango West

Introduction

This is part of the Durango Mountain Park and is located on its south boundary near the west side, but it is distinct enough to deserve special attention. It is the most challenging and most rewarding hike in the park. It's possible to do it on a long lunch break.

The Approach

Use the Leyden Street access. Reach Leyden from town by taking Twenty-Second Street west off Main Avenue. The street angles to the top of Crestview Mesa, where it becomes Montview Parkway; follow this west to Glenisle, then go south one block to Leyden and west again to the end of Leyden (N 37 17.054, W 107 53.264). As you drive up Leyden, you'll see both the Hogsback and Perins Peak beyond it.

The Hike

Take the trail over a large culvert and follow it along a usually dry gulch. In just over one-tenth mile, a trail branches at a 120-degree angle to the left uphill. You can take this, or you can go another two-tenths mile to a second left, which is a little less steep (N 37 17.126, W 107 53.557). Both of these trails top out to join a larger, more gradual trail that goes west toward Hogsback.

The trail twists and turns through some brush and eventually reaches open shale. The last two pitches are steep and can usually be done standing up—the shale has good footholds—but if it's wet or very dry, you'll probably slide a bit. Near the top is a very narrow spot where you must be careful not to slip, lest you take a steep, unscheduled glissade in the shale for 150 feet. The steep area is on the left part of the trail; it is a good idea to hold onto the brush on the right side. On the top (N 37 17.063, W 107 53.954) there is a nice single slab of sandstone that becomes your reward for huffing and puffing. It is a good place to lie down and rest or to sit and study the scenery: the city below, Perins Peak to the west, and the West Needles to the north-northeast.

You can return on the same route, or you can make a loop.

Options

A trail goes west off the Hogsback, and it's *really* steep for the first 30 yards. It's doable if you're careful. Follow this trail along a ridge for a quarter mile from the top, then take a right (east) off the ridge (N 37 17.177, W 107 54.105) and

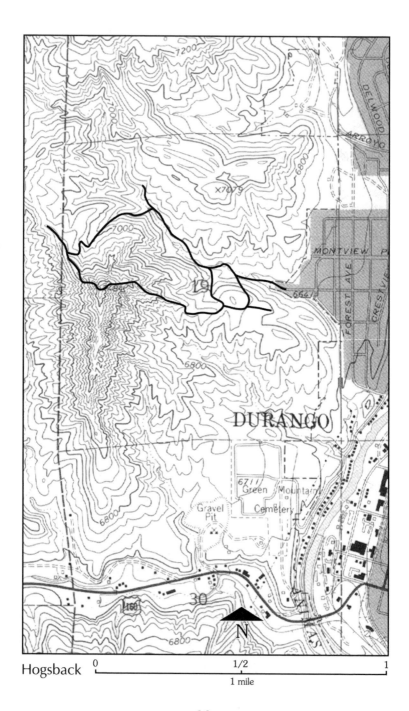

Hogsback

0   1/2   1

1 mile

drop down a winding trail for about a half mile, where the trail crosses Slime Gulch on a wooden bridge and comes to an intersection (N 37 17.286, W 107 53.781). Take a right, and follow this trail 0.6 mile to Leyden Street. Making this loop, which is all in the Durango Mountain Park, adds 0.3 mile to the trip.

If you go west off the summit, you can make an even longer loop by staying on the ridge longer, then dropping down at the head of Slime Gulch. *However*, know that this part of the loop, on Bureau of Land Management property, is open only from August 1 through November 30. The eight-month closure is to protect peregrine falcons, elk, and deer in the area.

❖ Perins Peak ❖

Distance: 5 miles (round trip)
Starting elevation: 6,660 feet
Elevation gain: 1,680 feet
High point: 8,340 feet
Rating: Difficult
Time allowed: 3 to 4 hours
Maps: 7.5′ Durango West; San Juan National Forest

Introduction

Perins Peak is included in the area restricted by the Colorado Division of Wildlife (DOW) in order to protect an endangered species, the peregrine falcon, as well as big-game

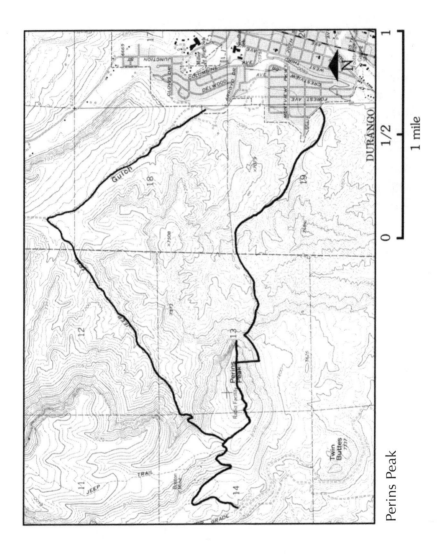

Perins Peak

1 mile

On Perins Peak after crossing the hazardous gully.

species whose young are born in this area. Human traffic is permitted on DOW land only one third of the year, from July 15 through November 15 (the end of hunting season), and is permitted on Bureau of Land Management (BLM) land in this area only from August 1 through November 30. But this is a good hiking area, and it's worth waiting for the open period. Also, it has the advantage of starting right out from the city limits.

The first part is quite easy, but the last thousand feet of altitude gain are difficult due to steepness and slippery conditions. It is a good, vigorous hike and is rewarding for the workout you'll get and for the nice view of both the La Plata Mountains and Durango from the top. Perins itself has a distinctive profile. Its top has a sharp, pointed cliff that faces east and looks down over Durango like a guardian.

The Approach

To start, take Twenty-Second Street west off Main Street in Durango. In a couple of blocks, Twenty-Second turns south and climbs Crestview Mesa. At the top, it turns west again and becomes Montview Parkway. Follow it to Glenisle, where you turn left (south). After one block, turn right on Leyden Street, follow it west until it ends, and park at the end (N 37 17.054, W 107 53.264).

The Hike

Begin hiking west up a drainage that the locals call Slime Gulch. You're now in the Durango Mountain Park. A well-defined trail follows a small stream (fortunately, it is dry most of the time) and crosses it several times. Stay on this trail for 0.7 mile, where it forks (N 37 17.286, W 107 53.781). Take the left trail, which crosses the gulch on a wooden bridge just past the fork.

Head up this trail for 0.5 mile to the top of a ridge (N 37 17.177, W 107 54.105) that comes down from the Hogsback, which is up above you to the southeast. Go right (northwest) on the ridge on a good trail for 0.3 mile, where an ill-defined, narrow trail takes off to the west along a lesser ridge (N 37 17.390, W 107 54.264). Take this trail, which traverses the lesser ridge on the south side of the head of a gully.

Just beyond the gully, swing toward the northwest and ascend toward a large shale rib coming down from the peak. You're now heading pretty much toward the Perins outcrop. There is a well-defined path in this area on up the rib. When it's pretty much impossible to go any higher on

14

Hikers on the Dry Creek to Durango Trail with the north point of
Perins Peak behind them.

this rib (N 37 17.436, W 107 54.675), there should be an
ill-defined path traversing the steep shale hillside to the
southwest. Follow this as best you can, watching your
footing. The next tricky part is crossing into and out of a
gully. There are a couple routes; pick the one that looks
best, and head up.

Now you should be pretty much due south of the cliff.
The going isn't quite so steep, but your new hazard is tightly growing oak brush and large rocks. Pick your way along
a contour toward the base of the cliff at its southeast corner. The best advice is to go as far west as necessary to
comfortably climb up to the next level. Once you are
beyond the cliff, going west, you can turn back to the north
for the final assault. In some places there's a sandstone wall

ten to thirty feet straight up. But if you're patient and careful, you can avoid this.

Once you are above the steep section, it is an easy 100 yards through oak brush to the top of the ridge. Find the old road and go east to the rocky point (N 37 17.443, W 107 54.707). Exercise care as you go out there, particularly to the north—you're a long way up, and while peregrines can fly from here, you can't.

The actual high point (N 37 17.439, W 107 54.991) is an easy quarter mile west of the cliff face. Since it is bare, you can get fine views in all directions. Also, you will find near the top two objects that look like large blank billboards. They are microwave reflectors.

Options

The mileage and time listed in the heading presuppose a return over the approach route. However, there is another option, to the north. If you make a loop, hiking up from the east and going down the northern route, you will have a two-mile hike back through town if you have not left a car there.

To take this approach to Perins, go west up Twenty-Fifth Street in Durango. Two blocks past Miller Middle School, go left on Clovis Drive and take it uphill to Borrego Drive (if you go straight, you'll end up being an uninvited guest in the Rockridge development). Go left on Borrego and park on the right side along a fence. There's an opening in the fence not far from the intersection, and that's the start of the trail.

Rockridge's developer has built this graveled hiking trail to traverse the full length of the property, heading toward

DOW land and following the route of an old four-wheel-drive road. When you reach the end of the graveled trail, go southwest up a drainage along the cut of an old road.

It should be apparent where you need to head—to a saddle between the northern and eastern points of the Perins massif. When you reach the saddle, continue southwest and look for an open meadow. You should find an abandoned road heading east upward toward Perins Peak. Follow this one-half mile to the top. It is four miles from the top back to the edge of town by this route versus the two and one-half miles on the first route described.

There is a possible route to or from the west, but this involves some serious bushwhacking through oak brush to get to or from Dry Fork Road. It isn't much fun and is definitely not recommended. But what you could do, if you're curious, is drop down from the top of Perins Peak toward the west and check out the old site of Perins City and the Boston Coal Mine. A quarter mile beyond the north-route turnoff, the road divides in a flat area. Take the left fork downhill. In another quarter mile, you come to another level spot. Go to the northwest end to find the site of the town and the mine.

No buildings remain here, but the place was once very busy, having been one of the largest coal mines in southwestern Colorado. It was active during the first quarter of the twentieth century. A railroad wound its way up the mountainside to carry out the coal.

Another option is to hike west and then north along the Perins massif and reach the northern point, which ends in a serious cliff at 8,682 feet—340 feet higher than the peak typically called Perins. For this route, go west from the top, and just past the split that goes northwest off the mountain, look for a path heading north. This route goes for two miles along a trail that is ill-defined or nonexistent. Again, this is not recommended for anyone other than adventurers with some time on their hands.

❖ Barnroof Point ❖

Distance: 5 miles (round trip)
Starting elevation: 6,960 feet
Elevation gain: 1,763 feet
High point: 8,723 feet
Rating: Moderate
Time allowed: 3 to 4 hours
Maps: 7.5′ Durango West; San Juan National Forest

Introduction

Two things you should know before attempting this hike:

One, Barnroof is heavily vegetated, especially with ponderosa pine and oak brush. The brush is from knee-high to ten or twelve feet high. It can be a real thicket, hard to get through, and it's hard to see where you're going near the top as it flattens out. Because part of this hike will require bushwhacking, you should probably wear long pants. No, you should definitely wear long pants if you plan on reaching the top. The last half mile is extremely thick.

Two, Barnroof Point is on Colorado DOW and BLM property and is closed to human traffic from late November (the end of hunting season) through March 31. Deer, elk, and grouse can often be seen on this mountain.

Barnroof is a low mountain east of the La Platas. It is interesting in that it stands as a single peak with valleys on all sides. This makes it a nice climb for presenting good views of surrounding territory, particularly the east side of the La Platas.

The Approach

Drive west of Durango three and one-half miles on U.S. Highway 160 to a right turn on Lightner Creek Road (County Road 207). Follow it 1.0 mile north to where Dry Fork Road, a gravel road, veers off of it to the right (north). Turn onto this gravel road, then park immediately in a large parking area to the left (N 37 17.647, W 107 56.381). This is Colorado DOW land.

The Hike

Begin your hike by crossing Dry Fork, which is usually a very small stream, and heading up the other side. Head northwest up an unmaintained path that becomes very steep, and in 0.2 mile you'll hit an abandoned road. Follow this uphill (north).

After 0.4 mile, this road ends; follow a trail that contours along for about a hundred feet, then goes very steeply uphill. You may need to use your hands along this stretch, and if it's muddy, it'll be slick enough that you may want to go do another hike. After this steep scramble, you'll have gained about a hundred feet in elevation, and you'll find yourself on the rim of what could be described as a gently uphill-sloping mesa top (N 37 18.033, W 107 56.713).

Once you are on this rim, it will be easy going for a while. The best bet is to stay close to the rim, but not so close that it scares the bejesus out of you—it's a long way down. There will be many fine views of the valleys below and the peaks beyond.

The farther you go, the tougher the going gets, and the less of a trail there is. After about 1.3 miles along the rim, the brush becomes very dense, and it's difficult to see where you're going. Just continue up, up, up, bearing northwest, pushing through the dense brush. Ultimately, in another 0.5 mile, you'll find yourself at the top (N 37 19.008, W 107 57.693).

The view of the La Platas from the high point—the northwest corner of this sloping mesa—is great. With a deep valley in between, foothills sweep upward to the rocky high peaks, forming a majestic view.

❖ Dry Gulch to Durango ❖

Distance: 5 miles (one way)
Starting elevation: 7,280 feet
Elevation gain: 400 feet
High point: 7,680 feet
Rating: Easy
Time allowed: 2 to 3 hours
Maps: 7.5′ Durango West; San Juan National Forest

Introduction

Please note that the DOW *prohibits* public access to this territory from November 15 to July 15 (eight months of the year) to protect the peregrine falcons, the deer, and the elk. The last month of the open period is mostly hunting season, but you should be safe if you wear a blaze-orange vest (and hat and gloves if you have them) required of hunters. This orange color is remarkably visible through the woods and brush. The route lies just outside the national forest boundary and traverses Colorado DOW property, a little BLM territory, and, for the last mile, private property.

The private property has been developed into the Rockridge subdivision for private homes. Fortunately, the developer is congenial to hikers—so much so that he has built a public hiking trail (mostly a wide gravel path) for the aforementioned mile, to just south of the intersection of Borrego and Clovis drives. It follows along the north side of a nice arroyo; hikers should stay on this trail for its entire length.

This is an easy afternoon hike, but it involves a car shuttle. It is routed west to east because this involves only 400 feet of altitude gain; east to west presents 1,000 feet of gain.

As a wildlife feeding spot, this area offers good opportunities to see game animals. Deer roam here year-round; elk are present mostly during the restricted winter period. You may also see bears here from time to time, and, on occasion, wild turkeys. If the high country is snowed in early enough, hunting for both deer and elk can be very good here.

The Approach

Drive west of Durango three and one-half miles on U.S. Highway 160 to a right turn on Lightner Creek Road (County Road 207). Follow it 1.0 mile north to where Dry Fork Road, a gravel road, veers off of it to the right (north).

21

This puts you into the wildlife area. Continue 2.0 miles north, and where the road splits in a "Y", go right. Go another quarter mile to a cattle guard. Turn right, and go downhill in front of the guard to a small parking area (N 37 19.442, W 107 56.576).

The hike begins here; it ends at the intersection of Clovis and Borrego drives on the west side of Durango, where another car can be parked. To find this spot from Durango, take Twenty-Fifth Street west off of Main Avenue about a half mile to a left-hand turn on Clovis; follow Clovis to the top of a hill, where you'll turn left onto Borrego. The trailhead is forty yards south of that intersection (N 37 17.774, W 107 53.154).

The Hike

From the western parking spot, start hiking east. The first task is to cross Dry Fork; it usually is a small stream and can be jumped, but you might get your shoes wet. Beyond the creek bank lies a nice meadow with a gently rising slope. Hike toward the east up this meadow; along its north side, just in the edge of the timber, you should find the remains of an old road, and a trail will become apparent. You follow it essentially all the way into Durango. The route rises now in less than a mile to its highest point (N 37 19.554, W 107 55.485) in some big ponderosa pines. Off to the right and high above is the sharp point of the north end of the Perins Peak massif. From here on it is downhill, alternating between tall pines and open meadows. At three and one-half miles you will pass the remains of some old ranch buildings with a nice cattail pond on the right followed by another meadow. The next meadow beyond that is usually

22

quite marshy; here it is best to cross to the south side. At four miles, you will come to private property. Take the developer's trail the last mile to Borrego Drive.

This is a good hike, but it is not a trail recognized by the U.S. Forest Service or the DOW for their maintenance. Therefore, in areas where the grass grows tall, it may at times be a little hard to follow. Usage helps to keep it defined.

Option

Use the trailhead near Clovis and Borrego drives and do an out-and-back, going as far as you feel like going. The obvious advantage of this is that you don't need to do the car shuttle.

❖ Dry Fork Loop ❖

Distance: 8.5 miles
Starting elevation: 7,390 feet
Elevation gain: 1,290 feet
High point: 8,680 feet
Rating: Moderate
Time allowed: 3.5 to 4.5 hours
Maps: 7.5′ Durango West; San Juan National Forest

Introduction

This loop trail is the result of two connections built to the Colorado Trail in the late 1980s and early 1990s. It starts along a drainage, then splits and moves up through big

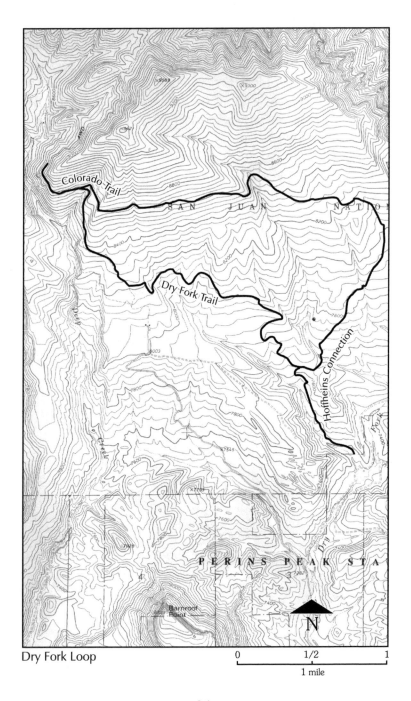

Dry Fork Loop

timber. The upper portion has a much different feel to it—thick woods with big timber—than the lower, drier portion.

This is a very busy trail in nice weather and is used by hikers, bikers, and horseback riders, with bikers predominant. It is a pleasant hike on good trail and is shady most of the way.

The Approach

Drive west of Durango three and one-half miles on U.S. Highway 160 to a right turn on Lightner Creek Road (County Road 207). Follow it 1.0 mile north to where Dry Fork Road, a gravel road, veers off to the right (north). Continue 2.0 miles north, and where the road splits in a "Y", go right. Take the right side for 0.8 mile and make a left-hand turn toward the trailhead; there should be a sign directing you to the Hoffheins Connection Trail. In a hundred yards you'll come to a large parking area (N 37 19.870, W 107 56.316), suitable for turning around a truckload of, say, cattle. (If you're lucky, you won't have such bad timing to be there when the cattle are unloading.)

The Hike

Start by crossing through a stock fence over a cattle guard. It's 0.7 mile of mostly uphill trail to a second cattle guard, then uphill another 0.1 mile to a three-way intersection (N 37 20.355, W 107 56.717). Your choice: You can go either way. The Dry Fork Trail was built with the mindset of having a relatively easy grade; Hoffheins Connection Trail is much steeper. For this description we'll go clockwise, heading up the mellower Dry Fork Trail.

Climb gradually, up through aspen and pine forests, along a fence line for a while. In 2.2 miles you'll join an abandoned road that comes up from your left. In another 0.5 mile there's a fork in this road, and it should be pretty obvious to veer right, continuing uphill. In another 0.4 mile you intersect with the Colorado Trail (N 37 21.355, W 107 58.295). Take a hard right, now heading east.

Climb some more, and in 0.2 mile you'll reach the hike's high point at 8,680 feet. Although you're not quite halfway, it's all (almost all) downhill from here. It's 2.3 miles from the high point to where the Hoffheins Connection Trail (N 37 21.131, W 107 56.110) splits off to the right (south). But if you have any energy left, you're going to want to make a short detour.

Just one-quarter mile east on the Colorado Trail is a spot called Gudy's Rest (N 37 21.185, W 107 55.900). It is a beautiful overlook where you can admire the continuing Colorado Trail far below in Junction Creek valley as it nears its Durango termination. A resting bench has been placed here (actually replaced many, many times due to vandals) to honor Gudy Gaskill, whose stubbornness and hard work helped to push through to completion in 1987 this enormous project connecting Denver to Durango by foot trail—a distance of 474 miles.

Back at the intersection, take the Hoffheins Connection Trail downhill 1.3 miles to the three-way intersection with the Dry Fork Trail, and continue the final 0.8 mile downhill to the parking area.

Options

It's not hard to make this a shorter or longer trip.

For a good short trip, just take the Hoffheins Connection

Trail 2.1 miles to the Colorado Trail, and take the detour to Gudy's Rest.

For a longer trip, extend your stay on the Colorado Trail in either direction. Going past Gudy's Rest takes you down to Junction Creek in about 1.4 miles. Oh yeah—you also lose about 600 feet in elevation that you'll have to regain on the way up.

Going west on the Colorado Trail at its junction with the Dry Fork Trail takes you as far as you'd ever want to go. Realistically, it's 3.5 miles of mostly uphill to a place called Road End Canyon. From here the trail drops down several hundred feet to Junction Creek. Unless you're looking for an epic hike, it's time to head back.

❖ Perins Peak Wildlife ❖ Area—Decker Tract

Starting elevation: 7,000 feet
Rating: Easy
Maps: 7.5′ Durango West; San Juan National Forest

Introduction

This is a little-used Colorado DOW area. It is west of the Perins Peak area and is part of it in name, although it is detached geographically. It is an elevated area between Lightner Creek and U.S. Highway 160 west of Durango. It is heavily wooded with big pines and some oak.

There is only one access—a rough four-wheel-drive road, the first mile of which is through private property (but legal to use).

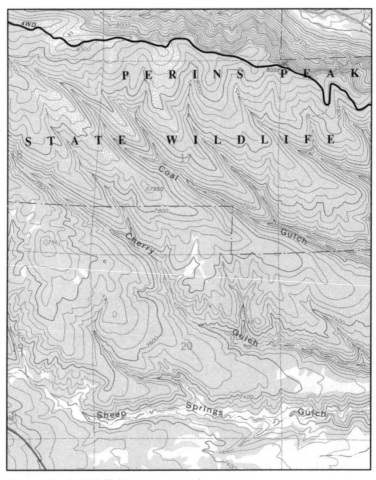

Perins Peak Wildlife Area—Decker Tract

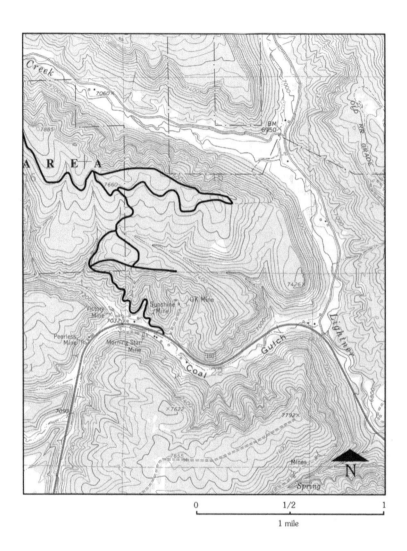

The Approach

Take U.S. Highway 160 west from town. From the bridge over the Animas River it's four and one-half miles, or one mile past the Lightner Creek turnoff. Here you will see a rough little road on the right. It is on the east end of an old mining spot. Go about 100 yards to a passable parking area (N 37 16.796, W 107 57.205). This begins the four-wheel-drive area. You could drive on, but this trail description assumes you've parked here.

The Hike

The road goes up above some old coal mines for 0.9 mile to the boundary of the wildlife area (N 37 17.194, W 107 57.362). A sign is posted here to identify the area. It will warn you that you can't have a dog off leash. Most of the roads inside are better than the approach road, but there are still some very bad spots. My advice is that if you're going to hike, and you're not out of your car by now, you should be.

The first road to the right goes for a half mile to a turn-around. There are trees close on each side but some good overlooks on the right down to the highway. Back on the main road, going north, you soon come to another right-hand road that is fairly good but that is currently blocked to vehicles by a steel cable. It still makes a good hike that goes east to near the dropoff; it then swings to the north side and goes back to the west, higher up to the main road. This is a good two-mile hike. You get close to the edge of a steep drop-off toward Lightner Creek in a couple of places. This affords some nice views on the right several hundred feet down into Lightner Creek with its many houses, and on north to Barnroof Point and northwest to the La Platas. The main road now curves to the west and, after negotiating some turns and hills, settles down to a slow, gradual rise mostly along the top of the ridge. You could drive about two more miles to a barrier for cars. The hiking trail goes on for more than a mile.

Other than during hunting season, you can generally enjoy the feeling of remoteness and solitude here, even though you are not far from town. On a nice summer weekend afternoon, you may meet other people, but not many.

❖ Animas City Mountain ❖

Distance: 5.5 miles (round trip)
Starting elevation: 6,700 feet
Elevation gain: 1,461 feet
High point: 8,161 feet
Rating: Easy
Time allowed: 2.5 to 4 hours
Maps: 7.5′ Durango East; San Juan National Forest

Introduction

This is an easy half-day hike near Durango. It is a good hike at any time of year, but it is especially appealing when the higher country is too deeply covered with snow for good hiking. This means November to June.

31

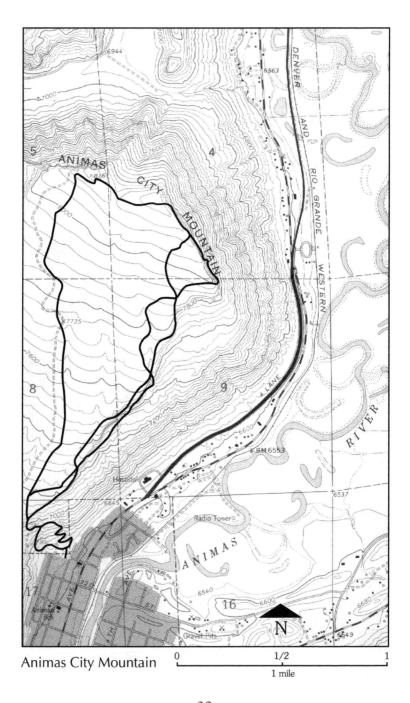

Animas City Mountain

0   1/2   1

1 mile

One caveat, however: There is a "conditions-based" closure on this BLM property from December 1 to April 15. What this means is that if snows get deep enough or the temperature gets extremely cold, and big game wander down from the high country, the BLM (in cooperation with the DOW) closes Animas City Mountain to give elk and deer a quiet place to go. If a closure is in effect, signs will be posted at the trailhead. In one six-year stretch, closures were made two times.

The east (right) side of the loop is two trails that parallel and occasionally cross each other. The purpose of the double route is to help separate bikers and hikers. The west side of the loop is an old four-wheel-drive road that is quite rough on the lower part.

The Approach

Take Thirty-Second Street west of Main Avenue in Durango to its west end on Fourth Avenue. Turn right here and follow it to the end, where there is good gravel parking for several cars (N 37 18.172, W 107 52.354). There's even a portable toilet in the summer.

The trailhead has a sign with a map of the loop, and maps are posted along the route at almost all intersections.

The Hike

Go north from the parking area; just past a power station you can go either left (steep uphill) or right (gentle uphill). I like taking the steep way, but let's say you go the easy way. This route switchbacks uphill. Go right at the first intersection, but then go left at the next one, about 0.6 mile from the start and 7,050 feet in elevation (N 37

18.301, W 107 52.556). That takes you in about fifty yards to the old four-wheel-drive road, which goes north fairly steeply another 1.8 miles to an overlook down the mountain's steep north side (N 37 19.683, W 107 52.329).

At this point, you can look down into the Falls Creek valley and northwest across the valley to the high La Plata Mountains. You can also see up the Animas River valley and the burgeoning town of Hermosa.

To continue the loop from here, go east up the trail. It climbs another 100 feet or so before finally topping out in about 0.2 mile. In another 0.3 mile the trail swings south, and you get some nice views of Missionary Ridge. Look for the rockfall that broke off the top of the ridge in 1998.

You'll begin to get nice views of the Animas Valley and the tortuous, winding river amid pastures populated with horses and cattle. There are also some old turns of the river now bypassed and disconnected, known as "oxbows." These usually have water in them from the snowmelt.

About 0.2 mile after the trail swings south, you'll come to the first of three junctions where two branches of the same trail cross each other down the east side of the mountain (N 37 19.429, W 107 51.687). This probably goes without saying, but the views are better if you stay closer to the rim, and the distance is approximately the same. It's 1.9 miles from the first junction to the intersection near the old four-wheel-drive road.

Options

There's one other way of accessing Animas City Mountain. From Main Avenue, travel west on Twenty-Fifth Street, which becomes Junction Street when it veers to the north.

Turn right on Birket Drive, and at the end of the drive, a trail begins. It's about a half mile from the Birket trailhead to the old four-wheel-drive road on Animas City Mountain, which you reach (N 37 18.193, W 107 52.533) at a saddle 0.2 mile from the Fourth Avenue trailhead.

❖ Log Chutes Trails ❖

Distance: Two loops, 4.7 miles and 6.3 miles
Starting elevation: 7,520 feet
Elevation gain: 880 feet
High point: 8,400 feet
Rating: Easy
Time allowed: 2.5 to 4.5 hours
Maps: 7.5' Durango West; San Juan National Forest

Introduction

This set of trails, reconditioned in the 1990s, is not far from Durango in the Junction Creek area. Two main loops are discussed here, but there are several other options off of these main loops.

The Approach

Take Twenty-Fifth Street west off of Main Avenue. This soon becomes Junction Creek Road. It's 3.0 miles to a "Y" intersection where you'll veer left; going right takes you up Falls Creek Road (County Road 205).

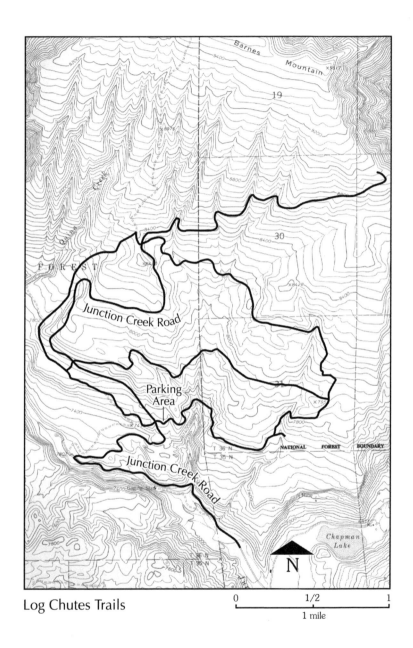

Log Chutes Trails

0   1/2   1

1 mile

In another 0.6 mile you'll reach the national forest boundary at a cattle guard; at this same point, the paved road becomes gravel. This is also the southern terminus for the Colorado Trail. The road soon turns into a twisting, climbing mountain road. From the boundary, go 1.8 miles (you'll pass Junction Creek Campground) and turn right into a parking area for the Log Chutes Trails (N 37 20.405, W 107 54.495). A closed gate bars the way to vehicles just past the parking area.

The Hike

Head east on a slight uphill grade on the closed-off road. You'll be using former roads of various widths most of the way. In 1.1 miles, turn left off of this road and go uphill to the northeast (N 37 20.343, W 107 54.753). There should be a brown plastic post that marks the way. In 0.6 mile of mostly climbing, you'll reach a flat spot where the shorter trail loop splits off to the left (west) (N 37 20.534, W 107 53.337).

For the long loop, continue another hundred yards to where another trail splits left (northwest) off of the old road. You should see another brown plastic post marked "more difficult" (to help mountain bikers decide the right route). From here, the trail climbs to the north for a half mile, then levels out and stays around 8,200 feet elevation for 1.3 miles as it again follows an old road. At this point, the trail takes off to the right (northwest) uphill on a single-track trail, and it climbs 200 feet more before reaching Junction Creek Road (N 37 21.367, W 107 54.668).

Go left downhill on Junction Creek Road for only about ten yards, locating the trail on the other side. This trail (actually an old road) heads slightly uphill for another 0.1

mile before coming to another old road, where you'll turn left and head steeply downhill (N 37 21.427, W 107 54.697). This trail has been used for downhill races, and it's possible that downhillers could be training on it. In any case, be aware that many mountain bikers use these trails.

From the road crossing, it's 1.5 miles to a corral that's on the right side of the trail. At this point, the short loop trail joins the long loop. You're hiking on a two-track old road. A hundred yards past the corral, as you turn from going south-southeast to almost due east, there's a trail that heads south. This trail takes you to the Colorado Trail near Junction Creek Campground. Instead, go another hundred yards due east and find a trail that heads south-southeast off of the two-track (N 37 20.647, W 107 55.106); if you reach Junction Creek Road, you've gone too far. As of my last hike here, in August 2005, neither of these junctions just mentioned were marked.

From here, it's 0.7 mile back to the parking area. At the end, you'll cross the road one more time and, voila, you're at your car.

Options

The shorter option was pretty well explained above. From where you take the left off of the longer loop, it's 2.2 miles to the corral. This trail dips and climbs a bit, but it mostly remains at approximately the same altitude.

There are several trails to the east of the main loops that you could take and add some more distance or see a new piece of land. It's a long way, but you can even follow the road that you split off of near the junction of the shorter loop and stay on it for a couple of miles all the way up to Junction Creek Road.

❖ Raider Ridge ❖

Distance: 4.6 miles (round trip)
Starting elevation: 6,600 feet
Elevation gain: 880 feet
High point: 7,480 feet
Rating: Easy
Time allowed: 2 to 3 hours
Maps: 7.5′ Durango East

Introduction

This is the first of four hikes that are part of the Telegraph Trail system—an interconnected set of trails just east of downtown Durango. Really, these four hikes are just suggestions and a way of introducing you to this system. The three that follow are Meadow Loop and Telegraph Trail, Carbon Junction Trail, and Sale Barn Canyon.

Raider Ridge is an easy hike out of Durango. It offers nice views over parts of the city, the college campus, the east side of the La Platas, and the south side of some of the San Juans.

The name "Raider Ridge" comes from the former mascot of the Fort Lewis College athletic teams. At one time, students maintained a big "R" on the campus side of this ridge. The Raiders are now the Skyhawks, but the ridge is often still called Raider.

Some of this ridge is private property; a big chunk is owned by Fort Lewis College and is open to the public. It is a steep sandstone uplift tilted ten to fifteen degrees to the southeast, known officially by geologists as a "hogback."

39

During mild winters, you can hike this trail in mid-winter. This route from Horse Gulch presents the sunny side of the ridge, where snow tends to melt fairly rapidly. It's even possible to scare up a deer or elk.

This has become a part of the Telegraph Trail system, an impressive set of trails east of town. Many of these trails were built in the late 1990s and early 2000s with the impetus of Trails 2000, a local trails-advocacy group. Raider Ridge is an older trail.

Mountain bikers are the main users of this system, but Raider Ridge does not get quite as many of them, particularly the "extended" ridge.

The Approach

From East Eighth Avenue, head east on Third Street a block to a small parking area (N 37 15.883, W 107 52.329). Be careful not to park in the way of a couple of local businesses. Third Street turns into a dirt county road that was closed to motor vehicles a few years ago by the county.

The Hike

Hike up Horse Gulch Road 1.0 mile (0.3 mile past the Meadow Loop turnoff) to where an old unmarked road splits from the main road at a 120-degree left turn (N 37 16.065, W 107 51.495). This trail heads west for 0.1 mile, where it splits again. Go to the right (north) uphill.

In another 0.3 mile, you'll reach another junction (N 37 16.314, W 107 51.573). Up ahead and to the left is a steep hillside of black dirt with a trail leading up it. This is the short way (about 100 yards from here) to the top of the ridge, and it's the route you'll come down if you follow these directions.

Instead of going up the black dirt hillside, go to the right, continuing on the remnants of the old road. From here, it's 0.8 mile and 200 feet up to the top of the "extended" ridge, from where you'll get an excellent view (N 37 16.763, W 107 50.966). Straight north, the Animas Valley opens in front of you, and you can see all the way to the West Needle Mountains. The La Plata Mountains rise west above the city. Down below are the golf course and the SkyRidge development.

Find the trail that heads to the west, go uphill briefly, and walk along the ridge to the high point of this hike at 7,482 feet. It's 0.8 mile to the black dirt mentioned previously. Enjoy the many splendid views along the ridge. From the black dirt, head downhill and retrace your route back to the trailhead.

Options

From the top of the extended ridge you have several choices. You could turn right, continuing up the ridge to the northeast until the trail peters out, then possibly bushwhack back down to Horse Gulch.

Or, from the black dirt, you can continue southeast on the ridge about three fourths of a mile, then loop back to the east and drop back down to Horse Gulch via one of several trails.

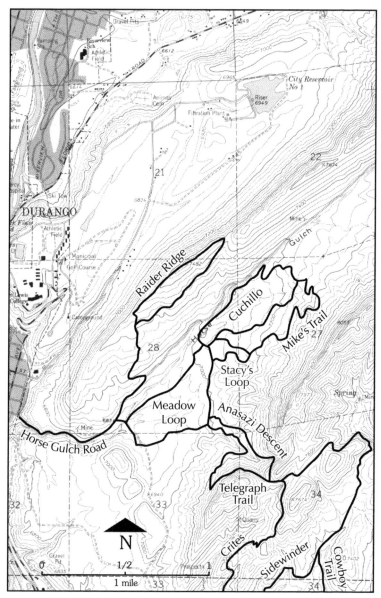

Raider Ridge/Meadow Loop/Telegraph Trail

❖ Meadow Loop and ❖ Telegraph Trail

Distance: 5 miles (round trip)
Starting elevation: 6,600 feet
Elevation gain: 880 feet
High point: 7,480 feet
Rating: Easy
Time allowed: 2 to 3 hours
Maps: 7.5′ Durango East

Introduction

This hike heads up Horse Gulch, just like Raider Ridge, but this time you head east instead of north, cruising the Meadow Loop and up Telegraph Trail. Options abound, and this is really just a suggestion for myriad hikes in the area. You could hike this area for weeks and not do exactly the same loop. The trailhead is just a few blocks southeast of downtown Durango. It's accessible nearly year-round—the only time it's not a decent place for a hike is when it's muddy.

It's a very popular spot for mountain biking, which you'll notice quickly. Be on the lookout. But most mountain bikers are courteous when they're not racing—as someone told me, a smile goes a long way.

The Approach

From East Eighth Avenue, head east on Third Street a block to a small parking area (N 37 15.883, W 107 52.329). Be careful not to park in the way of a couple of local businesses.

Third Street turns into a dirt county road that was closed to motor vehicles a few years ago by the county.

The Hike

Head up the dirt road, and soon you'll pass through the gate that closes the road to vehicles. In 0.7 mile, turn right off of the main road (N 37 15.850, W 107 51.681) onto the Meadow Loop, which follows the remnants of a road for 0.2 mile before turning off of it to the left and crossing the large meadow.

Keep right where there are trail options, and in another 0.5 mile head up the Telegraph Trail. There should be trail maps posted along the way to help guide you. Telegraph Trail climbs slowly as it contours east, west, south, and back east again, joining up finally near the top with the old "telegraph road" built early in the twentieth century. From the parking area to the top of Telegraph Trail (N 37 15.536, W 107 50.706) is 2.7 miles.

From the top, go another few yards and take a sharp left onto the Anasazi Descent. Veer right onto the Meadow Loop when you reach the bottom of the steep downhill. From the top of Telegraph Trail to the Meadow Loop to the intersection with Stacy's Loop is 1.0 mile. At the Stacy's Loop intersection (N 37 16.121, W 107 51.070), go left on Meadow Loop, and take two more lefts to stay on Meadow Loop; again, trail maps should help. From the intersection with Stacy's Loop, it's 0.7 mile back to Horse Gulch Road.

Options

So many options. Use the provided map, the posted trailside maps, or a free map provided by Trails 2000, which is available at local bike shops, to figure out the various combinations.

Stacy's Loop, Mike's Trail, and Cuchillo Trail are options in the Horse Gulch area. From the top of Telegraph Trail, the trail continues to the east, dropping into the Grandview area, and it's possible to make a loop involving Sidewinder and Crites Connection, or exit the trail system via Carbon Junction, or . . . .

❖ Carbon Junction Trail ❖

Distance: 4.2 miles (out and back)
Starting elevation: 6,460 feet
Elevation gain: 620 feet
High point: 7,080 feet
Rating: Easy
Time allowed: 2 to 3 hours
Maps: 7.5′ Durango East

Introduction

This is another trail that is very close to town, and it offers another option on the Telegraph Trail system. It's a nice hike, particularly in the spring and fall, and even in the winter if it's not muddy or covered by deep snow.

It is a popular route for mountain bikers, particularly on weekends.

45

The Approach

Take College Drive east from downtown Durango to East Eighth Avenue. Take a right (south) on Eighth Avenue, and go 2.3 miles to a small trailhead parking area on the left (east) side of the road (N 37 14.135, W 107 52.005). Eighth Avenue turns into Colorado Highway 3 a few blocks from College Drive.

You can also reach the trailhead if you're approaching Durango from the southeast. Turn right onto Colorado Highway 3 just after passing the light at Dominguez Drive (Wal-Mart turn). The parking area will be just ahead on the right.

The Hike

Begin uphill on the trail. It starts south but soon switches back; your bearing is generally east. It's a trail for a while, but soon you'll join an old road that heads briefly north. At the top of this hill—0.5 miles from the trailhead—you'll top out next to a large, flat field.

The trail goes back to the south, away from the old road, and skirts this field. Soon you'll find yourself between a gravel pit (left) and REA Canyon (right). In 1.0 mile after leaving the road, the trail splits, with Carbon Junction continuing to the left and the South Rim Trail going to the right (N 37 14.444, W 107 51.347). This presents one of many options, but this description assumes that you stay on Carbon Junction.

In another 0.6 mile of mostly gentle climbing, you reach a second intersection (N 37 14.732, W 107 51.136). At this point, Carbon Junction and this trail description end.

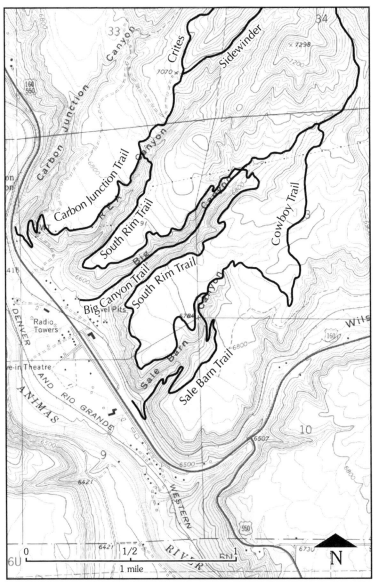

Carbon Junction/Sale Barn

Options

Where Carbon Junction ends, the Crites Connection goes to the left (north), and the Sidewinder Trail goes to the right (northeast). It's possible to do a 4.2-mile loop, going up Crites Connection 1.7 miles, right on Telegraph Trail for 0.5 mile, then right on Sidewinder Trail for 2.0 miles back to the three-way junction.

Another option: At the junction with the South Rim Trail, go right on the South Rim Trail about two miles, then go right onto Big Canyon Trail, which drops you in 1.1 miles onto a frontage road that parallels U.S. Highway 160. Hike along this frontage road about one-half mile back to the Carbon Junction parking area.

❖ Sale Barn/Cowboy Loop ❖

Distance: 8.2 miles (round trip)
Starting elevation: 6,480 feet
Elevation gain: 520 feet
High point: 7,000 feet
Rating: Easy
Time allowed: 3 to 4.5 hours
Maps: 7.5′ Durango East

Introduction

This is another Telegraph Trail system hike with many options. This one is located in the southeast part of the system. It offers views of the Grandview area, the La Plata Mountains, and even Wal-Mart.

There is some up and down to this hike, so the overall elevation gain is much more than 520 feet.

The Approach

Take U.S. Highway 550/160 south of Durango three miles from the Double Tree Hotel to Dominguez Drive. Go left onto Dominguez Drive; if you went right, you'd be headed toward Wal-Mart. After only a block on Dominguez Drive, just past the gas station, you'll turn right onto a frontage road. Go 0.4 mile along the frontage road, and just as it's about to turn back toward the highway, continue straight up a hill on a dirt road. Park in the good-sized lot ahead of you (N 37 13.443, W 107 51.382).

The Hike

Take the path at the east end of the parking area. It soon crosses a ditch and heads north. It stays briefly in Sale Barn Canyon, then climbs above. You'll reach the canyon top 0.7 mile from the trailhead.

Skirt a gravel-pit operation (it's on your right) through piñon-juniper forest. Note the variety of desert-type plants: sage, yucca, mountain mahogany, and several types of cactus. From the topping-out point, it's 1.0 mile to the end of Sale Barn Trail and a split (N 37 13.858, W 107 51.015).

Take the Cowboy Trail right (you'll return on the South Rim Trail, which goes left here). Follow the Cowboy Trail, crossing a gas-well road at 0.4 mile, and you'll come to a nice overlook of the Grandview area 0.4 mile after that. Here the trail turns from going south to heading northeast.

In 0.6 mile, you'll come to a road; go right (north) on this road fifty yards and find the Cowboy Trail again on the left-hand side. From here, it's another 0.3 mile to an intersection with the Big Canyon Trail (N 37 14.552, W 107 50.408); you'll drop about 100 feet to get there.

Take Big Canyon Trail left 0.5 mile, then at an intersection under power lines, go left onto the South Rim Trail (N 37 14.365, W 107 50.825). Hike uphill out of Big Canyon, then follow the trail as it winds along the mesa rim. Where the trail turns from going southeast, to heading northeast above Sale Barn Canyon, there's a shortcut you could take down the steep hillside (N 37 13.567, W 107 51.361). But if you continue on South Rim Trail, it's 2.5 miles from the Big Canyon junction to the three-way intersection with Sale Barn and Cowboy trails. Go right at the three-way and finish by hiking 1.7 miles back on Sale Barn Trail to the parking area.

Options

At the first trail split, go left onto South Rim Trail. Follow it 2.5 miles, dropping down into Big Canyon. Take the Big Canyon Trail left (southwest) 1.1 miles to its terminus. Follow the frontage road one-quarter mile, where you can find an old road that runs beneath the hillside behind Basin Co-op. Head southeast on this for 0.3 mile and link back up with the Sale Barn Trail. Take it downhill 0.2 mile to the parking lot. This whole loop is 6.1 miles.

Another possibility: At the first trail split, as in the option just described, go left onto South Rim Trail. Go 1.3 miles to the Well Road Cutoff (N 37 13.936, W 107 51.302), an ill-defined trail that goes southeast 0.2 mile to a gas-well road that in about a mile joins the Cowboy Trail. Go right on Cowboy Trail 0.4 mile back to that first trail split. This loop is about 6.3 miles.

HIKES UP AND ON MISSIONARY RIDGE

❖ Haflin Creek Trail ❖

Distance: 7.6 miles (round trip)
Starting elevation: 6,620 feet
Elevation gain: 2,880 feet
High point: 9,500 feet
Rating: Moderate
Time allowed: 4 to 5.5 hours round trip
Maps: 7.5′ Durango East; San Juan National Forest

Introduction

This is one of the better Missionary Ridge hikes for seeing changes wrought by the 2002 fire. Unfortunately, that means you're going to see a lot of black tree trunks with no needles or leaves.

It's still a nice hike—particularly early in the summer and early in the fall, when temperatures are a little cooler. It's a great early-summer warmup for Fourteeners. The altitude and mileage gained on this hike are similar to climbing a mountain; the big difference, obviously, is the altitude.

53

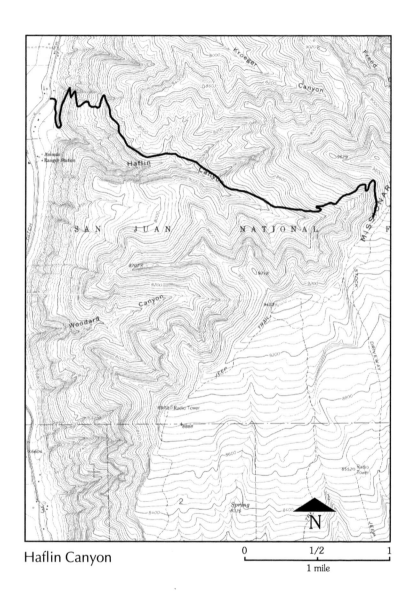

Haflin Canyon

Haflin is a small creek in a deep, rugged canyon that breaks through the west, steep side of Missionary Ridge. You start near the creek, hike high above it, later come even with it, cross it, and finally rise through an open brushy area to the top of the ridge above the stream source. In this brushy area, you can get good views to the west of the Animas River valley and the La Platas beyond.

Before the fire, this hike illustrated very well the different climatic zones. At the bottom, you started among piñon, junipers, oak brush, and yucca. Soon you reached a level of ponderosa pine; this gave way to quaking aspen and the beginning of spruce and fir. But the fire devastated this canyon, leaving few areas unscathed. It'll be decades before the burned conifers return. Aspen are already making a comeback—the first stage of succession.

Note: It's a good idea to stay out of this area during hard rains (flash floods and mudslides are possible) and high winds (if you see a falling tree, think fast).

The Approach

From Main Avenue in Durango, take Thirty-Second Street east about 1.2 miles to a left turn on East Animas Road (County Road 250). In 5.3 miles, you should see a sign on the east side of the road for Haflin Creek Trail. Off-the-road parking is available here (N 37 22.075, W 107 50.356). (A fenced-off forest service maintenance yard is just to the south.)

The Hike

The trail starts off nearly flat in an easterly direction but soon launches into a series of climbing switchbacks, some

Haflin Creek

of them a bit steep. The first switchback goes north in a quarter mile; if you miss it, you'll find yourself next to a small, windowless building in a few yards.

Continue climbing switchbacks and distancing yourself from the canyon bottom. In about 0.4 mile, you'll really start to notice the burned ponderosa. The good news is that you'll get views across the valley; you'll be able to see evidence of the Valley Fire, which occurred during the Missionary Ridge Fire but was not related to it.

At 1.1 miles from the start, you'll reach the end of the steep switchbacks and head southeast. (The trail rises only moderately for the next 1.5 miles.) At 1.5 miles from the trailhead, you'll begin to hear a waterfall. I know this will tempt some people, but it's very difficult to get to a place where you can see it. Best advice: Don't try. Enjoy the creek before it falls—there are several access points.

At 2.8 miles, the trail again steepens. It'll remain steep until the final switchback, after which the trail traverses south up an open hillside. At 3.8 miles, you'll hit the Missionary Ridge Trail (N 37 21.412, W 107 47.945). Enjoy views of the La Platas—Silver and Lewis are the most prominent mountains from here.

No part of this hike is difficult, but it is rated moderate because of the relatively large amount of altitude gain.

Options

This is listed as a half-day hike, but you could lengthen it by going either north or south on the Missionary Ridge Trail.

Going south, the hiking is good for a couple of miles, but beyond that the trail soon descends to private property.

North on this trail brings you to two easterly descents and one westerly descent within 6.2 miles. All three descents offer the possibility of making this a point-to-point hike. In 1.7 miles, you'll come to the First Fork Trail, and 3.0 miles after that you'll come to Red Creek—both of these go east off of Missionary Ridge. In 1.5 miles after Red Creek, you'll come to the Stevens Creek Trail, which heads west toward the Animas Valley.

All of these trails will be discussed separately.

❖ Stevens Creek Trail ❖

Distance: 11.4 miles (round trip)
Starting elevation: 7,750 feet
Elevation gain: 2,300 feet
High point: 10,050 feet
Rating: Moderate
Time allowed: 5 to 7 hours round trip
Maps: 7.5' Hermosa; San Juan National Forest

Introduction

This is called Stevens Creek, but you stay way above the creek and never really see it, or even come close enough to hear it. You are in the Stevens Creek valley, so that's good enough, eh?

This hike, like the Haflin Creek hike, goes up the west side of Missionary Ridge to the Missionary Ridge Trail across the top, but it is much longer because the route is less direct and because the Missionary Ridge Trail at the top swings to the east quite a distance. It passes through big-timber areas of pine, aspen, fir, and spruce, as well as through some open meadowland with streams in the valleys. But this trail is also like the Haflin Creek hike in that it travels through areas scorched by the 2002 Missionary Ridge Fire. It isn't all that pretty some of the time, but it does increase the view.

The route follows constructed trail and several old mountain roads, most of them closed to cars and trucks. Very little of it is rocky. There is nothing difficult about it except its length.

Access is a little tricky. There is a trailhead off of County Road 250, but it's *very* difficult to find and there's little or no parking. So instead, this description bypasses the lower part of Stevens Creek Trail and takes you up Missionary Ridge Road to a cutoff trail.

Also, be aware that this trail has become popular with downhill mountain bikers—they use it for practice. This shouldn't be a problem, because the mountain bikers stay mostly on the lower section. However, you definitely need to watch out for them.

The Approach

Take U.S. Highway 550 north of Thirty-Second Street and Main Avenue for 6.5 miles, and turn right onto Trimble Lane (County Road 252). Take Trimble Lane 0.9 mile and veer left (north) onto East Animas Road (County Road 250). Take East Animas Road 3.2 miles and veer right onto the gravel Missionary Ridge Road, heading uphill.

The Missionary Ridge Road winds its way uphill. To find this trailhead, it's a good idea to use your odometer and

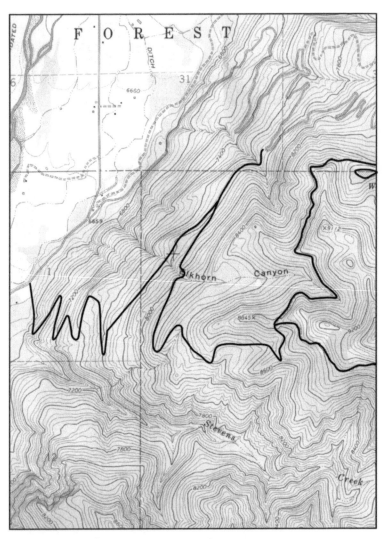

Stevens Creek

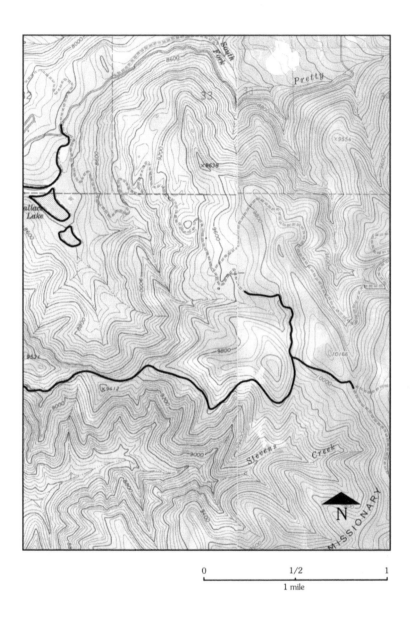

0   1/2   1

1 mile

your memory; it's 3.7 miles to the trailhead, which you'll find at the third sweeping left-hand switchback in the road. There won't be a whole lot to mark the trail, but after close inspection, you should see a brown plastic stake, or something, that tells you this is the cutoff trail to Stevens Creek Trail.

There's room for a couple of cars in a pullout off the switchback (N 37 25.460, W 107 46.982).

The Hike

Go south over a berm and find the trail heading slightly uphill. You contour in and out of one drainage, then turn south and join up with the Stevens Creek Trail in 0.5 mile (N 37 25.175, W 107 47.238). Go left uphill on an old road grade (still heading south). You're now at 7,860 feet, whereas the trailhead off of East Animas Road is at about 6,660.

The trail continues south for another quarter mile before it does a jog to contour the Elkhorn Canyon drainage. After heading south for another half mile, the trail turns east and heads generally east up to Missionary Ridge. Also during this stretch, the trail will widen as it joins another old road.

After 2.1 miles from where you joined the Stevens Creek Trail, and after a short climb north-northwest, you'll come to a junction (N 37 24.681, W 107 46.915). The trail left takes you to Wallace Lakes and back to Missionary Ridge Road. Continue right (east) on the trail. From here, it's another 3.1 miles to the Missionary Ridge Trail (N 37 24.507, W 107 44.392)—for the last half mile, you again join an old logging road.

The total hike from where you parked to the junction with the Missionary Ridge Trail is 5.7 miles.

At the junction with Missionary Ridge, the trail goes below the top on the west side; therefore, there is no view across to the valley below on the east side. If you want that view, you can go either right or left on the Missionary Ridge Trail, but it's about a half mile to the left and a mile to the right before you get decent views eastward. Or, just be satisfied with the good views looking west toward the La Platas.

Option

You could attempt to find the Stevens Creek Trailhead off East Animas Road. It's between 0.4 and 0.5 mile south from where Missionary Ridge Road begins.

From here, it's 2.8 miles and 1,200 feet in elevation gain to the junction mentioned above, where Stevens Creek Trail meets the cutoff trail that goes south from Missionary Ridge Road.

❖ Wallace Lake ❖

Distance: 1 mile (round trip)
Starting elevation: 8,200 feet
Elevation gain: 200 feet
High point: 8,400 feet
Rating: Easy
Time allowed: 1 hour round trip
Maps: 7.5′ Hermosa; San Juan National Forest

Introduction

This is a very easy hike in a nice, secluded area (except during hunting season). It is located well up on the west side of Missionary Ridge and is surrounded by big trees, mostly aspen. The hike itself is short, but the hiking area is several miles from Durango. Still, it is a pleasant drive.

The Approach

Take U.S. Highway 550 north of Thirty-Second Street and Main Avenue for 6.5 miles, and turn right onto Trimble Lane (County Road 252). Take Trimble Lane 0.9 mile and veer left onto East Animas Road (County Road 250). Take East Animas Road 3.2 miles and veer right onto the gravel Missionary Ridge Road, heading uphill.

After a little less than six miles, you come to the Wallace Lake turnoff. There should be ample parking here (N 37 25.687, W 107 46.086).

Missionary Ridge Road is often plagued by a washboard effect. It also climbs steeply up a series of many switchbacks. It yields fine views of the Animas Valley from a higher and higher perspective. Westward across the valley, the Hermosa Cliffs and La Plata Mountains grow ever more impressive as you continue to climb.

The Hike

Actually, four-wheel-drive vehicles can go on to the lake, but the hike is pleasant and short. Shortly after the trail begins, the road branches. Go to the right, and you will soon be at the lake. There are two other small lakes in the vicinity. You reach the main lake first, with the others to the right

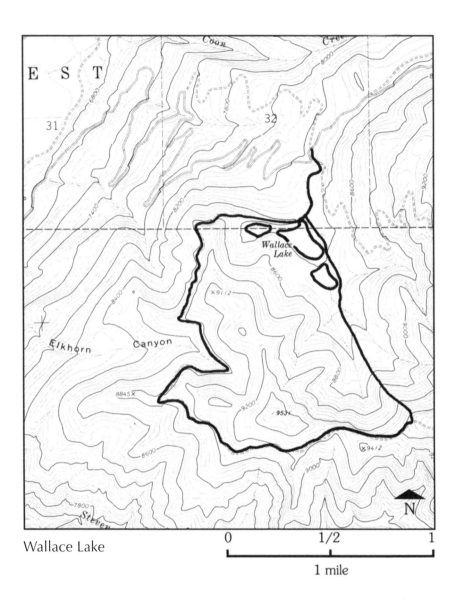

Wallace Lake

0   1/2   1

1 mile

and left of it. All of these lakes are shallow. In dry years, they sometimes dry up completely. It is a peaceful and lovely spot, although it should be noted that Wallace Lake is not exactly your picturesque high-country lake. It can be brackish with no defined boundary—not a great place to go down to the shoreline and wade in, or throw sticks for the dog. During the fall, it is surrounded by golden-clad aspen.

Options

Those who want a more vigorous hike can follow the jeep road on around to the right alongside two of the lakes. It twists and turns and climbs another mile and a half to meet up with the Stevens Creek Trail (N 37 24.681, W 107 46.915). Return the way you came.

You could continue up the Stevens Creek Trail another mile and a half, then take a shortcut northwest back to Wallace. It's one mile northwest, but you must bushwhack down the steep side of the basin, following the creek to the uppermost of the three lakes.

❖ Mountain View Crest ❖

Distance: 9.2 miles (round trip)
Starting elevation: 11,480 feet (11,080 feet)
Elevation gain: 1,518 feet (1,918 feet)
High point: 12,998 feet
Rating: Moderate (long and high but not difficult)
Time allowed: 6 to 8 hours
Maps: 7.5′ Mountain View Crest, San Juan National Forest

Introduction

The trailhead is northeast of Durango, reached via twenty-four miles of gravel road (which can be washboarded) and two miles of four-wheel-drive road. It'll take ninety minutes to two hours of driving from Durango. The end of the trail offers some of the most fantastic scenery in Colorado. I am going to suggest some variations that will cause differences in time, mileage, and altitude. The statistics given above are from the end of the four-wheel-drive road to Overlook Point and back by the same route. Once you are in the area, you will want to take advantage of the full range of views. You can make this hike in a half day, but a long, full day is much better to allow you to get a good exposure to its riches.

The Approach

Take U.S. Highway 550 north from town several miles to Trimble Lane, where you'll take a right. Take Trimble Lane (County Road 252) one mile to East Animas Road (County Road 250), and turn left (north). From there, it's 3.2 miles to Missionary Ridge Road, a gravel road that veers right and uphill off of County Road 250. This climbing gravel road (Forest Service Road 682) has many switchbacks and goes through areas badly scarred by the 2002 fire.

Follow Forest Service Road 682 about nineteen miles and take Henderson Lake Road when it branches off to the right. In 2.9 miles there's a large parking area on the right. Most cars should be able to make it another 0.3 mile, where the road becomes four-wheel-drive. From here, it's 2.1 miles to the end of the road at the wilderness barrier, where you will find plenty of parking space (N 37 31.828, W 107 40.857).

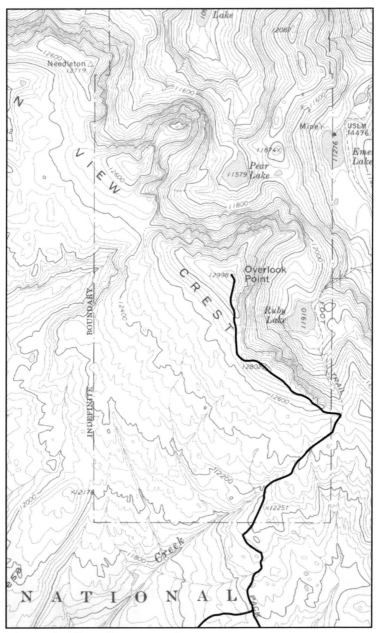

Mountain View Crest   (North segment)

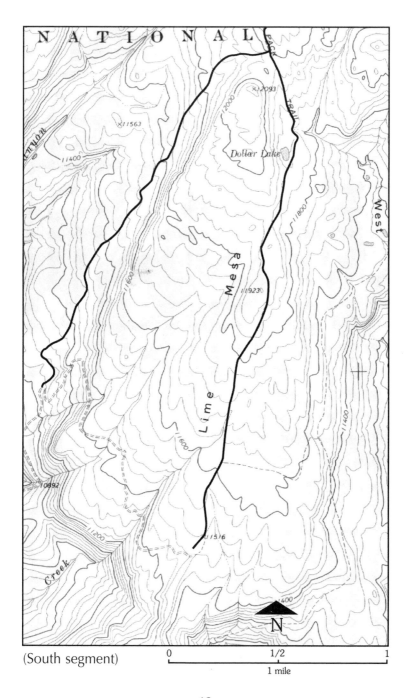

NATIONAL

X 12093

2000

Dollar Lake

West

11563

11400

Canyon

11600

Mesa

11800

11923

Lime

11600

11400

10992

11200

11516

Creek

11400

N

(South segment)

0   1/2   1

1 mile

Lunch stop on the way to Mountain View Crest; Lime Mesa is on the left, Dollar Lake is just ahead.

From the point where the road turns to four-wheel-drive, it's only 0.4 mile to the alternate trail route described below which skirts the west side of Lime Mesa. Driving to the wilderness boundary takes fifteen to twenty minutes more and gains you about 400 feet in elevation.

The Hike

From the end of the road, cross into the Weminuche Wilderness and hike straight north along the east side of Lime Mesa, following the old, rutted-out jeep road. The trail is right at timberline, and in a while you'll begin to get wide-open views. It's 1.9 miles to Dollar Lake (N 37 33.327, W 107 40.367). Another mile past the lake, the trail turns northeast and steepens.

70

Pigeon and Turret peaks across Needle Creek Valley from
Mountain View Crest.

At 3.5 miles, to the south of a ridge, two trails split (N 37 34.414, W 107 40.075). One goes right, almost due east. Take the one going left (north) uphill to the ridge, and in one-tenth mile, you'll reach a saddle at the east end of Mountain View Crest. Don't let the view take your breath away.

The views become even more dramatic as you climb left along the ridge one-half mile to the top of the first rise (12,802 feet). The second rise, another half mile beyond, is called Overlook Point, and it stands at 12,998 feet (N 37 35.020, W 107 40.577).

The drama is below and beyond in the form of four beautiful lakes. To the right and below Overlook Point lies, first, Ruby Lake, and a little farther north and lower, Emerald Lake. Walk northwest and down from Overlook Point and you'll see both Pear and Webb lakes. All of these provide excellent trout fishing. To go down to them commits you to an overnight stay; they're farther away than they appear.

But the view down to the lakes is only the start of the scenery. Far below them is Needle Creek—too far down to see—but across Needle Canyon and abruptly above rise Pigeon and Turret peaks. These two miss being Fourteeners by a small margin, but there is no more dramatic view in the San Juan Mountains. Viewing the east face of Pigeon Peak can send shivers up and down your back.

The Needle Fourteeners are easy to spot if you know what you're looking for. The Wilsons, to the northwest, dwarf Engineer Mountain in the foreground. Almost due north, on the far horizon, is the unmistakable summit of Sneffels, another Fourteener.

Options

You really don't have to drive all the way to the wilderness barrier. From where the road turns rough (see the approach), it's 0.4 mile to a switchback. Just where this sweeping switchback begins climbing toward the south, look for a blocked-off road heading north (N 37 32.454, W 107 41.612). This road/trail heads north-northeast and meets up with the trail described above north of Dollar Lake.

The route becomes less defined the farther you go but should be fairly easy to follow. The best advice is to not stray too far from Lime Mesa. If you veer west into the trees too far, you'll get bogged down. In 1.7 miles, you come to the north end of Lime Mesa and reach timberline; swing right (east) here across the tundra. In about 0.2 mile, you should intersect the trail described above. Take it left another 1.1 miles to the saddle at the east end of Mountain View Crest.

If you take this alternate route along the west side of Lime Mesa, and begin from the switchback, it's about one-half mile shorter with 400 feet more in elevation gain than the route described from the end of the road.

Also, it's possible to climb Mount Kennedy. From where the trails split at mile 3.5, take the the trail going east, and hike three miles. You can end up climbing north off the trail to the top of Kennedy. It has a double top, with the farthest being the highest (13,125 feet). Either top will give about the same view.

The view here is to the north into Chicago Basin, surrounded by the Needles Fourteeners. They are, from west to east, Eolus, Sunlight, and Windom. This is one of the most popular backpacking areas in the state. People ride the Durango & Silverton Narrow Gauge Railroad to Needleton and hike six miles up Needle Creek, where a base camp can be established for climbing all three peaks.

❖ Red Creek Trail ❖

Distance: 6.2 miles (round trip)
Starting elevation: 8,020 feet
Elevation gain: 1,780 feet
High point: 9,800 feet
Rating: Easy, except for the last half mile
Time allowed: 3 to 4 hours round trip
Maps: 7.5′ Rules Hill; 7.5′ Lemon Reservoir; 7.5′ Hermosa; 7.5′ Durango East; San Juan National Forest

Introduction

Red Creek Trail is a nice hike any time the snow is not too deep, but it is especially good on a warm summer day. For most of the way, it follows a nice gurgling stream at the bottom of a narrow canyon in the shade of big fir, spruce, and aspen trees. Like other Missionary Ridge hikes, you'll notice evidence of the 2002 fire. However, the east side of the ridge was not as severely scorched as the west side (Haflin Creek and Stevens Creek trails, for instance). So there are places you'll see no damage at all, and some spots of severe damage.

The trail is easy to follow. It climbs quite gradually for 2.7 miles, then, steeply, it proceeds up a series of switchbacks the last half mile to the top of Missionary Ridge.

74

The Approach

To get to Red Creek from Durango, take East Third Avenue north to its end and turn right (northeast) onto Florida Road. Take this road 9.7 miles to a left-hand turn onto County Road 246, also the way to Colvig Silver Camps.

Follow this gravel road past the camps; in 1.0 mile, the road becomes Forest Service Road 599, and it gets much rougher and heads into the 2002 burn area. This road can get very potholed and difficult, especially when it's been raining a lot; you can probably do it in any car, but four-wheel-drive is not bad to have if you get into a jam. In another 0.3 mile, you'll have to go through a fence and may have to open a large swinging gate.

In 0.6 mile beyond the gate, you may notice the trailhead for the First Fork Trail. (To get to First Fork Trail, you have to ford Red Creek.) There's not a lot of room to park here, but there is a small pullout for a couple of cars. Go beyond this spot another 0.3 mile, where the road swings west briefly and ends in a large parking area (N 37 21.552, W 107 44.590).

As you can deduce from the above description, it wouldn't be the end of the world to park your car at the swinging gate or at First Fork trailhead and walk up the road the rest of the way to the Red Creek trailhead.

The Hike

Begin northwest through a forest of tall aspen and fir that escaped the 2002 fire. You'll cross to the west side of Red Creek in the first tenth of a mile and will continue to cross and recross it.

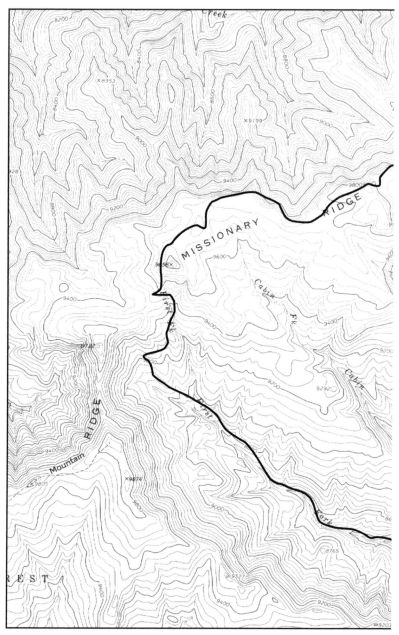

Red Creek Trail

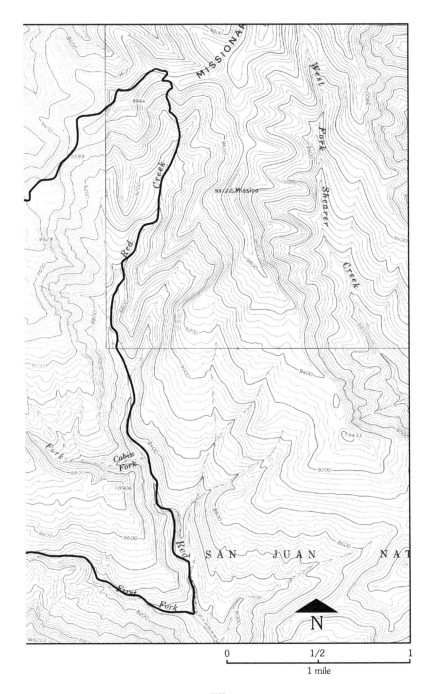

0   1/2   1

1 mile

This area didn't fare badly in the fire, but it is prone to flash floods because of the conditions noted above. You may notice a few places where the trail has been washed out and repaired.

In 0.9 mile from the start, you'll pass through a forest service gate on the west side of the creek. At 2.6 miles, the trail is overgrown and hard to follow; in other places, the trail is a deep trench. At 2.7 miles, the trail steepens noticeably, and a quarter mile beyond that you come to a clearing from where can look back south from where you came and get a nice view into the distance. You can also look up from this clearing and see the ridge that is your destination.

It's another 0.1 mile from the clearing (3.1 miles from the start) to the top of the ridge, where you'll meet the Missionary Ridge Trail, here going east-west on the ridge top (N 37 23.739, W 107 44.716). The distance figure of 6.2 miles round trip in the trail description assumes turning around at the union with the Missionary Ridge Trail.

Options

This hike can be extended into a 10.1-mile loop that brings you back to the starting point via First Fork Trail. From the junction of Red Creek and Missionary Ridge trails, go west. There's a lot of up and down, some of it steep. In 0.8 mile, you drop to a low point on the ridge (9,600 feet), then climb back up immediately. From the low point, it's 0.7 mile to a thick aspen forest where, curiously, trees were badly burned on one side and left unscathed on the other.

In all, it's 3.1 miles along Missionary Ridge from Red Creek to First Fork trails. You'll find First Creek Trail taking off to the east at a low point on the ridge (9,500 feet). The little wooden sign doesn't exactly scream at you, but you probably won't miss it (N 37 22.616, W 107 46.886).

Take First Fork Trail downhill, making sure in a little over one-tenth mile to take the switchback going right (south). Another trail goes straight (east) here, and people have been known to wander for a while. A lot of trail rebuilding was done on this stretch after the fire. In 1.5 miles from the top, the trail levels out a bit and begins a numerous set of creek crossings. In another 2.2 miles from the first creek crossing, you'll come to the end of the trail and have to ford Red Creek to reach the road (N 37 21.314, W 107 44.527). Go left (uphill to the north) on the road 0.2 mile back to the parking area.

Obviously, another loop option is to go up First Fork Trail and down Red Creek Trail. Amazingly, this is also a 10.1-mile loop.

Another option from the Red Creek Trail junction with Missionary Ridge is to go out and back northeast along the Missionary Ridge Trail. It's only 1.6 miles along the ridge to the junction with Stevens Creek Trail (N 37 24.507, W 107 44.392). This opens up the possibility of a point-to-point hike (consult the Stevens Creek description for more details, but it could make about a 10.4-mile hike). Along the stretch from Red Creek to Stevens trails, the spruce-and-fir forest is well-burned. Chances are you'll be okay, but dead trees have been heard falling. Best advice: Don't travel along here when it's windy.

❖ Shearer Creek Trail ❖

Distance: 16 miles (round trip)
Starting elevation: 7,560 feet
Elevation gain: 2,640 feet
High point: 10,200 feet
Rating: Easy, but long
Time allowed: 7 to 9 hours round trip
Maps: 7.5′ Rules Hill; 7.5′ Lemon Reservoir; San Juan National Forest

Introduction

This is a delightful, but long, hike to the top of Missionary Ridge from a southeasterly approach. It starts out climbing a hill above Florida Road and in 1.3 miles joins Shearer Creek, which it follows closely almost all the way to the top. The rise is quite gradual most of the way except at the top.

This trail was closed for a couple of years after the 2002 fire because portions of the trail were washed out by heavy rains, leaving near-cliffs into and out of the creek bed. It finally reopened in late 2004. Do not use this trail when it's raining hard because of potential flooding from water and mud.

The Approach

From the intersection of East Third Avenue and Fifteenth Street in Durango, go northeast on Florida Road (County Road 240) 11.9 miles to a turnout and trailhead parking area on the north side of the road (N 37 20.797, W 107 42.199).

The Hike

The first two miles are through private property, so you must stay on the trail. The forest service has legal access for the public through this area. The first few miles of trail are well marked and fairly easy to follow uphill through the large ponderosa pines still standing after the fire.

Begin uphill through a spring-loaded wooden gate. You'll climb, passing through several more gates that you'll have to open and shut. As the trail drops about 150 feet to the creek, you'll begin to pass through the burned section. In 1.3 miles from the start, the trail crosses the creek (N 37 21.617, W 107 42.053) and takes a sharp left onto a dirt road. The trail crosses and recrosses the stream many times. It is a gurgling, pleasant little stream in the summer and fall and is easily crossed on the rocks. In the spring and early summer during the snowmelt, the stream is higher and much harder to cross. Therefore, this trail is not recommended until the major snowpack is gone at levels of 10,000 feet and lower.

The trail eventually joins a fairly level road (at about N 37 24.485, W 107 42.697). From here, you'll head northwest on a side ridge that leads to the Missionary Ridge Trail and, in about two miles, to the top of Missionary Ridge. The point of this side ridge overlooks Lemon Reservoir 2,000 feet below, but it is heavily wooded, making it hard to see the lake.

The return is by the same route as the climb. There is one problem on the return. In the last mile after you leave the stream, there are enough cow paths to possibly obscure the main trail. If you keep a close eye on the trail and head basically southwest, you should make it back to the parking area, happy but tired.

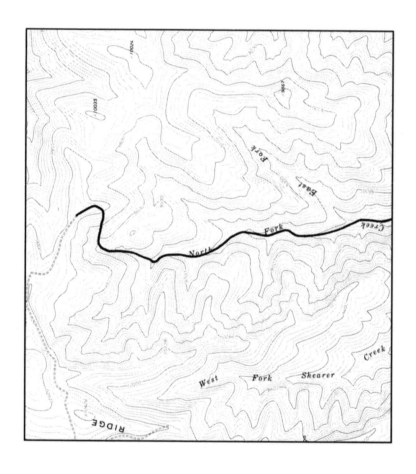

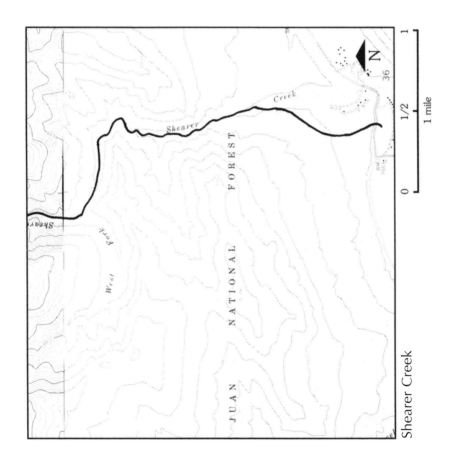

Shearer Creek

Options

Returning via the Stevens Creek or Red Creek trails is possible. These routes assume that you have a second car waiting to pick you up at the bottom of these trails.

From where Shearer Creek Trail reaches the top of Missionary Ridge, it's about 1.5 miles west (left) to the junction with the top of Stevens Creek Trail. It would be another 5.7 miles on Stevens Creek Trail, taking the cutoff toward Missionary Ridge Road (mentioned in the Stevens Creek description). Total for this hike: 15.2 miles.

Or, you could continue south past the Stevens Creek junction another 1.6 miles along the Missionary Ridge Trail to the Red Creek Trail, then 3.1 miles on the Red Creek Trail. Total for this hike: 12.7 miles.

❖ Burnt Timber Trail ❖

Distance: 6.5 miles (round trip)
Starting elevation: 8,500 feet
Elevation gain: 2,500 feet
High point: 11,000 feet
Rating: Easy
Time allowed: 3.5 to 4.5 hours round trip
Maps: 7.5′ Lemon Reservoir; 7.5′ Mountain View Crest; San Juan National Forest

Introduction

Some hikers may think that the easy rating for this trail is underrated because of the climbing, but there is nothing difficult about any part of it. It just goes steadily upward at a good incline and requires a slower pace and more rest for some hikers than other easy trails.

This is a rewarding hike that traverses genuine back-country and stays near the rugged Florida River canyon. The east side of this canyon presents a high, imposing wall of timber and rock. Most of this hike is in the trees along the base of the east side of Missionary Ridge, but there are frequent views eastward through the trees. The last mile shuts off the eastward view while passing through a high-altitude open, but steep, meadow.

The Approach

To find the trailhead from Durango, take East Third Avenue north to its end, and turn right (northeast) on Florida Road. Follow this out of town thirteen miles to Lemon Reservoir Road (County Road 243). This spot is easily recognized: The main road here turns right at a ninety-degree angle around a little country store and crosses the Florida River. Lemon Reservoir Road goes straight.

A couple of miles up this road, you come to the dam, behind which is impounded beautiful Lemon Reservoir. This is an irrigation supply filled by melting winter snows. It is peaceful and inviting, nestled as it is at the base of high wooded hills on each side. Lemon Reservoir is a favorite fishing and picnicking spot with several good sites along its banks.

To reach the trail, drive along the side of the lake and two miles beyond its north end. Here you cross a cattle guard; one road goes straight on up Miller Mountain, but

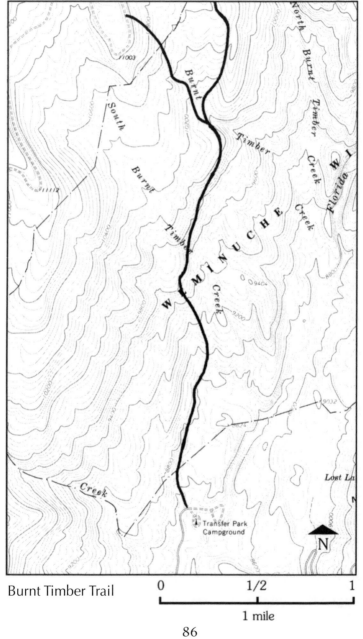

Burnt Timber Trail

0   1/2   1

1 mile

you should turn left into the Florida Campground. In a quarter mile you cross Florida River, then immediately turn left. The road winds on around south, west, and north again for a mile and comes to an end at Transfer Park Campground, tucked into a flat spot next to the river.

Plenty of parking space is available where you first enter the campground, at the northwest corner. The trail begins at the north side of this area (N 37 27.790, W 107 40.906).

The Hike

The trail is a good one—well maintained and easy to follow. It is used by horseback riders as well as hikers. The three and one-fourth miles (one way) given in the heading takes you to the old Burnt Timber Road along the top of Missionary Ridge. Some may wish to turn back shortly after entering the meadow instead of climbing on up to the road, which is a mile farther and 800 feet higher; you would then have to follow the trail still farther to get good views of surrounding peaks. Others may want to go even farther, for the trail continues, eventually coming to a crossover to Lime Mesa Trail west and north or going on to a turn eastward that takes you to Durango City Reservoir, some thirteen miles from Transfer Park. This is beautiful country but carries you into backpacking instead of day-hiking distances.

The projected 6.5-mile hike presupposes returning to Transfer Park from Burnt Timber Road by the same route as you came.

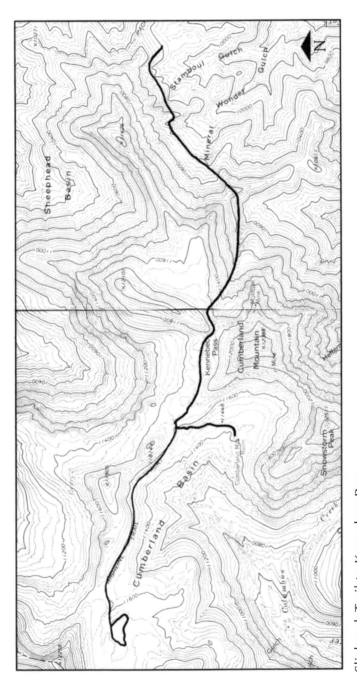

Slickrock Trail to Kennebec Pass

LA PLATA MOUNTAIN CLIMBS

❖ Slickrock Trail to ❖ Kennebec Pass

Distance: 4 miles round trip; 7.6 miles round trip
including Taylor Lake
Starting elevation: 10,340 feet
Elevation gain: 1,420 feet
High point: 11,760 feet
Rating: Moderate
Time allowed: 2 to 3 hours
Maps: 7.5′ Monument Hill; 7.5′ La Plata;
San Juan National Forest

Introduction

This is a relatively short hike following a long drive on a gravel road, but both the drive and the hike are well worth it. The drive starts at 7,000 feet and slowly winds its way up to the trailhead at 10,340 feet. It rises through piñon-juniper country, up through ponderosas. Eventually, tall aspen close in on the road, along with spruce and fir.

When I hiked this trail in early August, the wildflowers were abundant; open places displayed great patches of blue larkspur and alpine asters, punctuated with yellow daisies. Columbine are profuse up higher. When I hiked this trail in early October, the aspen trees were aflame with gold.

This is great deer and elk country. Your chances of seeing deer are quite good; elk occasionally appear, but they are more apt to stay farther away from the road. One foggy morning, a bear ran across the road in front of us.

The Approach

To reach the trailhead, take Main Avenue in Durango to a west turn on Twenty-Fifth Street. In a couple of blocks, this curves off to the northwest and becomes Junction Street. Take this out of town, where it becomes Junction Creek Road. The road follows Junction Creek all the way to the national forest boundary. The boundary is easily recognized, for the blacktop stops here with a cattle guard. (It's about 3.5 miles to the cattle guard from the Main Avenue turnoff.) Driving on a gravel road from here on will be slow due to many curves, a steady uphill climb, and often a washboard effect in the surface.

Check your speedometer at this point. It's about seven miles to Animas Overlook, where you can stop and get great views up the Animas Valley and of the mountains to the north. At about eleven miles, you come to Rand's Point, where there is a turnout on the left side of the road. Stopping here is well worthwhile, for you look far down into Junction Creek canyon and across its headwaters to the steep sides of Cumberland Mountain, Snowstorm Peak, and Lewis Mountain. Kennebec Pass, the hiking objective, is also visible between Cumberland Mountain and a high, flat ridge north of it.

Looking down the west ridge below Mount Baker toward La Plata Canyon and across to the western La Plata Mountains.

At about 17.5 miles (allow for some variation in speedometers), take a spur road to the left (southwest). There may be a sign here pointing out that this is the way to the Slickrock Trail, or the Colorado Trail. Follow this road 0.8 mile to the trailhead. The Colorado Trail is coming up from its origin west of Durango; it crosses the road at this point and joins the Slickrock Trail. Here, a wide spot a few yards north of the trailhead provides suitable parking space (N 37 26.933, W 107 59.162).

The Hike

Begin hiking uphill through a nice forest. As you near the pass in about 1.5 miles, the trail traverses an open rocky area that yields a view southeastward down the entire

91

Junction Creek canyon to Durango. The canyon is heavily wooded in dark green; a glance upward toward the pass and Cumberland Mountain shows the light green of tundra above timberline. Every view from this trail is different and beautiful. Another 0.5 mile brings you to the pass (N 37 26.886, W 108 00.153). Here, the views north and northeast give the best skyline panorama in Southwest Colorado. You see the Needles, Twilight and the West Needles, the Grenadiers, Sultan, Engineer, Grizzly, and many others. If you hike 150 yards down the other side of the pass, you see around the west side of the ridge on the north side of the pass, and more of the panorama opens up: Lizard Head, the Wilsons, Dolores Peak, and Lone Cone. Just as you go through the pass there, an unnamed ridge rises on your right (north) 300 feet in a quarter mile. The view is enhanced even more if you climb it.

If you are interested in mining history, you can hike a quarter mile southeast from the pass to an old mine, the Muldoon, that is in a better stage of preservation than some. It is in an exposed area above timberline, so the views are excellent.

The four miles specified in the heading are based on a return from Kennebec Pass to the starting point. This is a fairly easy hike, but it is a bit steep.

Options

Taylor Lake can also be included in this hike. It adds another 1.8 miles (3.6 miles round trip) to the distance but not much elevation change. To go to Taylor Lake, continue from Kennebec Pass along the Colorado Trail, which uses a closed two-track road, then links up with a four-wheel-drive road coming up through the La Platas. Where the four-wheel-drive road turns left and down the hill to Cumberland Basin, the trail goes on straight (west) to the lake.

Trails continue southwest and northwest from Taylor Lake. The one heading southwest climbs a ridge, drops down into Bear Creek canyon, and goes up the other side to the pass between Sharkstooth and Centennial peaks. This is described as Sharkstooth Trail and is approached from the west—a much shorter and easier route for that area. The one going northwest is the Colorado Trail, which soon joins Indian Trail Ridge for more excellent views.

❖ Tomahawk Basin– ❖ Diorite Peak

Distance: 5.2 miles (round trip)
Starting elevation: 9,900 feet
Elevation gain: 2,861 feet
High point: 12,761 feet
Rating: Moderate to difficult
Time allowed: 3.5 to 4.5 hours
Maps: 7.5′ La Plata; San Juan National Forest

Introduction

This is another hike out of La Plata Canyon. You can chop some distance and altitude off the climb by driving up the rough four-wheel-drive road as far as 1.5 miles. Eventually,

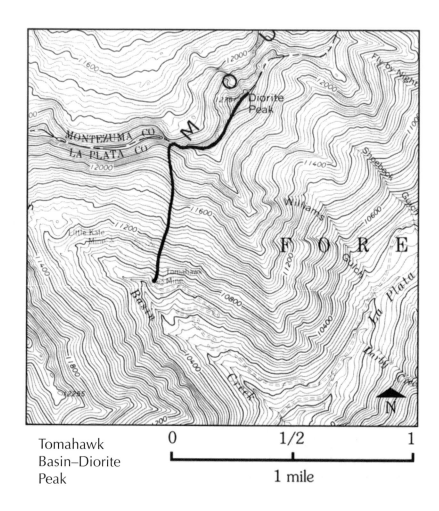

Tomahawk
Basin–Diorite
Peak

0   1/2   1

1 mile

the road becomes too rough for any vehicle, and you'll have to start winding your way on foot up the mountainside.

The hike is without benefit of trail but is easy to follow because it quickly gets above timberline, where everything is visible. Above timberline, most of the hike is on loose talus rock.

The Approach

To make this climb, take La Plata Canyon road 10.7 miles from U.S. Highway 160 to the Tomahawk Basin road. To break this down a little better, it's 6.1 miles from where the pavement ends, or 1.3 miles from the Lewis Creek turnoff. The Lewis Creek turnoff is the road that crosses the La Plata River on a bridge. The last 1.3 miles to the Tomahawk Basin turnoff are very rough in spots, and you may need four-wheel-drive for the last part.

The Tomahawk Basin turnoff (N 37 25.489, W 108 02.600) is a 120-degree turn uphill to the left. The Tomahawk Basin road is very rough and narrow—two-wheel-drives should not attempt it.

The Hike

Begin up the road. It'll be easy going for a while and steeper the higher you go. In 1.2 miles, you'll come to the remnants of a huge old mill (N 37 25.717, W 108 03.404). It is very picturesque in the fall.

Keep following the remnants of an old road. In another 0.3 mile it becomes too rough for vehicles. When you run out of road, hike north up the mountainside toward the low spot in the saddle at about 12,300 feet. A few hundred feet below the saddle is the site of an airplane crash from the early 1960s. This was a military flight in which two men were killed. The tragedy was all the more ironic since 300 feet more of altitude would have allowed them to clear the ridge. The crash and many snows have scattered the wreckage over a wide area. Most of it has been salvaged, but climbers will no doubt see some scraps of aluminum skin, wires, and other smaller parts as they climb through the area.

Once you are at the saddle (N 37 26.256, W 108 03.333), turn right, climb to the high point of the ridge, and follow it around northeast to Diorite Peak. This is a half mile from the saddle.

The views from the top (N 37 26.398, W 108 03.048) are breathtaking. Immediately below, steeply down on the west side, you look into Bear Creek basin. On the far side of the basin are Mount Moss and Centennial Peak. The connecting ridge between them is extremely rough and forbidding. Across this ridge and a little beyond is Hesperus Peak at 13,232 feet—the highest point in the La Platas. North of Centennial Peak, Sharkstooth rises steeply to a sharp point. To the north there is a complete panorama of peaks, including, from west to east, the San Miguels with their three Fourteeners and the distinctive Lizard Head shaft, Grizzly Peak, Engineer Mountain, the Twilights, the Needles, and many more. To the east, near at hand, are La Plata Canyon and the east ridge of the La Plata Mountains.

Return by the same route you ascended.

❖ Centennial Peak ❖ and Sharkstooth

Distance: 4.4 miles (round trip); 5.0 miles for both peaks
Starting elevation: 10,900 feet
Elevation gain: 2,162 feet (plus 526 feet for Sharkstooth)
High point: 13,062 feet
Rating: Moderate (Sharkstooth is difficult)
Time allowed: 3 hours (add another hour for Sharkstooth)
Maps: 7.5′ La Plata; San Juan National Forest

Introduction

This hike is described as a climb to the top of Centennial Peak with an optional side trip to the top of Sharkstooth.

A fairly long drive is involved; the last eight miles of it are through tall aspen forest with occasional breaks in the trees to reveal the western profile of the La Platas. These are the highest peaks in the range but are not often seen because lower peaks block the view from all directions except from the west. This territory is unpopulated for a number of miles. As you approach from the west, the glimpses that you get include Hesperus (at 13,232 feet, the highest peak in the La Platas), Moss, Spiller, Centennial, and Sharkstooth; all except Sharkstooth are higher than 13,000 feet. Although a bit shorter, Sharkstooth captures your attention because of its sharp triangular shape thrusting abruptly into the sky above the pass. From this angle it definitely looks like a shark's tooth.

97

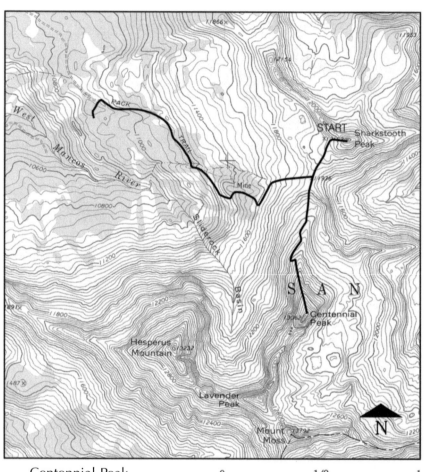

Centennial Peak
and Sharkstooth

The Approach

To take this hike, go north out of Mancos on the Dolores road, Colorado Highway 184. Just a quarter mile north of Mancos, turn right and go uphill on the road marked for Jackson Reservoir and Transfer Campground. After it enters the national forest, this road is labeled Forest Service Road 561 and is a good gravel road. Follow it twelve miles (two miles past Transfer Campground) and take a right onto Forest Service Road 350 (Spruce Mill Road), heading east. It is still a good gravel road, although narrow and winding at times. In about 6.5 miles, a small road labeled "Twin Lakes, Sharkstooth Trail" drops off to the right. This road takes you 1.5 miles, past Twin Lakes, to the trailhead, where it ends. This road is rough and rocky, and small lakes tend to form in it in places; when the road is dry, ordinary cars drive on it with a little care. At the trailhead (N 37 27.757, W 108 05.800) there is room to park several cars.

The Hike

The trail begins in big spruce and fir and moves steadily uphill to the saddle between Sharkstooth and Centennial. This is an easy and well-defined trail. Partway up is an old mine on the left. Near this same area, at the south end of a switchback, is a breathtaking view of Hesperus Peak on the right and Centennial Peak on the left. A very jagged ridge and Lavender Peak are in between.

Centennial is a bit shorter than Hesperus and is distinguished from the sharper peaks by a roll top. Both Centennial and Hesperus are characterized by bands of different-colored sedimentary rocks. In fact, Centennial was

Climbing Centennial from the saddle on the trail, with Sharkstooth in the background.

called Banded Mountain until its name was officially changed July 30, 1976, in celebration of the Colorado state centennial. This was, of course, the same month in which the United States was celebrating its bicentennial.

At the saddle (N 37 27.429, W 108 04.577), turn south (right) off of the trail, which at that point goes east and drops deeply into Bear Creek canyon. When you turn right, there is no more trail to follow, but you cannot get lost—just climb upward seven-tenths mile to the summit (N 37 26.837, W 108 04.614). You start up steeply over talus; after 150 yards, you come to a much more gradual slope over tundra. Stay near the high point of the ridge. As you get near the top, it will be rocky again. There are some paths showing in this area.

100

Each time I have climbed this mountain, there has been a strong, cold west wind; it seems to be a regular pattern for the area. Be sure to have warm clothes along, including gloves, even in the summer. At the top, you can take a few steps down to a ledge on the east side for shelter.

From the top, you can see a long way in all directions except south, where the neighboring peaks are the whole view. To the southeast toward Durango, you cannot quite see the city, but you can see Fort Lewis College, which is located on a mesa 300 feet above town. To the north, you can see the full sweep of the San Juans, from the Needles northeast to the San Miguels northwest. Even farther west are the Abajos in Utah, and to the southwest the Sleeping Ute Mountain.

The return trip should be made to the saddle and back down the trail you ascended.

The climb up Centennial Peak is not really difficult, but talus and the altitude make it deserve a moderate rating.

Option

If you wish to climb Sharkstooth on this same excursion, be aware: Its shale rock coating is extremely loose, and this will not be the most fun you've had on a climb. Frequent communication is essential to avoid kicking rocks on your buddy below. No member of a climbing party should be immediately below another. Near the top, every handhold and foothold must be tested before trusting your weight to it. Dogs probably shouldn't climb this one—as much for your sake as theirs. They don't listen when you tell them to bark a warning when they dislodge a rock.

That said, Sharkstooth can be climbed fairly quickly. Simply attack its south side from the saddle. It is only 526 feet above the saddle. It starts over ordinary talus but gets steeper and steeper as you rise. There are plenty of rocks to grab, but the trouble is that most of them are loose.

The top (N 37 27.593, W 108 04.378) is very small, and the north face drops even more precipitously than the south face. The views are much the same as from Centennial Peak. The descent must be done with even more care than the ascent.

❖ Hesperus Mountain ❖

Distance: 5 miles (round trip)
Starting elevation: 10,900 feet
Elevation gain: 2,332 feet
High point: 13,232 feet
Rating: Difficult
Time allowed: 4 to 6 hours
Maps: 7.5′ La Plata; San Juan National Forest

Introduction

Hesperus Mountain is the highest point in the La Plata Mountains. It makes a good one-day hike and climb; its summit gives almost a complete 360-degree view. To the south and southeast, nearby peaks cut off some valley views. Hesperus is a handsome mountain and well worth the climb. It is seen mainly from the west. The eastern and southern parts of the La Platas and other San Juan peaks cut off views of it from the populated areas and highways.

The peak is to be climbed from the west ridge. This can be done from the north or the south side of the ridge. The south side is approached via the Echo Basin road, two miles east of Mancos. The more usual route is by the north side of the ridge; this route is described here.

The Approach

The best route for a north-side approach to the mountain is the Sharkstooth trailhead (N 37 27.757, W 108 05.800). This access is described in the previous hike, "Centennial Peak and Sharkstooth," so it will not be repeated here.

The Hike

At the small Sharkstooth Trail parking area, take the West Mancos Trail south toward Hesperus Mountain, now quite visible and dominating the southern view above the forest. The trail starts on an old road but soon becomes a very good trail through the woods. From the point of view of the Hesperus climber, two unfortunate things happen: The trail swings east for some distance and then begins to lose altitude. It swings east in order to cross the North Fork of the West Mancos River at a good spot—about three quarters mile from the start, over a good log bridge. Then the trail immediately swings to the west. Shortly after crossing the stream and before renewing its descent, the trail comes into a clearing where the north face of Hesperus, beginning almost at your feet, confronts you in all its massive grandeur.

At this point, experienced climbers looking for a challenge may want to try the short but more difficult route and start the ascent immediately. It saves considerable distance

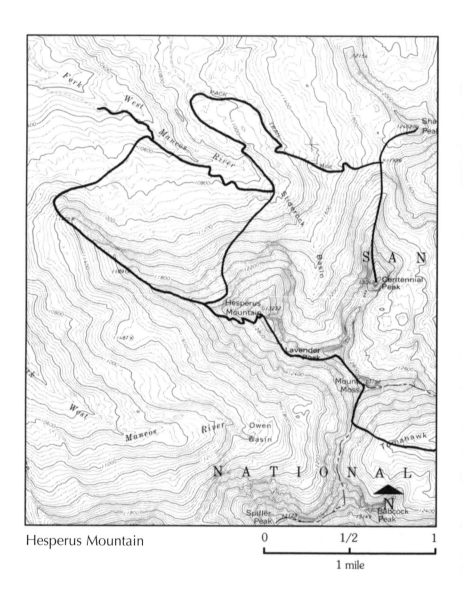

Hesperus Mountain

0   1/2   1

1 mile

Hesperus Mountain from the western-approach road: Centennial Peak is off its left shoulder and Sharkstooth is at the far left.

over the easier route described below. You can work out your own approach, but it is better to move up southwest on a course that is less steep and later more directly south toward the top of the main west ridge. This ridge ascends gradually up to a point where the predominant gray of the rocks turns to a dark red and an abruptly steeper grade. If you can strike the top of the ridge here (N 37 26.743, W 108 05.822), you will find a trail coming up along the crest of the ridge. (Skip the next two paragraphs for more directions.)

For climbers of more modest accomplishments, it is best to go much farther west and start up the west ridge of the peak near timberline. Unfortunately, this presents a dilemma, for the West Mancos Trail continues to descend fairly rapidly. One choice is to abandon the trail, climbing up

Glissading off Hesperus.

toward the face to near tree line and then proceeding west for most of a mile, largely on talus rock. This will take you to a point where the ridge can be climbed at a much lower and easier level. This route is nearly level, but talus, though not difficult, is much slower to hike on than trail.

The other option is to follow the West Mancos Trail down another mile and a quarter to an old timber cut. Here, the trail joins an abandoned logging road. (The main problem with this route is that by this time you have descended another 400 feet.) Anywhere within the next couple hundred yards, you should leave the trail and start uphill, finding your own route through the band of big timber (which is several hundred yards wide at this point). You should emerge into the same talus area after twenty to thirty minutes. Here, choose a route of ascent toward the lower end of the west ridge. Once you are on top of the ridge, you should find a route worn into a trail, heading left for the summit. It is easy for three-quarters mile, up to 12,400 feet—basically to the point experienced climbers would hit the ridge if they followed their previously recommended directions.

At the 12,400-foot level, you are confronted with a steep rise through a red formation. The last 800 feet will be steeper and rocky but not extremely difficult, so take heart. There is a good trail up this steep rise on the left side; then the trail crosses over to the right side and stays there the rest of the way to the top. Part of the time you will be on loose rock, part of the time on ledge. The small rocks here make an enjoyable musical clinking sound. But as you enjoy the music, take care, especially in places where someone is below you, not to dislodge rocks. (I nearly killed a good friend along here.)

The summit (N 37 26.702, W 108 05.336) is not large but is enough of a roll to support several people comfortably as they eat their well-earned sandwiches and absorb the great panorama.

The return trip for the main route described here is the same as for the approach—back down the west ridge. However, a little way to the west of the red ledge there is, in the early summer, a snowy chute that can provide a good glissade for those equipped with ice axes and proper experience. The top is quite steep and can be hazardous for the novice. It does offer a quick and exciting way down the steep part of the ridge.

Because of the talus, the steepness, and the total altitude gain, this hike is rated difficult. However, almost anyone in good health and with patience and some carefulness should be able to make it and enjoy it.

Options

From the summit, there is a connecting ridge to Mount Lavender, and from Lavender southeast to Mount Moss and northeast to Centennial. The ridge to Centennial Peak looks impossible, but a technical climber reported that he had done it.

It's possible to begin from Tomahawk Basin off the west side of La Plata Canyon, climbing to the head of the basin then across Moss and Lavender to Hesperus. This is a much more difficult route, but it can be done in a day. Moss and Lavender are not too bad until the last pitch on Lavender, which is close to straight up but possible because of the broken character of the rock. It gives rewarding views. From Lavender across to Hesperus is difficult and a bit discouraging due to several gashes in low points, some of them difficult though not technical.

❖ Transfer Trail ❖

Distance: 3.8 miles (loop)
Starting elevation: 8,930 feet
Elevation loss: 700 feet
Low point: 8,230 feet
Rating: Easy
Time allowed: 2 to 3 hours
Maps: 7.5′ Rampart Hills; San Juan National Forest

Introduction

This hike begins on the Transfer Trail at the Transfer Campground northeast of Mancos but includes parts of

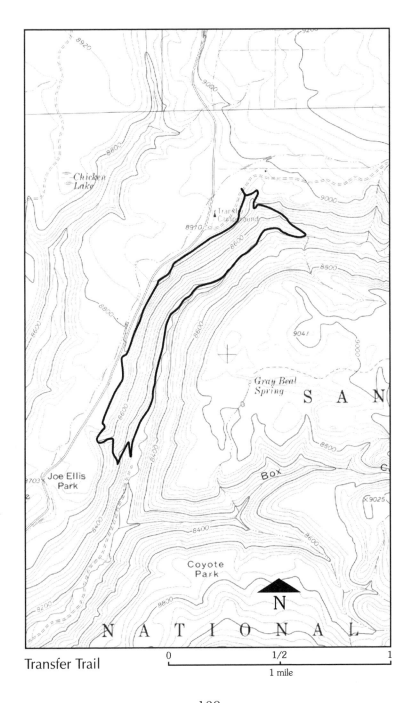

Chicken
Lake

Transfer
Campground

Gray Beal
Spring

S A N

Joe Ellis
Park

Box

Coyote
Park

N

N A T I O N A L

| 0 | 1/2 | 1 |

1 mile

Transfer Trail

four different trails. It's a gem in the western La Platas that has much to offer. If you do this in the fall, you'll want to bring a camera for gorgeous shots of the colorful foliage, with the sheer West Mancos Canyon and the La Platas (already snow-covered, if you're fortunate) in the background.

That's when you're up on top. When you drop down, you'll feel the temperature drop, and you'll be hiking next to a noisy river towered over by tall spruce and fir. It's never flat and it's rocky in places, but it's a nice half-day trip.

The Approach

Take U.S. Highway 160 from Durango twenty-eight miles to Mancos, and turn right at the town's one stoplight onto Colorado Highway 184. Take Colorado Highway 184 just 0.3 mile and turn right (east) on West Mancos Road, which is paved for about a mile and then turns into a good gravel road. It's 10.0 miles (even though the sign says 9) on the West Mancos Road to Transfer Campground, where you'll veer right into the campground. Park in the ample clearing near the large campground sign. Walk back across the campground road to the trailhead (N 37 28,100, W 108 12.476), which should be marked by a brown wooden sign that gives mileages to places as far as the Colorado Trail.

The Hike

Head southeast down the Transfer Trail. You'll already be hearing the river (west fork of the Mancos) below—assuming the ubiquitous cattle aren't too loud.

In 0.3 mile, the Transfer Trail meets the West Mancos Trail (N 37 28.039, W 108 12.316). Go right, continuing downhill and downstream. After another 0.3 mile, you'll be walking right alongside the West Mancos River. The trail, as you soon learn, doesn't stick to the river but meanders above it and back down to it repeatedly. This shaded canyon holds its moisture, as witnessed by moss-covered tree trunks and rocks. Many places along the stream are excellent picnic or wading spots.

After 1.4 miles along the river, just after passing new water-project construction and a concrete platform, you'll join a two-track road. Another one-tenth mile brings you to the Box Canyon Trail (N 37 27.121, W 108 13.004). This is the low point (in elevation) of the hike. Turn right onto a single-track trail heading north uphill toward the West Mancos Road. (If you continue straight, the Box Canyon Trail turns left off of the road in 100 yards, crosses the West Mancos on a flattened log, and heads toward—whatdya know?—Box Canyon.)

The brunt of the uphill climb toward West Mancos Road lasts about 0.5 mile, with a gain of nearly 500 feet. At that point, the trail reaches the rim, joins a dirt road for fifty yards, then veers right off of the road, again as single-track. This is the Rim Trail, and it's the finest stretch of this hike for photos of the La Platas. You'll see the sharp, but small, summit of Sharkstooth on the left, then Centennial, Hesperus (the most prominent), several others, and the smaller Helmet Peak on the right.

It's 1.1 miles along the rim to the Transfer Campground road, which you then follow right for another one-tenth mile to the parking area.

Options

Transfer Campground can be a starting point for several hikes, large and small.

The Big Al Trail begins here; it's a 0.3-mile, handicapped-accessible hike to an overlook of the West Mancos Canyon. The trail is named after Al Lorentzen, a local forest service employee who was disabled by a falling tree while fighting a fire near Yellowstone National Park in 1988.

After the first 0.3 mile on the Transfer Trail, you could take a left on the West Mancos Trail and go east to your heart's content. It's about 4.5 miles to Golconda, an abandoned town with virtually no remnants, and another dozen or so to join the Colorado Trail.

A final option: At the low point, take the Box Canyon Trail the other way, across the West Mancos on the flattened log. Go far enough (seven miles) and you'll connect with the Echo Basin Road. It's probably better to go until you feel like turning around.

❖ Parrott Peak ❖

Distance: 7.0 miles (round trip)
Starting elevation: 8,500 feet
Elevation gain: 3,307 feet
High point: 11,857 feet
Rating: Moderate to difficult
Time allowed: 4 to 5 hours
Maps: 7.5′ Hesperus; 7.5′ La Plata; San Juan National Forest

Introduction

This is an interesting climb early in the season or in the fall, when higher areas are snowed in. It has the advantage of a southern exposure, which keeps the snow off later in the fall and takes it off earlier in the spring. It is also quickly accessible from Durango.

Without a high-clearance vehicle, you may need to do some extra hiking. Drive as far as you feel comfortable doing so, and park.

The hike is basically bushwhacking, although there are some trails from time to time that can be followed profitably. They are not official national forest trails and are not maintained. They're just paths maintained by traffic, both bovine and human.

The Approach

To reach this area, take U.S. Highway 160 west of Hesperus 5.5 miles to the Cherry Creek National Forest road. A short uphill brings you to a wide-open area; head for a little four-wheel-drive road that goes northwest uphill through a gate (which is closed in the winter). Two-wheel-drive vehicles can make it all or most of the way up this road if you're careful, but it climbs steeply in places and has a couple of rough spots. In one mile, this road reaches an old railroad right-of-way. Turn right, and follow this east-northeast about another mile, where it's closed off to vehicles (N 37 20.320, W 108 06.459).

The Hike

Begin by continuing along the railroad grade, on foot. Go about three-fourths mile, then begin heading north-north-

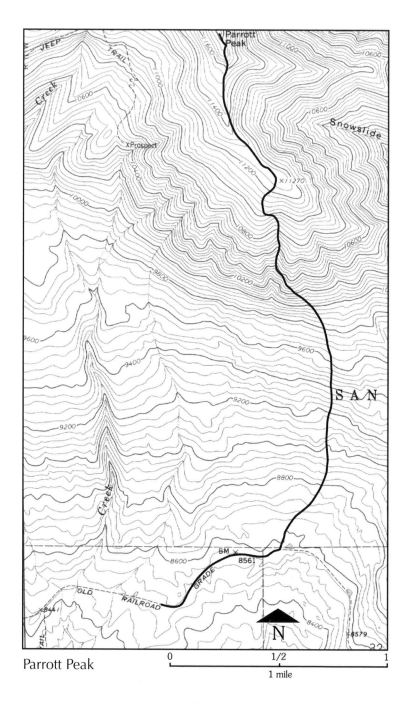

Parrott Peak

0   1/2   1

1 mile

east through the timber. If you start heading up into the timber too soon, you'll end up climbing through huge downfalls, or huge piles of rock, or near-cliffs. It's better to aim a little more east for a broad shoulder that extends south from the summit. In any case, the going is steep and not easy.

The higher you go, the easier it gets, because the timber is less dense. It might be easier at some point to drop down into an open ravine and climb up that.

At last you hit the top of a partially cleared ridge at 11,200 feet (N 37 21.983, W 108 05.971). The actual top is another 0.8 mile northwest along this ridge, most of it easy hiking. The top (N 37 22.499, W 108 06.176) is above timberline and affords fine views down into La Plata Canyon and across the canyon to the eastern range of the La Plata peaks. There are also good views south to the mesa country and on into New Mexico.

The return trip should follow the same general route as the approach. There is nothing extremely difficult about this trip, but not having a trail and having to bushwhack can be frustrating. And the total altitude gain is substantial; consider the rating moderate-plus.

Options

There is an alternate route you may want to consider that is easier and also offers the option of climbing Parrott and Madden peaks in the same trip. It lies principally on the 7.5' Thompson Peak USGS topo map but cuts through a piece of Hesperus and ends up on La Plata.

To take this route, drive to the top of Mancos Hill on U.S. Highway 160, about ten miles west of Hesperus and about a mile past the entrance to Target Tree Campground. At the top of Mancos Hill, turn north onto a gravel road (Madden Peak Road, or Forest Service Road 316). Where there is a choice of roads, continue on Forest Service Road 316. In 6.5 miles, a road goes left up to prominent radio towers. In wet weather, two-wheel-drive vehicles may find it advisable to stop here. Others can go on most of another mile and park in a big meadow.

Start hiking on up this same road another half mile to a split in the road. Either branch of it can be taken from here. The left fork takes you to the top of a ridge, where you should turn right off the road and follow the ridge directly to the summit of Madden Peak (11,972 feet, N 37 22.939, W 108 06.360), in about a mile. There is a trail along much of this ridge; it is an easy climb. Overall, from the big meadow to the top of Madden is a little more than two miles.

To climb Parrott Peak from the top of Madden Peak, go down a ridge to the right (south). Here, you drop down to a saddle at 11,560 feet before ascending another 300 feet to the top of Parrott.

If you choose the right fork of the road at the split, you will stay in a basin below the Madden ridge and head straight for the saddle; this is mostly to the east with a little bias to the north. The route is basically easy. At the saddle, you have a choice as to which peak to do first. Madden is to the left, Parrott to the right.

❖ Madden Peak ❖

Distance: 6.4 miles (round trip)
Starting elevation: 9,000 feet
Elevation gain: 2,972 feet
High point: 11,972 feet
Rating: Moderate to difficult
Time allowed: 4 hours
Maps: 7.5′ La Plata; San Juan National Forest

Introduction

We've discussed routes up Madden and Parrott peaks from the south and west. This route is from the east side, out of La Plata Canyon, with a totally new perspective. During the ascent, there are great views from time to time into the canyon and across it to the eastern ridge of the La Plata peaks. At first you are in the seclusion of deep timber.

. One tip: There are no tried and true trails up either Madden or Parrott peaks from this direction. You're going to end up on some steep ground, and you may have to stop a few times to get your bearings. The result, I predict, will be worth the hardship.

The Approach

For this ascent, take the La Plata Canyon road one-third mile west of Hesperus; it goes north off of U.S. Highway 160. From U.S. Highway 160, it's about 4.0 miles to the village of Mayday and 4.7 miles to where the road turns to gravel and enters the canyon.

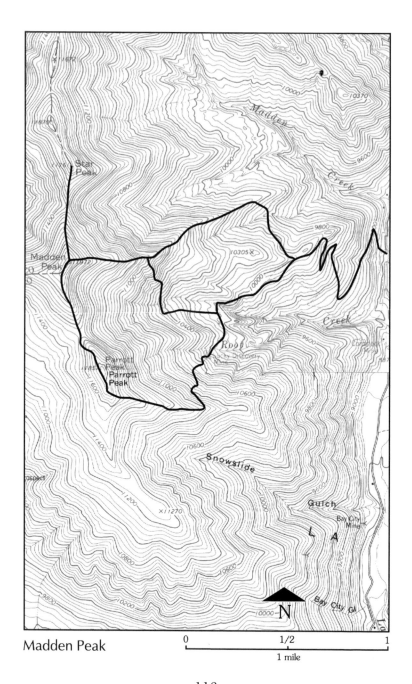

Madden Peak

You'll pass Snowslide and Kroeger campgrounds. A little farther, you'll pass a private picnic ground operated by the Odd Fellows Lodge. Just past the lodge, as you come to the top of a short hill, a little mining road turns left and goes uphill. A dilapidated green bus here was once used as a cabin. This is your trailhead (N 37 22.989, W 108 04.638). It's 2.2 miles on gravel road to this point.

You could drive this road with four-wheel-drive or a high-clearance vehicle, but why not hike it? Distances given in the heading assume you will be hiking all of this road.

The Hike

Begin a steady climb up the west side of the La Plata valley. It's 1.3 miles and 900 feet in elevation gain to the fifth major switchback, from which you get a nice view down into Madden Creek and up to Gibbs Peak. (Don't be confused; Madden Creek's headwaters are between Star and Gibbs peaks.)

At 1.5 miles from the start, you'll come to a split in the road (N 37 22.975, W 108 05.159). The left route seems to be the easier of the two, and we'll detail that one in a moment. The right route goes northwest, and you'll lose a little bit of elevation. In about 0.3 mile, the route divides; take the one bearing left and uphill, which takes you to the crest of a ridge in a hundred yards or so. Follow this ridge to the top of Madden Peak. There are a few steep spots and some downed timber, but it's doable.

Back to the split at 1.5 miles. If you go left, the road also drops downhill before climbing again. Eventually, it swings south to cross a creek, heads briefly uphill, and levels out in a clearing 0.6 mile from the split. Before the road goes downhill into the woods, find the two-track road that heads steeply uphill almost due west (N 37 22.744, W 108 05.554). (This road has re-emerged in the last decade thanks to the diligence of four-wheel-drivers and ATVers.) Take this two-track 0.3 mile to its end; here you might find a faint cut heading north-northwest. In any case, head northwest, eventually leaving the faint cut, and head up a steep slope 0.4 mile to the ridge coming down from Madden Peak.

Once you reach the ridge, it's another 0.4 mile along this ridge to the top (N 37 22.939, W 108 06.360). Near the top, the going gets very rocky and a bit slower, but there's nothing extremely difficult. The mileage given assumes you'll retrace this route back down to the valley bottom and your car.

Options

Options aplenty here. To climb Parrott first: Instead of taking the two-track road that goes steeply uphill to the west, continue on the road back down into the timber. You may stumble across the ruins of an old mine just as the road ends. A trail continues briefly but isn't easy to follow. Eventually, you'll be bushwhacking. Head south-southwest as best you can up to a ridge, then follow that west and north to the peak.

To climb the saddle between Madden and Parrott peaks: Take the steep two-track road to its end (N 37 22.752, W 108 05.868), and instead of bearing northwest, continue west and southwest to the saddle at 11,550 feet (N 37 22.655, W 108 06.294). It looks as if the ridge south to Parrott Peak is nearly impossible, but it works out if you pass through the saddle and around the cliff. Getting up to Madden Peak from here is easier.

❖ Gibbs Peak ❖

Distance: 7.8 miles (round trip)
Starting elevation: 9,080 feet
Elevation gain: 3,206 feet
High point: 12,286 feet
Rating: Moderate
Time allowed: 4 to 5 hours
Maps: 7.5′ La Plata; San Juan National Forest

Introduction

Compared to many La Plata hikes, Gibbs Peak is an easy one because it has a road most of the way up and at least a semblance of a trail from where the road ends. And it only has a few steep spots to the summit.

Every hike in the La Platas is steep, and a drive up the canyon shows why. It's a narrow valley that rises steeply on both sides. The good news: The valley floor gets most of the traffic, so when you rise above it, you'll likely get some solitude—assuming that's what you seek.

The Approach

From Durango, it's eleven miles on U.S. Highway 160 to Hesperus, then another one-third mile to the La Plata Canyon road, which goes north off of U.S. Highway 160. It's about 4.7 miles to where the road turns to gravel, just past Mayday.

You'll pass Snowslide and Kroeger campgrounds. It's 3.2 miles on gravel road to the Gibbs Peak road, a four-wheel-

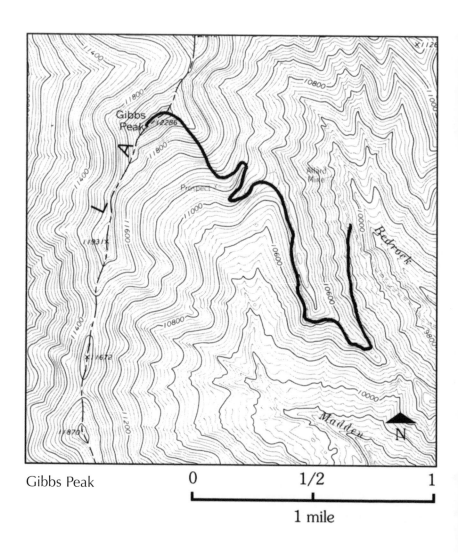

Gibbs Peak

0	1/2	1

1 mile

drive road that heads left (northwest) uphill (N 37 23.495, W 108 04.294). If you cross Bedrock Creek, you've gone too far.

The Hike

Begin up a four-wheel-drive road that varies between sections of steep climbs and sections of gentle rises. One little glitch has developed recently. In about one-quarter mile, you'll come to a cabin tucked into the earth on the left side of the road. The landowners here at one point closed the gate to shut off traffic and posted "no trespassing" signs, but as this book was being completed, they'd posted a sign that allowed hikers and vehicles to pass through.

So it might be possible to drive up this road, and it might be okay to hike through here. Or, you may have to detour around to the north of this private land—but not very far. If you stay down by Bedrock Creek, or a little north of there, until you get past the private property, you should be okay. The forest service is attempting to work out a public easement through here, or at least an understanding with the landowners. The mileage for this hike assumes that the landowners are allowing people to pass through their property on the road.

In 1.4 miles, you'll come to a major switchback (N 37 24.256, W 108 05.270), with the road going uphill (south) to the left, and a less obvious road continuing straight to the Allard Mine. Go uphill to the left, and in another 0.6 mile, a major switchback changes your direction to the west, then to the northwest. The road becomes a bit rockier for a while.

After a flat section that heads north-northwest, the road heads west and begins to climb up the mountain. At a point where downfall blocks the road (3.3 miles from the start of the hike), it's best to begin hiking west and southwest of the mountainside. There should be a hint of a trail here. Soon, you'll again turn northwest and climb a rocky ridge toward the summit (N 37 24.590, W 108 06.132). You may have to use your hands in a couple of places, but there's little exposure.

Options

If you can find it, there's a little trail that leaves the road just north of Madden Creek. You can follow that trail and eventually end up going north on a little-used road that connects with the Gibbs Peak road described above at about 10,800 feet. That would be one way to avoid the private property on the road.

There's also a road on the north side of Bedrock Creek, and it would be possible to take this far enough west to avoid the property. This would mean some bushwhacking at some point to get back up to the road and a journey up and down a steep ravine, but it could be done.

As stated in the introduction, private-property issues continue to crop up in the San Juans, particularly in the La Platas. Don't trespass, but if you have questions, talk to officials with the U.S. National Forest.

HIKES BETWEEN DURANGO AND SILVERTON

❖ Hermosa Trail ❖

Distance: 8 miles (round trip), with additional options
Starting elevation: 7,800 feet
Elevation gain: 240 feet
High point: 8,040 feet
Rating: Easy
Time allowed: 3.5 to 4.5 hours
Maps: 7.5' Hermosa; 7.5' Monument Hill; 7.5' Elk Creek;
San Juan National Forest

Introduction

Hermosa Trail is in the heart of a very large roadless area. There are high ridges and many canyons. The whole area contains many thousands of acres. The main trail is nineteen miles long, and there are many side trails. To explore this area thoroughly would take many days of backpacking. However, good day and half-day hikes can be done from both the south and north ends quite easily.

This is excellent elk-hunting territory and has good trout streams as well. There are also many deer.

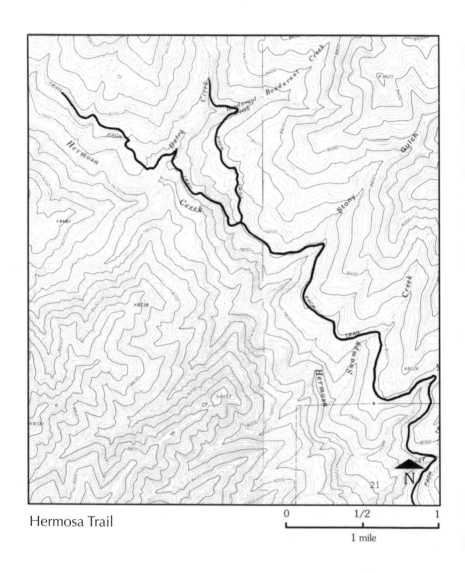

Hermosa Trail

0   1/2   1

1 mile

The trail at first follows the contour of Hermosa Creek but is several hundred feet above it so that you look down into the canyon below and up at the heavily wooded mountains. Across the canyon, the hills rise up above timberline to the 13,000-foot peaks of the La Platas.

The trail is one of the widest, best maintained, and most heavily used in southwestern Colorado. You can encounter mountain bikers, cattle, and even dirt bikes, which are allowed on the southern section. It is also one of the easiest to hike, for there is no major altitude change. Along the trail are big trees, open vistas, and wildflowers.

The Approach

From Thirty-Second Street and Main Avenue in Durango, take U.S. Highway 550 north 8.8 miles and turn left onto County Road 203. This turn is 0.4 mile past Hermosa village and just after the highway crosses Hermosa Creek, before the railroad crossing. Go a hundred yards to a "T" intersection and turn right, onto the Lower Hermosa Road, which parallels the highway briefly.

Follow this paved road, which eventually turns to gravel, uphill 3.7 miles to the Lower Hermosa Trailhead, a forest service campsite and trailhead on the left. Follow signs to trailhead parking (N 37 27.351, W 107 51.471). In actuality, it's easier to ignore this new official trailhead and start at the end of the road (N 37 27.568, W 107 51.393), just 0.3 mile after the turnoff to the official trailhead.

The Hike

The trail stays at approximately the same elevation as it crosses several side streams that may be fairly well dried

Hiking on the Hermosa Trail.

up, or they may be flowing and muddy, making hiking boots useful though not needed on other parts of the trail.

At four miles, the trail divides (N 37 28.963, W 107 52.698). The left branch descends 500 feet in the next mile to a good footbridge (N 37 29.344, W 107 53.188) across Dutch Creek. Just beyond here, you can step off to the left to Hermosa Creek itself. Both of these are good fishing streams. Hiking beyond this brings you back up to the previous level. You can continue on as far as interest and time permit.

If you take the right branch at the trail split, you are on the Dutch Creek Trail, although you do not see the creek itself until you go up the trail a mile. There is one fairly steep hill of about 250 feet that you go down before reaching the creek. Again, you can hike on this trail as far as time and interest permit. There is a small, open, grassy meadow where you first come to the stream.

Whichever trail you take, return by the same route to the road and your parking place.

Options

Those who may want to consider doing the entire length of the trail have two options. One is to backpack, spending at least one night on the trail; the other is to spend a long day hiking at a good pace with only a few short rest periods. This is best done from the north end, because there is a net drop of 1,000 feet from north to south. It is not all downhill, however; there is the 500-foot climb out of the Dutch Creek crossing described above, plus two other rather large hills. It is a very rewarding hike, with ever-changing scenery. You start out in a wide meadow bounded by forest on the mounting sides of the valley, followed by low canyon walls. You end by doing a traverse of the mountainside with the creek far below and the top high above. The scenery is spectacular, especially during the fall color season, from the last week of September through the first ten days of October.

For access to the north end, see the following hike description for Corral Draw–Hermosa Trail.

❖ Corral Draw– ❖ Hermosa Trail

Distance: 10 miles (one way)
Starting elevation: 10,400 feet
Elevation loss: 2,400 feet
High point/Low point: 10,900/8,500 feet
Rating: Moderate
Time allowed: 5 to 6 hours
Maps: 7.5′ Hermosa Peak; 7.5′ Elk Creek; San Juan
  National Forest

Introduction

This is a partial loop or point-to-point hike. The Corral Draw Trail makes a good hike combined with the northern end of the Hermosa Trail. This description starts at the top and descends to the Hermosa Trail with a gentle climb out to the Hermosa trailhead. Of course, it could be hiked the other way, but Corral Draw is a substantial climb. It stays near the drainage except near the top and is mostly in heavy timber. The part of the Hermosa Trail used here starts out in a canyon with timber above and then moves out into a wider, graceful meadow at the upper end.

The Approach

From Thirty-Second Street and Main Avenue in Durango, take U.S. Highway 550 north twenty-five miles and turn left (west) into the main entrance for Durango Mountain Resort. At the northeast corner of the large parking lot, pick up the gravel road (Forest Service Road 578) going north; it soon turns back west and climbs in several switchbacks up the ski hill, with some of the runs visible to the south. At the top, the road turns north; in a half mile, it turns left downhill (Relay Creek Road goes north). Follow the road west down into Hermosa Park—a nice, secluded, meadowed valley. Where the road reaches the bottom of the valley, there is a little road that turns off to the left (south) and soon fords the East Fork of Hermosa Creek, usually a small stream. Just beyond the stream there is a nice trailhead area with generous parking, a corral, and toilet facilities. Park your extra car here (N 37 37.792, W 107 54.952).

Take the other car back to the main road and continue west on it. The gravel stops at this point, and the road goes on the rest of the way over dirt; the steep parts can be difficult when they are wet.

The road swings northwest, and in a little over a mile, it fords the main stream of Hermosa Creek. This is a wide crossing with a rocky bottom. After the spring snowmelt

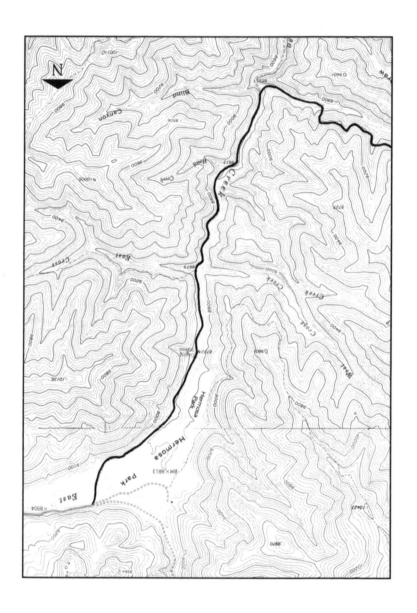

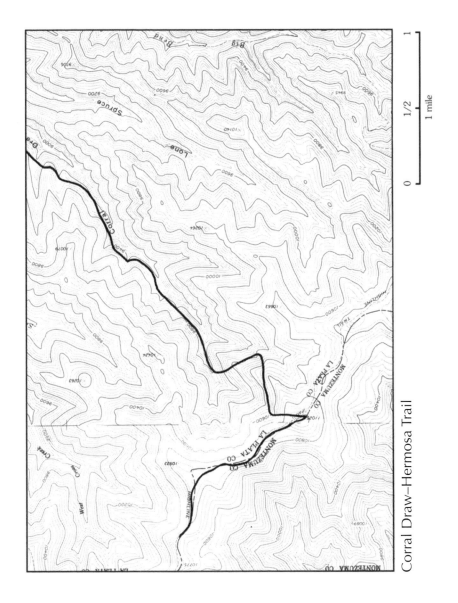

Corral Draw–Hermosa Trail

0   1/2   1

1 mile

133

(the third week of June or later in some years), most cars can make this—don't lose momentum through the water. Four-wheel-drives are better here, but except for this problem, other cars should be able to get up the road when it is dry.

About a mile beyond the ford, turn sharply left on the Hotel Draw road (Forest Service Road 550). Follow it through a valley and to the top of the ridge in three and one-half miles. Continue following the road, now going south along the ridge, to a split. The right side (Forest Service Road 550) goes down the west side of the ridge via Scotch Creek to the Dolores Valley. The left side (now Forest Service Road 564) is your road; follow it a little more than a hundred yards to the Colorado Trail. Park here (N 37 38.401, W 107 58.060).

The Hike

Take the trail south, at first steeply uphill, for about 1.4 miles to where the Corral Draw Trail starts off to the left, downhill (N 37 37.729, W 107 58.807). Corral Draw now descends 2,400 feet in 5.5 miles in a well-defined trail, much of the time through a meadow but sometimes in large timber. Hunters like this trail in the fall.

At the bottom of the route, Hermosa Creek must be crossed (N 37 35.564, W 107 56.186). It is a large stream and may have to be waded. There is a usable log to the north a couple of hundred yards, but that leaves you on the west side, where a cliff comes down to the stream edge. There are some stepping stones along here, but you still may have to step in the water a time or two. South of the regular crossing there was at one time a pile of debris that you may still be able to use for crossing. Almost immediately after crossing the creek, you will find the Hermosa Creek Trail. Take it to the left (north) gently uphill for three miles to its start, where your extra car should be parked. The climb out provides more than 300 feet of elevation gain, well spread out over the entire distance—just a pleasant hike.

Options

Hikers who want to approach this trail from the west side should take the Roaring Forks Road east off of Colorado Highway 145, some seven miles south of Rico. It starts out as Forest Service Road 435; later it meets Forest Service Road 564—take this to the left. In several more miles, it meets the Colorado Trail one and one-half miles north of Orphan Butte. Stay with the road another four to five miles, where it should meet the Colorado Trail again. (They have been paralleling each other for these miles.) Here, you can park and hike the Colorado Trail northeast about a mile to the Corral Draw trailhead, which will now be a right turn.

❖ Jones Creek Trail ❖

Distance: 8.6 miles (round trip)
Starting elevation: 7,720 feet
Elevation gain: 1,560 feet
High point: 9,280 feet
Rating: Moderate
Time allowed: 4 to 6 hours
Maps: 7.5' Hermosa; San Juan National Forest

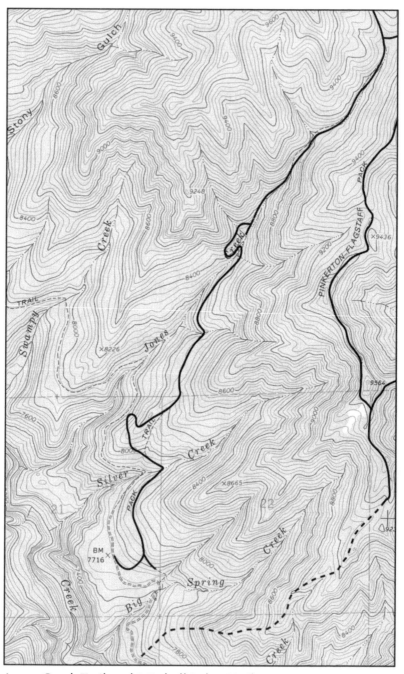

Jones Creek Trail and Mitchell Lakes Trail

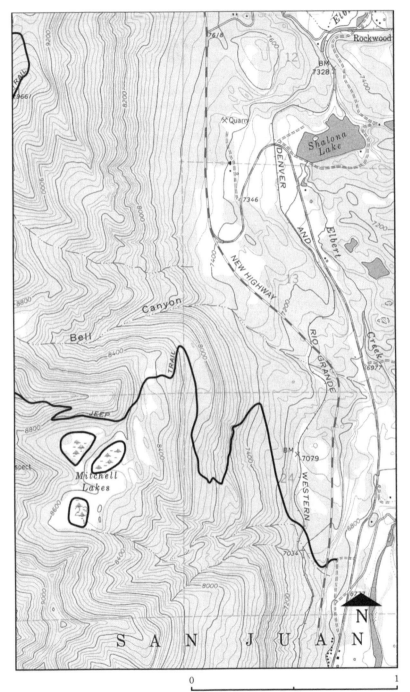

Rockwood

BM
7328

X Quarry

Shalona
Lake

7346

Canyon

Bell

TRAIL

JEEP

8800

spect.

Mitchell
Lakes

BM
7079

7034

S A N   J U A N

N

0   1

1 mile

Introduction

Jones Creek Trail is an old trail that was recently rebuilt and partially rerouted, taking out the steepest and most rutted sections. The new one is delightful, mostly in big timber—ponderosa pine, fir, and spruce—with a small meadow at its terminus. It is located in much the same area as the Hermosa Trail.

The Approach

From Thirty-Second Street and Main Avenue in Durango, take U.S. Highway 550 north 8.8 miles and turn left onto County Road 203. This turn is 0.4 mile past Hermosa village and just after the highway crosses Hermosa Creek, before the railroad crossing. Go a hundred yards to a "T" intersection and turn right, onto the Lower Hermosa Road, which parallels the highway briefly.

Follow this road uphill 3.7 miles to the Lower Hermosa trailhead, a forest service campsite and trailhead on the left. Follow signs to the unobtrusive trailhead parking area. The road ends just 0.3 mile past the official trailhead.

Walk back out to the Lower Hermosa Road, and go uphill a short distance to find the Jones Creek Trailhead (N 37 27.378, W 107 51.413), going uphill on the right side of the road.

The Hike

The trail climbs rather rapidly through switchbacks at first, levels out, climbs again, drops some, and then mostly climbs when it meets up with Jones Creek. The trail hugs the creek's west bank and ends in a large clearing, where it meets the Pinkerton–Flagstaff Trail (N 37 29.464, W 107 49.931). Along the way, the trees are high enough and close enough in some places to give an air of mystery. The abundance of shade makes it a good hot-weather hike. Unfortunately, this means that often the view is obscured. When you do get views, you can see down into the rugged Hermosa Creek area.

The trail is fairly popular with mountain bikers, who can pop around sharp corners suddenly. Most mountain bikers are very courteous and slow down immediately.

With more than eight miles in the round trip, many hikers will be satisfied by just going out and back, but several other options are available for those who want a longer hike.

Options

At the top, you'll meet the Pinkerton–Flagstaff Trail, which goes along the top of the ridge in basically a north-south direction. This is the spine of the main high ridge east of Hermosa Creek. The trail runs along much of the top to the west above the Hermosa Cliffs, with the Animas River to the east. There is a lot of wild, roadless area between these two streams. On the ridge, the trail spends most of its length higher than 9,400 feet, going up to 9,661 feet at one point.

Going left on the Pinkerston–Flagstaff Trail takes you in several miles up to the Dutch Creek Trail. The right fork is more practical—in 2.6 miles, it curves southeast and parallels Jones Creek at a higher level and at a gradually widening distance. In this distance, it intersects the trail coming up from Mitchell Lakes and the east side of the major ridge. The top of the ridge has quite a bit of open space, presenting long-distance views into the high peaks of the La Plata Mountains to the west and to the top of Missionary Ridge to the east. It is a good place to take a well-earned rest from the climb and drink in the splendor of nature's best. You could get down to U.S. Highway 550 in another 4.4 miles. See the Mitchell Lakes Trail description below for this east side.

❖ Mitchell Lakes ❖

Distance: 8 miles (round trip) to the top of the ridge above the lakes
Starting elevation: 6,800 feet
Elevation gain: 2,600 feet
High point: 9,400 feet
Rating: Moderate
Time allowed: 4 to 5.5 hours
Maps: 7.5' Hermosa; San Juan National Forest

Introduction

The Mitchell Lakes as such are not much to brag about. There are four little lakes in the group, located on private land. They are shallow and filled with marsh grass, but they occupy a secluded shelf surrounded by meadow, which, in turn, is surrounded by ponderosa pine and some aspen. There are perhaps a hundred acres of open space; here you can get a feeling of both spaciousness and insulation from the rest of the world. The hike itself yields rewarding views of the Animas Valley and Missionary Ridge beyond.

The Approach

From Thirty-Second Street and Main Avenue in Durango, follow U.S. Highway 550 twelve miles north to a right turn downhill on County Road 250. Go 0.2 mile and turn left onto what's called County Road 250 North. It's another 0.1 mile to a gravel road on the left-hand side, Forest Service Road 740, going west. Drive another hundred yards or so and park wherever there's a good spot (N 37 27.364, W 107 48.238). A four-wheel-drive vehicle could go all the way to the lakes, but it is not recommended because the road is very rough and steep in places.

The Hike

Begin hiking up the four-wheel-drive road, crossing under the highway in a huge metal culvert. In a quarter mile, you'll cross the Durango & Silverton Narrow Gauge Railroad tracks.

Follow the road all the way to the lakes area, which is three miles. The lakes themselves are private property; if you keep to the road at the north side of the lakes, you will be on public property. (The forest service is considering a land swap that would put more of this area in the public domain.) The road is closed to automotive travel about here, but it continues as a trail to the top of the ridge. The lakes are very shallow, but they add a nice touch to the scene in their open-meadow surroundings, a kind of respite from the heavy timber and steep road both below and above them.

At the top of the ridge, you strike the Pinkerton–Flagstaff Trail going north and south along the top of the ridge. There are excellent views both east and west from the top. If you want to go back the way you came, you will have eight total miles of good hiking through variable terrain—a good half-day hike.

Options

The other option is to go down the west side with another car parked near the beginning of the Hermosa Trail. There are two ways to do this. Turn right at the top, and you will have a good trail all the way, mostly downhill, but it will be about seven miles. (See the Jones Creek Trail description for the way down to the Lower Hermosa Road via the Jones Creek Trail.)

Turn left at the top, and you can be down to the road in two, but more adventuresome, miles. The first 0.3 mile is on trail, but it quits, and the rest of the hike is a bushwhack that must be navigated. To do this, follow the crest of the ridge to where it begins to go down; stay with the crest until it disappears in a steeper descent. Big Spring Creek will be the first drainage off to the right and will be quite some distance down at first. Cliff Creek is a smaller drainage to the south of Big Spring. Follow the highest part of the ridge on down to the road between these two drainages. Most of the time you will be in timber with a few open places. In a few spots, there will be small, low brush, which can be a nuisance. There will also be a fairly steep descent of about 200 yards not very far from the bottom. This will bring you to the road below the Hermosa Creek trailhead perhaps as much as a quarter mile. Therefore, some bias to the right would be useful if that is where you parked your second car.

❖ Goulding Creek ❖

Distance: 6 miles (round trip)
Starting elevation: 7,900 feet
Elevation gain: 2,170 feet
High point: 10,070 feet
Rating: Moderate
Time allowed: 3.5 to 4.5 hours
Maps: 7.5′ Electra Lake; San Juan National Forest

Introduction

Ten miles north of Durango, a series of high bluffs begins on the west side of U.S. Highway 550. These bluffs, known as Hermosa Cliffs, continue on north for sixteen miles. In places they are precipitous and look invulnerable. But they can be breached via three good trails. Near the south end, ahead of the genuine cliffs, is the Mitchell Lakes Trail; near the middle is Goulding Creek; and near the north end is Elbert Creek.

Goulding Creek Trail approaches from an area that looks nearly impossible from below, but it turns out to be a very good trail and not terribly steep, thanks to many switchbacks. It is a trail satisfactory for horses. Horse-riding hunters use it in the fall, and cattlemen use it through the summer.

This is a beautiful hike at any time, but especially during late September and early October, when the aspen leaves are at their golden best.

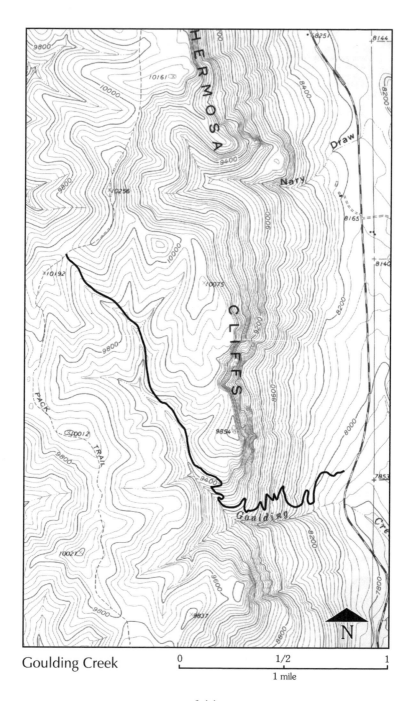

Goulding Creek

The Approach

From Thirty-Second Street and Main Avenue in Durango, go 16.5 miles north on U.S. Highway 550, and look for a small wooden sign on the left side of the road that says "Goulding Creek Trail," and a dirt road heading up. It's not prominent, so you'll have to look for it—and be careful of the traffic. This should help: It's almost exactly one mile past the entrance to Tamarron, a resort with a golf course and condos on the east side of the highway.

Once you find the road, drive up it about fifty yards to where it makes a "T", and turn left. Go downhill 0.2 mile to the end of this road and park. The road is a little rough but usually is no problem for any vehicle. The trail should be obvious where it heads uphill to the west from here (N 37 30.715, W 107 49.176).

The Hike

The trail heads fairly steeply uphill to the west, then swings back south and is almost flat for a quarter mile before heading back uphill, tending to the west as it switches back numerous times (thirty-two by one count) up through a beautiful aspen grove. It's steep in parts and can be treacherous if wet. At some points, there are open spots in the trees that provide good views of the valley below and Missionary Ridge beyond.

This trail is always slightly above Goulding Creek until you break through the Hermosa Cliffs at 1.5 miles up the trail and after 1,500 feet of altitude gain. At about that point, you'll come to a stock gate; one gate "post" is a large fir tree. In a matter of yards, you're right next to the creek, and the trail does not climb nearly as steeply as it follows the valley bottom. Goulding Creek during much of the summer is just a trickling stream; it sometimes ceases to flow altogether.

When you get through the cliffs, you are ushered into a peaceful green valley surrounded by tall timber on the hillsides. A couple of old log cabins are located in the valley. One near the top of the ridge is a cattleman's line camp.

For a short hike, you could terminate here, but it is worth going on. The main trail stays fairly close to the stream most of the time, moving northwest to the top of the ridge, where it ends by joining the Pinkerton–Flagstaff Trail, a north-south trail at the crest of the ridge (N 37 31.578, W 107 50.639). This is between Dutch Creek and Jones Creek.

The last quarter mile to the top is surrounded by acres and acres of lupine. During much of the summer, beginning quite early, this is a sea of blue floral display, well worth the hike by itself.

At the top, you look westward down into the Dutch Creek drainage and on across the vast Hermosa Creek roadless area. This is one of the best elk summering grounds in Southwest Colorado.

Options

The three miles given in the heading presuppose a return back down the same trail. However, those who want a long hike have a couple of other options. Either of these would mean coming out at or near the end of the Lower Hermosa Road, where you would need another car or someone to pick you up, for you would be nearly fifteen miles by road from the original parking place.

The first and shortest route is to go left down to Jones Creek Trail. To do this, first follow Pinkerton–Flagstaff Trail south for 3.0 miles to the top of the Jones Creek Trail, and take Jones Creek on down another 4.3 miles to the Hermosa Road, joining the road below its upper end. Or, instead of going to the Hermosa Road, you could skip the Jones Creek route: Go south beyond its start on the Pinkerton–Flagstaff Trail another two miles and head down the Mitchell Lakes Trail on the east side. This would reduce the highway distance between parking places to only five miles.

The second option is via the Dutch Creek Trail. The easy but long way to join this trail is to go right (north) up the Pinkerton–Flagstaff Trail 1.5 miles to where the Dutch Creek Trail joins it from the west. It is about 6.5 miles down this trail to the Hermosa Trail and another 5.0 miles down (left, or southeast) that trail to the Lower Hermosa Road.

❖ Forebay Lake ❖

Distance: 3.4 miles (round trip)
Starting elevation: 8,150 feet
Elevation gain: 220 feet
High point: 8,370 feet
Rating: Easy
Time allowed: 1.5 to 2.5 hours
Maps: 7.5′ Electra Lake; San Juan National Forest

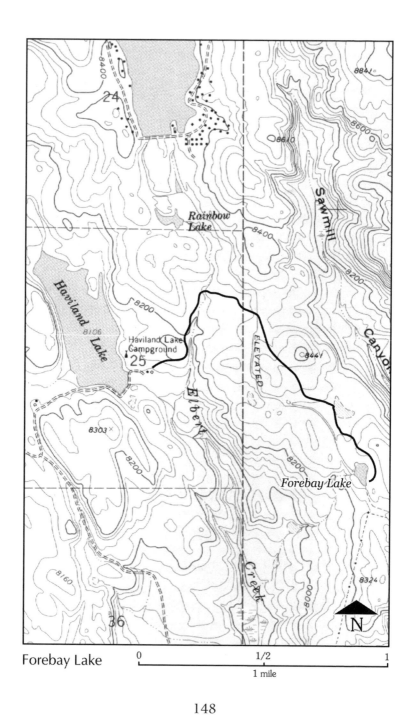

Forebay Lake

0   1/2   1

1 mile

Introduction

This is a very easy hike, good for the whole family, with little elevation change. It follows a four-wheel-drive road through rather dense vegetation, which makes it a bit unique in this part of the state. Forebay Lake is a good fishing spot. It has been a supply lake for the power plant at Tacoma along the Animas River but is currently being bypassed for that purpose.

The Approach

From Thirty-Second Street and Main Avenue in Durango, take U.S. Highway 550 north 17.5 miles to a right turn (east) on the Haviland Lake Road. Haviland Lake is a lovely larger lake with a nice forest service campground and good fishing. Drive in from the highway about a mile; shortly after crossing the bridge at the southeast corner of Haviland, veer to the right instead of following the main road to the campground. In another 0.1 mile, veer to the right onto a dirt road and park here in a large area for cars (N 37 31.974, W 107 48.334). The road gets rough after this spot. Four-wheel-drive vehicles could drive all the way to Forebay Lake, but that's not what we're here for.

The Hike

Head east up the road. In 0.4 mile, you'll have to ford Elbert Creek as it comes down from Electra Lake to the north (N 37 32.224, W 107 48.115). It's usually possible to do this without getting wet; just north of where the road crosses the creek, there's a small waterfall and a log or two that should get you across.

Just after you cross Elbert Creek, a trail heads right (east) off the road; this is a shortcut that'll save you a few minutes. The trail cuts through a meadow under a power line, then rejoins the road.

From here, you will be following a big pipe that carries the water supply for Tacoma from Electra Lake, a mile farther north. (Electra Lake is a large and attractive place but is a private area.)

In about 1.4 miles from the start, you'll hike past a small lake/pond on your left (east). This is not Forebay Lake; continue on 0.3 mile to Forebay (N 37 31.640, W 107 47.390), where a huge round metal tower looms above the lake, reflecting off of it.

Just southeast of Forebay, you can stand at the top of the bluff overlooking the Animas River and the power plant a thousand feet below. At the right time of day in the summer, you might even see the little narrow-gauge train at the bottom of the canyon carrying sightseers between Durango and Silverton. Across the Animas Valley, the view is up the steep, high western side of Missionary Ridge.

The road stops at Forebay Lake, so the return must be made back the way you came.

❖ Elbert Creek ❖

Distance: 8 miles (round trip)
Starting elevation: 8,800 feet
Elevation loss: 1,650 feet
Low point: 10,450 feet
Rating: Easy, but fairly long
Time allowed: 4 to 5 hours
Maps: 7.5′ Electra Lake; 7.5′ Elk Creek; San Juan
National Forest

Introduction

The Elbert Creek Trail breaks through the Hermosa Cliffs a couple of miles south of Durango Mountain Resort (formerly called Purgatory Ski Area). Cattle are a fairly constant fixture on this trail, particularly at the beginning. But it's a nice trail, especially when aspen change in the fall.

The Approach

From Thirty-Second Street and Main Avenue in Durango, go twenty-two miles north on U.S. Highway 550 to Needles Country Square, a small business area with a gas station, a liquor store, a café, and more. Park at the south end of this business area; there is trailhead parking adjacent to a wooden fence that is part of a corral.

The Hike

Enter the corral (N 37 35.534, W 107 49.446) through a metal gate, heading west, and leave the corral through a

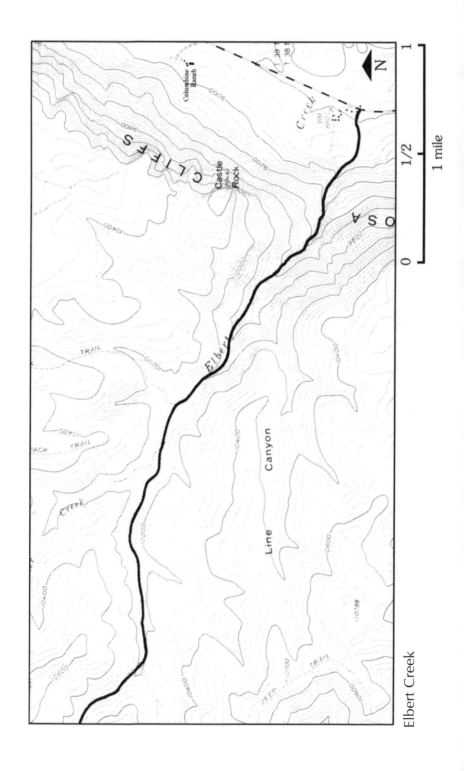

Elbert Creek

second gate. The trail is somewhat indistinct as you continue west along the south side of a barbed-wire fence. Eventually, the trail becomes more obvious. You'll enter the national forest boundary in a couple of hundred yards, and 0.2 mile from the start, you come to Elbert Creek. During the spring snowmelt, it can be a good-sized stream and a problem for crossing. You may elect just to wade it; later on in the summer it may be completely dry. It has to be crossed again higher up, but this first crossing is the only difficult one.

The trail turns north, and in another 0.1 mile, you'll pass a large house owned by someone with great views of the Needle Mountains—Pigeon and Turret are distinct from here. The trail then turns south and west, rising through some long switchbacks and soon entering a deep canyon that makes its way through the Hermosa Cliffs. It climbs gradually through big timber in four miles to the top of the ridge that separates this drainage from the Hermosa drainage. It is a good trail most of the way. At one point, it joins and follows a road for a few hundred yards. It follows along the south side of the creek at this point. You should be able to pick it up again where the road turns north to cross the creek. It is another one and one-half miles to the top of the ridge.

This hike description only takes you to the top of the ridge; the return is by the same route. The trail, however, turns south along the top and eventually follows Little Elk Creek down to the Hermosa Trail in six miles. This route is not recommended unless you are prepared to stay overnight.

Options

The road that you cross before reaching the top of the ridge is a good dirt road. It is possible to terminate the hike there, only three miles from its beginning. This road is reached from Durango Mountain Resort. To get to it, turn off of U.S. Highway 550 at the ski-area entrance. Go uphill on this road until you see a gravel road (Hermosa Park Road, Forest Service Road 578) heading right (north). Take this as it rises above the ski area in a series of switchbacks to the top of the ridge. Where Forest Service Road 578 turns right in a flat spot, take a left turn instead onto Elbert Creek Road (Forest Service Road 581). In about 5.4 miles of twisting road, you come to the spot where the Elbert Creek Trail joins it. This road is on the whole pretty good. Two-wheel-drive vehicles can use it when it is dry, although there are a few rough spots. Those who want an easy hike could drive to this point and hike down.

You could drive on another three miles to the northern trailhead for the Dutch Creek Trail. You could do an out-and-back on the trail. It would be about a fourteen-mile hike from this trailhead, taking Dutch and Hermosa Creek trails, to the southern terminus of the Hermosa Creek Trail.

❖ Purgatory Flats ❖

Distance: 8 miles (round trip)
Starting elevation: 8,800 feet
Elevation loss: 1,100 feet
Low point: 7,700 feet
Rating: Easy
Time allowed: 3.5 to 4.5 hours
Maps: 7.5′ Engineer Mountain; 7.5′ Electra Lake; San
  Juan National Forest

Introduction

This hike is a reverse climb: You begin at the top, hike
down to the Animas River below (a drop of more than
1,000 feet), then climb back out of the canyon. It's a good
half-day hike, but the views, which are great by many
standards, are not quite as dramatic as those afforded by
the Molas Trail into the same canyon several miles
upstream. Cascade Canyon is deep and narrow with a
rugged beauty all its own.

The Approach

Durango Mountain Resort is in the process of developing
land around the highway, so you may have to play a little
bit of find-the-trailhead. The trailhead used to be at
Purgatory Campground, but because of a land swap, the
campground no longer exists. The good news is that the
Purgatory Flats Trail will survive and will remain accessible
to the public.

155

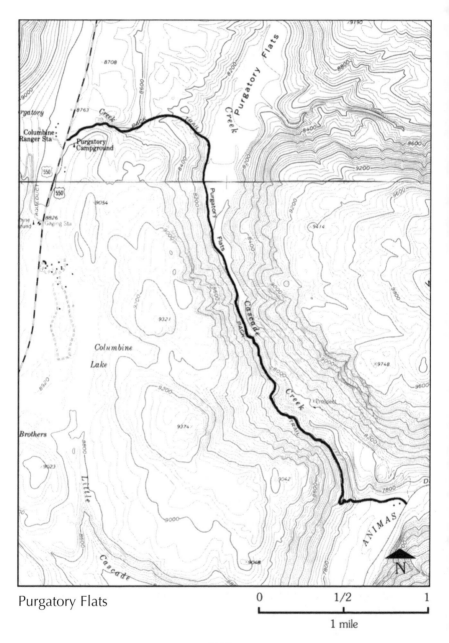

Purgatory Flats

0   1/2   1
1 mile

Here's how to find it: From Thirty-Second Street and Main Avenue in Durango, go 25.0 miles north on U.S. Highway 550. When you see the entrance to the ski resort (west of the highway), begin scanning for the trailhead on your right (east side of the highway). The forest service said it will have to move the trailhead around, probably for several years, as development (homes, condos, commercial space) continues. However, there should be signs along the road pointing you to the trailhead.

In the fall of 2005, the trailhead and parking area (N 37 37.719, W 107 48.486) could be found by taking the Tacoma Village entrance across the highway from the main Durango Mountain Resort entrance and going about 200 yards to the end of that road.

The Hike

The trail heads eastward, dropping down along little Purgatory Creek and soon crossing the creek. You'll begin to get views of the Twilight Peaks (West Needle Mountains) to the northeast and Purgatory Flats below. In about 1.3 miles, the trail reaches the flats (N 37 37.793, W 107 47.608) and heads almost due south, now following along Cascade Creek.

In another three-quarters mile, the creek enters its narrow canyon in its final plunge to the river. Most of the hike is close to the west side of Cascade Creek, but it sometimes moves up to 250 feet above the stream in search of an adequate bench. At the end, the trail zigzags back and forth down to the Animas River just below the mouth of Cascade Creek. There is a nice flat area on both sides of the river for resting and picnicking. The east side is larger than

Looking out of Cascade Canyon along Purgatory Trail with
Engineer Mountain in the distance.

the west side and has some good tree coverage. There is a good bridge across the Animas River (N 37 35.869, W 107 46.574) for hikers and horses.

Option

At the river crossing, the planned half-day hike returns back up the same trail. The trail itself, for backpackers, quickly crosses the train tracks and continues northeast along the east side of the river, always near to it, for another five and one-half miles. There, it joins a trail heading up Needle Creek. That trail goes up into Chicago Basin for access to Fourteeners Eolus, Sunlight, and Windom, and on up farther to Columbine Pass.

❖ Potato (Spud) Lake ❖

Distance: 2 miles (round trip)
Starting elevation: 9,360 feet
Elevation gain: 440 feet
High point: 9,800 feet
Rating: Easy
Time allowed: 1 hour
Maps: 7.5′ Engineer Mountain; San Juan National Forest

Introduction

Spud Lake is a short, easy hike and a rewarding one. The lake is officially named Potato Lake. Rising as a steep cliff

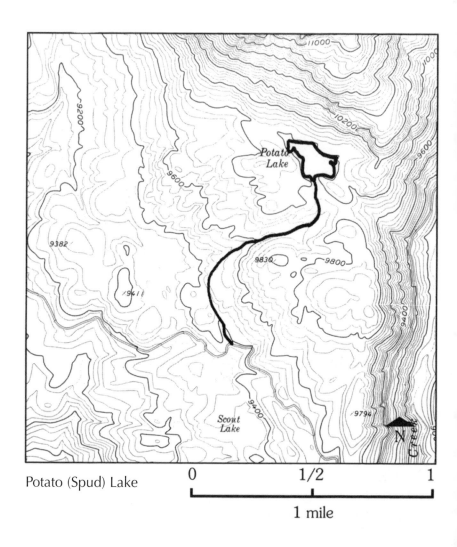

Potato (Spud) Lake

0   1/2   1

1 mile

out of the north side of the lake is Potato Hill. The lake and cliff are known popularly as Spud Lake and Spud Mountain.

The Approach

From Thirty-Second Street and Main Avenue in Durango, take U.S. Highway 550 north about twenty-seven miles. In 2.3 miles after passing the entrance to Durango Mountain Resort, and just as you make a sweeping right-hand turn to cross Cascade Creek, turn right onto Lime Creek Road. The road is rocky in places but can be driven in a two-wheel-drive if you go carefully.

Take Lime Creek Road 3.5 miles to where the road passes a lily pond. Just as the road turns sharply east to go by the north side of the pond, there is a turnoff big enough to park two or three cars. The trail begins here (N 37 39.153, W 107 46.403).

The Hike

The trail bears generally north. It passes through aspen trees and, shortly before the lake, goes past several interesting beaver ponds, some still active.

The lake (N 37 39.731, W 107 46.004) provides several acres of good fishing. It is a lovely spot, with Spud Mountain very close on the north, the Twilight Peaks to the east across Lime Creek, and Engineer Mountain to the northwest. Engineer Mountain cannot be seen from the lake, but it can be viewed from several points along the trail. This is a beautiful hike during the summer, but it is

161

Spud Lake with large beaver lodge and a view of the south side
of Spud Mountain.

especially beautiful during the early fall, when the aspen leaves are in full color. This is usually around October 1, but the colors are likely to be good ten days before and after this date.

Option

There is another smaller but beautiful lake nearby (it is unnamed) for those who have time to explore a little more. To find it, start up the same trail from the parking lot. In 100 yards, veer left off of the trail, following the remnants of an old trail for two-tenths mile (count from the parking area). At that point, the old trail (it's the former trail to Spud Lake) swings to the right and starts up steeply; for the other lake, turn left at this point on an old road and follow it generally west and gradually downhill for about a half mile to a nice opening where the lake and surrounding meadow are located. It is a lovely, quiet spot, not often visited.

When you're done hiking, you might consider driving along Lime Creek Road all the way around to its north terminus, at the lowest spot between Coal Bank Pass and Molas Pass on U.S. Highway 550. This takes you steeply down to Lime Creek, then back up again to rejoin the highway. If you're careful, you should be able to do it with two-wheel-drive.

❖ Potato Hill ❖ (Spud Mountain)

Distance: 5 miles (round trip)
Starting elevation: 10,600 feet
Elevation gain: 1,271 feet
High point: 11,871 feet
Rating: Difficult
Time allowed: 3 to 5 hours
Maps: 7.5′ Engineer Mountain; San Juan National Forest

Introduction

Spud Mountain is short compared to its neighbors—
Engineer Mountain to the west and the Twilight Peaks and
West Needles to the east—but it stands alone and makes a
good half-day hike. The view south from the top is impressive. It includes the Cascade and Animas valleys and
Electra Lake far below. Durango Mountain Resort is to the
southwest.

Spud Mountain is best climbed from the north, from the
top of Coal Bank Hill. This requires bushwhacking a lot of
the way, through large spruce and fir trees. There are traces
of trail along the ridge that other hikers and elk have used.

The Approach

Take U.S. Highway 550 north from Durango to the top of
Coal Bank Hill—thirty-three miles from Thirty-Second
Street and Main Avenue, and 5.5 miles from the crossing

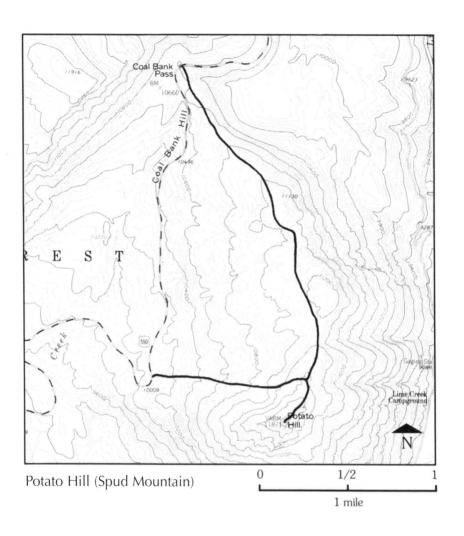

Potato Hill (Spud Mountain)

0   1/2   1

1 mile

Spud Mountain from the northwest, showing the highway just
below Coal Bank Pass.

of Cascade Creek at the bottom of the hill. Park at the rest
stop at the top of Coal Bank Hill—out of the way of
tourists, if you can.

The Hike

From the parking area (N 37 41.937, W 107 46.630), strike
out in a general south-southeast direction, keeping as high
as you can on the expansive ridge. You'll find some trail,
but you'll also have to bushwhack through some spots. Go
to the right (west) around one bump on the ridge to reach
a saddle (N 37 40.734, W 107 45.805) at about 11,100 feet.

From here, you'll be on a rocky slope heading up the
last 700 feet, south and then southwest, to the summit (N
37 40.350, W 107 45.993).

Option

You can also climb Spud Mountain from the west, beginning at a switchback in the highway (N 37 40.543, W 107 46.805) just after you pass the sign that tells you you're at 10,000 feet. Park the car near here and begin a steep ascent through downed timber. This is by no means an easy ascent, although it is shorter.

Head almost due east to the 11,100-foot saddle previously described, or to just south of that saddle.

❖ Engineer Mountain

Distance: 7.0 miles (round trip)
Starting elevation: 10,660 feet
Elevation gain: 2,308 feet
High point: 12,968 feet
Rating: Difficult
Time allowed: 4 to 6 hours
Maps: 7.5′ Engineer Mountain; San Juan National Forest

Introduction

Engineer Mountain is one of the most photographed peaks in the San Juans. As you approach from Durango about ten miles south of the peak, it appears as a symmetrical cone rising straight ahead as if it were growing out of the highway. From Jarvis Meadows just north of the Purgatory Ski Area turnoff, it totally dominates the northerly view.

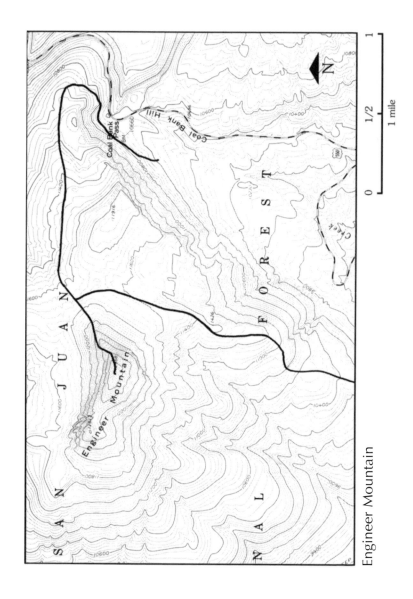

Engineer Mountain

The climbing route up the northeast ridge of Engineer Mountain rises out of the tundra.

The Approach

The shortest and easiest way to climb Engineer Mountain begins at the top of Coal Bank Pass. Take U.S. Highway 550 north from Thirty-Second Street and Main Avenue in Durango 33 miles to the top of the pass. Just north of the large parking and rest area there, turn in on the opposite side of the road (west), going a little less than 200 yards to the trailhead, labeled "Pass Creek Trail." There is parking here for a few cars (N 37 41.956, W 107 46.751).

The Hike

Start north on the trail. It moves up a steep, grassy slope northeastward into the big spruce-fir timber. Once inside

169

the timber, the trail swings back gradually westward. Some new trail has been built recently in this area to improve the grade and to avoid some of the muddy spots. Two lovely little lakes lie on the left side of the trail.

At 2.5 miles, the trail emerges out of the timber onto the tundra, and you reach a trail junction with the Engineer Mountain Trail, which goes south and north here. At about this point, you should leave the trail and head for the northeast ridge of the mountain. There are many braids of the trail, but to avoid damaging this area, please stay on the main branch.

The tundra area here has many beautiful wildflowers. As you move up the beginning of the cone, the tundra rises steeply, later giving way to rock—mostly talus with a few small ledges. Take the right side of the ridge at first, then move up onto the ridge itself. The ridge is narrow—only two to four feet wide in places. Much of the rock is loose, and there is much exposure here. Therefore, you must test each handhold before trusting it. A little higher up, you emerge out onto the cone itself. The top (N 37 41.957, W 107 48.392) is not far beyond.

Since Engineer Mountain stands alone, even though it is a little less than 13,000 feet, the panorama of peaks and valleys to be seen is great in all directions. The north face of Engineer is a sheer drop of 800 feet. Looking down this direction, you can see a fine example of a rock glacier at the head of one of the branches of Engine Creek.

Rock glaciers are somewhat unique to the San Juan Mountains. They look like a giant pudding flowing in slow waves. In fact, they are talus rocks that do move in a very slow pattern. Geologists say they are taken for a slow ride by ice in and under the rock.

Options

If you have an extra couple of hours, you might want to go west from the top, over the small shoulder peak, around to the north side, and back to the tundra and trail across the rock glaciers. The west descent beyond the shoulder is over steep talus but is quite doable. Hiking the waves themselves involves some up-and-down work, all on loose rocks. You must be especially careful crossing leading edges of the waves, because the rocks are typically at the maximum angle of repose; hiking over them can start a hazardous rock slide. At several places along this area, you can hear underground streams gurgling through the rocks.

As mentioned before, there is an Engineer Mountain Trail that approaches from the south. It is about twice as long as the Coal Bank Pass route and involves 3,920 feet of altitude gain. This is a favorite trail for elk hunters in the fall. Hikers might be interested in it as an alternate or a return route, keeping in mind that the south end of it joins U.S. Highway 550 some five miles down from Coal Bank Pass, at the U.S. Forest Service's Engineer Mountain Work Station.

This trail is in good condition. Going south from the intersection described above, it soon drops into heavy timber and goes mostly south four miles to a junction with the work station road, 200 yards west of U.S. Highway 550.

If you want to start up this route from the south end, measure up one mile from where the highway crosses Cascade Creek, and turn left for that 200 yards. From the north, it is the first right turn a little way below the runaway-truck turnoff.

❖ Grizzly Peak ❖

Distance: 7 miles (round trip)
Starting elevation: 11,200 feet (N 37 43.523, W 107 51.705)
Elevation gain: 2,538 feet
High point: 13,738 feet
Rating: Difficult; very difficult by alternate return route
Time allowed: 6 to 7 hours
Maps: 7.5′ Ophir; 7.5′ Engineer Mountain; San Juan National Forest

Introduction

Grizzly Peak is a challenging and rewarding climb. It rises out of the west side of the Cascade Creek valley five miles northwest of Engineer Mountain. It is ten miles back from the road and can only be seen from U.S. Highway 550 thirty miles north of Durango, between the ski-area turnoff and the Cascade Creek crossing.

It can be climbed from Cascade Creek valley, but this is a long route and involves two days. The easiest route is the one described here.

The Approach

Turn west at the ski-area entrance twenty-five miles north of Thirty-Second Street and Main Avenue in Durango. As you approach the ski area, go north up a gravel road

172

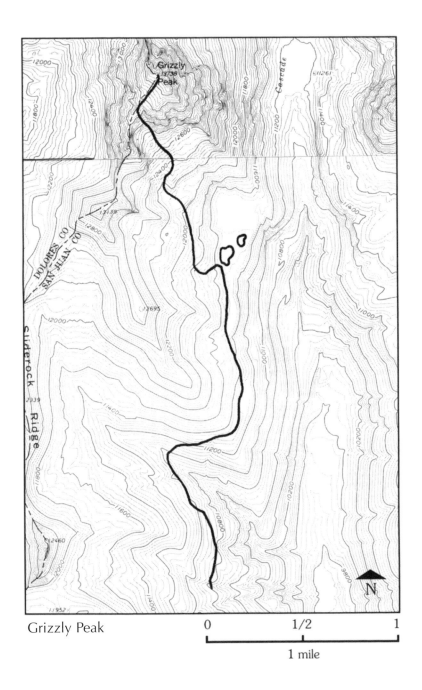

Grizzly Peak

Grizzly Peak; the trail goes around the base of the high foreground ridge.

(Forest Service Road 578) at the north end of the parking lot. This road soon climbs back to the west and overlooks the ski area. At the top of the climb, the road turns north and descends slightly; in 0.5 mile, the main road makes a ninety-degree turn to the left and heads downhill to Hermosa Park. Go straight onto Forest Service Road 579, the Relay/Cascade Divide Road.

In 1.3 miles past that intersection, veer right onto Cascade Divide Road at a well-marked split. (The Relay Creek Road goes to the left.) You're now on a former logging road that is in good shape at first, but it soon narrows and gets rougher. It should be doable most of the way for two-wheel-drive if you drive cautiously, but four-wheel-drive is highly recommended.

Grizzly Peak from across the Upper Cascade Canyon.

The road hugs the shoulder of Graysill Mountain, with Cascade Creek far below and Engineer Mountain beyond to the northeast. Go all the way to the end of the road—about ten miles.

The Hike

Take the well-defined path at the end of the road (N 37 43.523, W 107 51.705) another couple of hundred yards to where you strike the Colorado Trail. Take it right (north) to a crossing of an unnamed creek, where the trail swings sharply right (east). At this point, it goes around on a contour of a high, steep ridge that comes off the south side of Grizzly. Go on around the end of the ridge to where the trail begins to enter the woods.

The climbing chute above the lakes on Grizzly Peak.

Leave the trail here and continue on about the same contour level going straight north, nearly paralleling the Colorado Trail. There should be a fairly obvious route from previous climbers.

In about a mile, you should come to a delightful shelf with some small lakes and marshy areas. A stream fills this area from above, and another drains it, plunging over the side down to Cascade Creek.

At the southwest side of this area, climb steeply upward toward the northwest. Soon you should see a steep chute of big rocks with cliffs on each side. The right side of this is a shoulder of Grizzly Peak, the top of which you cannot see from here. Climb the chute, bearing northwest. It is somewhat tedious but better than the alternatives.

176

At the top of the chute, you will find yourself on a rocky ridge; turn right for a fairly easy quarter-mile climb over talus to the top of Grizzly Peak (N 37 45.370, W 107 51.717). The top itself is very rocky, but it affords excellent views of many rugged peaks that lie between South Mineral Creek on the east and Trout Lake on the west. The near ones in this area (north) include, west to east, Sheep Mountain, San Miguel Peak, and Rolling Mountain. A bit farther north, to the left of Rolling Mountain, are Vermilion Peak and U.S. Grant Peak. Farther to the west and a little north are the San Miguel Mountains. These include three Fourteeners—Wilson Peak, Mount Wilson, and El Diente—in addition to Lizard Head and its distinctive shaft rising 400 feet straight up out of the top of the mountain.

An eastern view shows the many peaks around Silverton and, farther south, the rugged Needles area of the Weminuche Wilderness.

Option

For the return trip, the same route is recommended. But for those interested in rock climbing, instead of taking the chute down to the marshy area, continue south along the ridge. This is farther and slower. On this route, you will move up and down over various sizes of rocks. At times, there is considerable exposure and slow rock climbing. The route is not recommended for the inexperienced or faint of heart. Once you are over this tricky ridge, climb to the highest point (still going south) and proceed down the steep south side to a more gentle tundra area. Hike southeast and back to the end of the road.

177

An alternate starting route begins near Bolam Pass. This route involves a very steep, rocky climb up the west side of Grizzly Peak, and the hike is long and slow. (Four-wheel-drive vehicles are advisable for this route, but when the road is good, high-clearance two-wheel-drives can make it; you do have to ford Hermosa Creek, which can be risky for two-wheel-drives in the early summer when the creek is still swollen with snowmelt.) For this route, take the main road above Durango Mountain Resort down into Hermosa Park. At its west end, the road turns north and follows Hermosa Creek up to its headwaters.

About two miles up this road after leaving Hermosa Park, there is a division in the road, with the left turn going to Hotel Draw and Scotch Creek. Do not take this turn; rather, go straight on. Eventually, you should come to the ghost town of Graysill. Go another 0.3 mile and park at a small lake where the Colorado Trail crosses the road (N 37 42.801, W 107 54.216). Hike east along the trail, then veer east-northeast off the trail when the trail heads south. Keep going up to the top of the ridge, and take the ridge north. There is an unnamed peak a mile south of Grizzly Peak. You will find it easier to climb over this unnamed peak from a saddle southwest of it than to climb directly up the west side of Grizzly. If you do this, you will then have to follow the tricky ridge, described above, on over to Grizzly.

❖ Graysill Mountain– ❖ Grayrock Peak

Distance: 6.6 miles (round trip)
Starting elevation: 10,400 feet
Elevation gain: 2,104 feet
High point: 12,504 feet
Rating: Moderate
Time allowed: 4 to 5.5 hours
Maps: 7.5′ Engineer Mountain; San Juan National Forest

Introduction

Graysill Mountain is a formation in the shape of a horse-shoe, facing eastward; it peaks out on its southeast corner, and at that point it is called Grayrock Peak. It is not a high peak compared to many of the others in the San Juans, but since it is the highest point for several miles in any direction, it is impressive and yields fine views. It is located west of Cascade Creek and southwest of Engineer Mountain.

This climb, done from the east side, demands some bushwhacking, route-finding, and slow hiking over rocks. But the hard part is not long, and the summit is surprisingly exhilarating.

The Approach

Graysill Mountain lies north of Durango Mountain Resort (known by locals as Purgatory Ski Area). To reach it, take U.S. Highway 550 north from Thirty-Second Street and

179

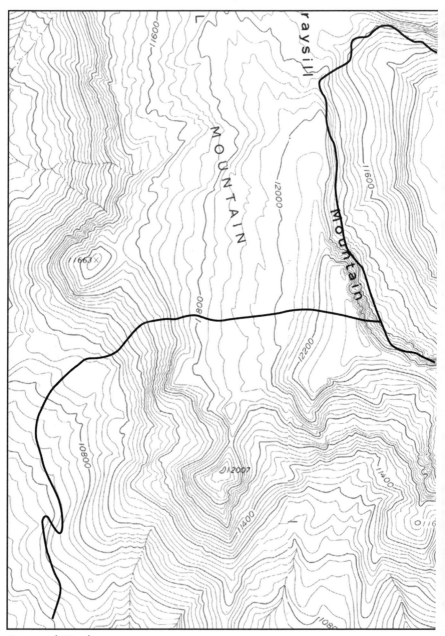

Grayrock Peak

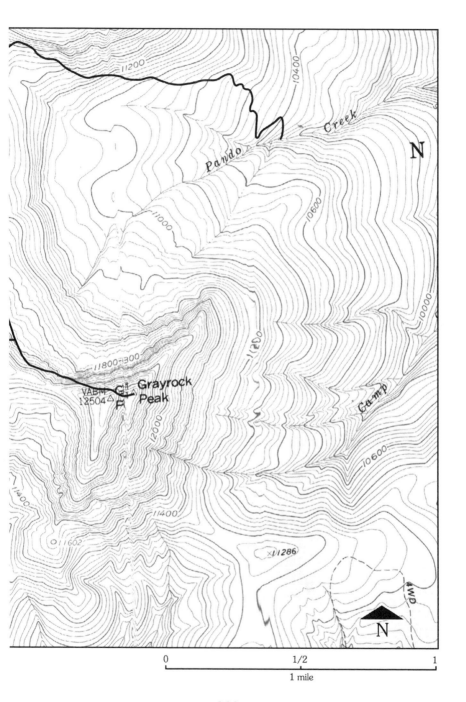

Main Avenue in Durango for twenty-five miles, and turn left (west) at the ski-area entrance. Go 0.5 mile on pavement on the main road, then look for a gravel road going right (north), away from the ski area.

This road is flat as it heads north, but it then heads south and west and climbs in a series of switchbacks. In 3.3 miles, it tops out and then turns north (the Elbert Creek Road goes south here). In a half mile, there is a left turn down into Hermosa Park. Do not take this; rather, go straight onto Forest Service Road 579/580 (the Cascade Divide/Relay Creek roads). In another 1.2 miles, the Cascade and Relay roads split; go right onto Cascade Divide Road.

The road gets rougher and rougher the farther you go, and it's nice to have four-wheel-drive, although careful two-wheeling should get you through. In 5.3 miles from the split, the road swings northwest and tends slightly downhill. (At this point, you are northeast of Grayrock Peak, which only helps you if you know what the peak looks like.) The road crosses two braids of Pando Creek, then swings back uphill toward the northeast. Keep going a couple of hundred yards to where the road turns almost due north, and park at the junction of an abandoned road (N 37 41.236, W 107 51.145).

The Hike

Start up the abandoned road. It tends northwest, then switchbacks to the west. Ultimately, you want to go nearly due west up to a ridge that's part of Graysill Mountain. For this lower part, however, these roads can help you get started and avoid the thick forest by going around it to the north.

When it looks like the roads aren't helping, head west. You'll have to bushwhack, going over downed timber and through some thick brush. In about 0.8 mile from the start, a slope of shale rock comes down the mountainside above you to the north. There may be another way, but you can walk carefully across the shale and skunk cabbage, keeping the saddle on the ridge as your goal.

In 1.5 miles from the car, you'll reach the ridge at 11,600 feet. Head southwest, then go south up a mellow, tundra slope on the ridge (Graysill Mountain). Keep gaining altitude, and stay fairly close to the steep drop-off to your east. The going gets rockier, and the ridgeline turns southeast, then east, and then it drops to a saddle (N 37 40.485, W 107 51.998) just below Grayrock Peak.

The ridge narrows, and from a distance this looks kind of hairy. But fear not: It works out when you reach it. Hike up the last 300 feet of elevation to the summit. The rocks underfoot are small and noisy, sometimes with a musical sound and sometimes with just a clunk. From where you reach the ridge, it's 1.8 miles to the summit, which is marked by a large cairn (N 37 40.437, W 107 51.771).

Grayrock Peak features its own special thrill—a sheer cliff on its north side practically straight down for a thousand feet. After recovering from the sight of this plunge, you will want to enjoy the more distant views. Engineer Mountain rises as a fine, stalwart warrior out of Cascade Canyon 3.8 miles to the northeast. Grizzly Peak is a sharp and dominant point six miles to the north and is even higher than Engineer Mountain. Northwest are Hermosa Peak and, farther beyond, Lizard Head and the Wilsons. On the southwestern skyline are the La Plata Mountains, and you can even see Sleeping Ute Mountain, which is southwest of Cortez.

The return should be made by the same route as the climb.

Options

Grayrock Peak can also be climbed from a western approach. This is actually easier than the route given above, but it is longer, and it is harder to find the starting point. The access road is the same until the junction of Cascade and Relay roads.

Take the Relay Creek road (Forest Service Road 580) to the left; it goes west and northwest, passing under the shoulder of Grayrock Peak on the south side. The road is a good gravel road, but it does a lot of switching around.

In 6.2 miles, there will be a huge, man-made, cleared flat area on your right. Park here (N 37 39.697, W 107 53.551) and begin hiking up a closed-off road that heads to the north, just off of the Relay Creek road.

These old logging roads wind up the mountain for a while; they're well defined, but it won't be perfectly clear which ones to hike on. Go north as best you can, then northeast up through trees to an obvious green saddle between talus slopes.

Climb east into the open and seek out the crest of the ridge to your left when you can. If you find the route to the saddle, turn right at the top of it. Follow the above description southeast and east toward the summit of Grayrock.

❖ Hermosa Peak ❖

Distance: 3.6 miles (round trip)
Starting elevation: 11,520 feet
Elevation gain: 1,059 feet
High point: 12,579 feet
Rating: Moderate
Time allowed: 2 to 3 hours
Maps: 7.5′ Hermosa Peak; San Juan National Forest

Introduction

Hermosa Peak involves traveling some backcountry roads, but it is one of the easiest and quickest high-altitude climbs in southwestern Colorado. It offers fine views of even higher peaks from its top; even driving the road to it is a worthwhile experience.

The climb is quite short but is rated moderate because it is high and because some 250 yards of it are steep, with one short hazardous spot.

The Approach

Access is via the Bolam Pass four-wheel-drive road. This road, however, is usually in better condition than many such roads. Under dry conditions, two-wheel-drive cars and trucks can usually make it if they have good clearance and a good low gear for the steep hills. You'll also need to ford Hermosa Creek at one point—pick a good route and keep your momentum.

185

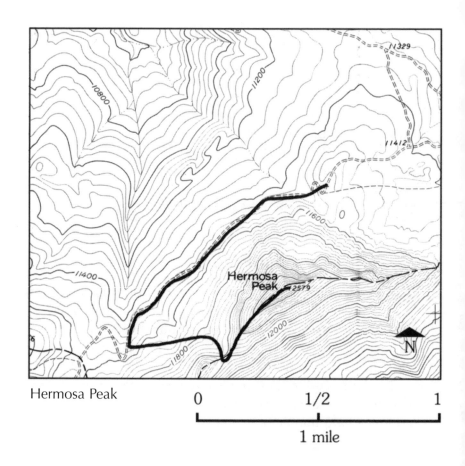

Hermosa Peak

This hike may be approached on Forest Service Road 578 from the east or west. For the eastern approach, take U.S. Highway 550 twenty-five miles north of Durango and turn left (west) into the main ski-area entrance. Go north 0.5 mile and find a gravel road (Forest Service Road 578) going north. Take that, and stay on it to the top of Bolam Pass, and past the top of the pass 0.7 mile to a left turn onto Forest Service Road 149. (In all, you're on Forest Service Road 578 for eighteen miles.)

Take Forest Service Road 149 for 0.8 mile, where it's blocked off (N 37 42.963, W 107 55.511). Hermosa Peak dominates the southern skyline.

The Hike

Hike on down the road about a mile. You will be following the Colorado Trail, which joins the route just beyond the barrier. The right place to leave the road/trail is a point just west of a saddle between Hermosa Peak and a smaller, unnamed peak south of it.

The climb starts out east up an easy, grassy slope. (There may be a few trees at first, depending on your choice of where to start up.) The grassy slope heads toward the saddle, 0.4 mile uphill. This is quite easy climbing except just below the saddle, where it gets steeper and you must negotiate talus.

At the saddle (N 37 42.364, W 107 55.991), go left (northeast) toward the top 0.4 mile beyond. A hundred yards above the saddle there is one small cliff to get over, but almost anyone can make it with care and a little boost from a companion. Once you are above this, it is a short but steep climb to the ridge; the top (N 37 42.599, W 107 55.711) is a few hundred yards beyond.

Our hiking group climbed Hermosa Peak during the foliage color season a few years ago. We had along a guest from the Midwest who had come out to photograph the aspen. This was his first time on a mountain; with some encouragement, he made the top with no difficulty, but on the steep part near the top, he insisted on crawling on his hands and knees because he was so frightened of the height and steepness. There really was no serious risk; going down he was braver.

The top of the mountain does furnish some beautiful views. All the same mountains that you can see from Bolam Pass can be seen even better from here, plus more. There is a fine view of Engineer Mountain to the east. Blackhawk is the nearest to the southwest. The La Platas loom on the southern horizon. The north face of Hermosa Peak is practically straight down. (Hint from experience: Don't set a pack too close to the edge; it could roll down and disappear over the steep face, necessitating a hairy rescue on the steep north side.)

Options

Access from the west route is via Colorado State Highway 145. On this side, the road is called Barlow Creek Road, but it is the same road as Bolam Pass Road. It turns east off of Highway 145 six miles north of Rico, or six miles south of Lizard Head Pass. Just across the Dolores River, a very nice forest service campground is located north of the road along the river. Barlow Creek Road turns right, whereas the road straight ahead goes on into the campground. It is seven miles and 1,800 feet of elevation gain on up to the route that turns off to Hermosa Peak. This junction is in an open space in a flat area, so it should not be hard to find.

❖ Jura Knob ❖
(Coal Creek, Deer Creek)

Distance: 9.6 miles (loop trip plus climb of Jura Knob)
Starting elevation: 10,300 feet
Elevation gain: 2,314 feet
High point: 12,614 feet
Rating: Moderate
Time allowed: 5 to 6 hours
Maps: 7.5′ Engineer Mountain; 7.5′ Snowdon Peak; San Juan National Forest

Introduction

Coal Creek and Deer Creek trails each provide fine half-day hikes into big timber, but this book has combined them into a very good full-day hike that includes a climb of Jura Knob. The trailheads are both on U.S. Highway 550 and are 1.6 miles apart; therefore, this highway distance will need to be provided for in hiking, or some other arrangements will have to be made. This is in addition to the time and mileage given above. Good parking space is available near both trailheads.

The easiest way to do this hike is to have a car at each end and begin at Coal Creek, since it is 500 feet higher. This high-altitude hike involves considerable altitude gain. Otherwise, it is easy, with only one spot (near the top of Jura Knob) where rock scrambling is involved.

189

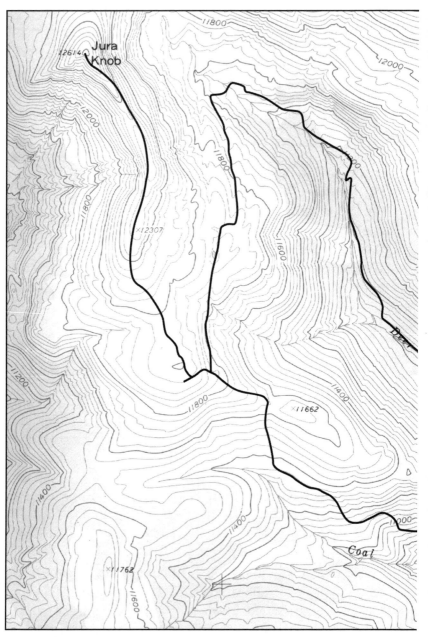

Jura Knob

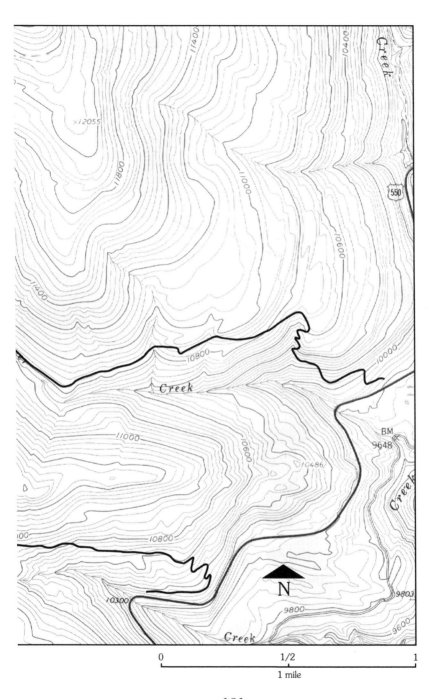

The Approach

Coal Creek is the first drainage north of Coal Bank Pass. Just below where U.S. Highway 550 crosses the creek, 1.2 miles from the top of the pass, park on the south side of the road (N 37 42.513, W 107 46.204) and walk down the highway about 200 yards to where the trail starts sharply upward to the east.

If you have a second car, shuttle it another 1.8 miles down to where Old Lime Creek Road turns off to the right (south) from the highway. There is plenty of parking in the vicinity.

The Hike

The trail soon angles northeast into the trees, then curves back around westward. At about two miles, the trail emerges into a grassy clearing. Timberline can be seen a few hundred yards above this to the north.

You may find two or three trails in this area. What you want to do is head basically north to a saddle on the ridge at 11,640 feet (N 37 43.094, W 107 47.329). A trail heads up this way but peters out. There should be dark-brown wooden poles you can follow to the ridge top, where you'll find a trail running east-west along the ridge. This is actually still the Coal Creek Trail.

Upon reaching this high point, you can look northeastward across Deer Creek valley, hundreds of feet below, to two peaks about the same size. Neither of these is Jura Knob. Continue up (west) on the ridge, following the trail another 0.3 mile to the junction of the Coal Creek and Deer Creek trails, 2.7 miles from the start. It should be marked, with signs on two tiny trees at a rocky promontory (N 37 43.176, W 107 47.571).

Jura Knob: The shoulder-high ledge is on the left side. Rolling Mountain is in the center, and the shoulder of Twin Sisters is on the right.

Continue briefly on the Coal Creek Trail, but then veer off of it to the north, following the easy ridgeline up toward Jura Knob, one mile beyond. One obstacle of some difficulty remains. It is a ledge a short distance below the top, where there is one shoulder-high vertical climb. Most adults can make this by themselves with proper placement of the feet. Anyone can make it with a boost from a partner.

The top (N 37 44.238, W 107 48.119), lying a short distance beyond the ledge, is a smooth roll with small, flat rocks for its surface. It is a good place to stretch out for a rest or to eat a sandwich while enjoying views of peaks in all directions. Immediately to the north are the Twin Sisters on the right and Rolling Mountain to the left.

193

Farther north between these is the Ice Lakes area, with U.S. Grant Peak immediately beyond. Ice Lake itself cannot be seen. To the west, Grizzly Peak majestically guards over the Cascade Valley, but there is a low ridge in between that keeps you from seeing down into that valley.

Retrace your route from Jura Knob back to the junction of Coal Creek and Deer Creek trails. Take Deer Creek Trail to the left (north). Just so you know, from here it's 4.9 miles to the highway via the Deer Creek Trail. The trail drops slightly, then climbs again and reaches a high point at a tarn at about 11,950 feet (N 37 43.560, W 107 47.547). Now you'll drop down, gently and then more steeply, northward to cross Deer Creek at 11,500 feet (N 37 44.118, W 107 47.488). Just after this crossing, a trail goes up to the left, but for now, veer to the right, staying near the creek. There is a riot of wildflowers along this trail up to where it enters the heavily wooded area. Eventually, the trail ends up well above Deer Creek, climbing a bit before dropping steeply back down to the highway. Once you cross Deer Creek, the trail always stays on the north side of it.

The final descent drops you 1,000 feet to the highway in about a mile, and the trail enters an aspen grove just before its finish. Once you hit the highway (N 37 43.187, W 107 45.197), it's about 0.2 mile downhill to Old Lime Creek Road and your car.

Options

Most options are probably fairly obvious: Park at the Coal Creek trailhead, hike up Jura Knob, and hike back the same way, avoiding Deer Creek Trail entirely. It's still a nice hike.

Or, take a stroll up the Deer Creek Trail as far as you wish, and return the same way. The upper end of the creek is in a beautiful, high valley, with lots of wildflowers at the right time of summer, as previously mentioned.

❖ Crater Lake– ❖ Twilight Peaks

Distance: 11.0 miles to Crater Lake (round trip); 13.4 miles to North Twilight Peak (round trip)
Starting elevation: 10,750 feet
Elevation gain: 890 feet to Crater Lake; 1,435 feet additional to North Twilight Peak
High point: 11,640 feet at Crater Lake; 13,075 feet at North Twilight Peak
Rating: Easy but long to Crater Lake; difficult to North Twilight Peak
Time allowed: 4 to 6 hours to Crater Lake; 2 to 3 hours additional to North Twilight Peak (round-trip times)
Maps: 7.5′ Snowdon Peak; San Juan National Forest

Introduction

This is a combination hike with two possible destinations, both of which are highly worthwhile. This is a fairly popular area, but the farther you go along the trail, the fewer people you will see. It's a long day if you add the climb of North Twilight Peak, but it is doable.

The Approach

The trailhead is at Andrews Lake, which is reached via U.S. Highway 550 about thirty-nine miles north of Durango, one mile south of Molas Pass. Turn southeast off of the highway onto a paved road that winds less than a mile to Andrews Lake. There is plenty of parking in the vicinity of the lake, along with restroom facilities.

The Hike

Pick up the trail on the west side of the lake (N 37 43.695, W 107 42.649), and head around the south side of the lake, heading east. The trail moves beyond the lake and soon turns to the south, zigzagging up 400 feet.

After this, it continues south to Crater Lake, rising sharply only for short distances. The trail moves in and out of the edge of the timber, affording fine views northward toward the mountains surrounding Silverton and westward across Lime Creek valley to Engineer Mountain and Grand Turk. The high spruce-fir bands of forest on both sides of this valley are excellent elk-hunting areas.

The last clearing, where the trail turns east for a half mile, affords a distinctive view of the steep north face of the Twilight massif. About a mile beyond this, you reach the lake (N 37 40.520, W 107 42.790), a lovely little high-altitude gem surrounded by tall trees; timberline is just above it.

The hike into the lake and back can be done in a long half day. Some may want to take advantage of the excellent camping sites here and perhaps do a little fishing and relaxing. The hike to Crater Lake and back is rated fairly easy, but it is long.

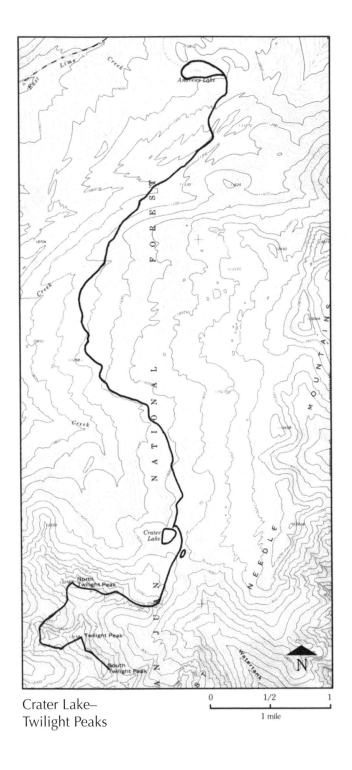

Crater Lake–
Twilight Peaks

The Twilight–West Needles massif from the open-meadow ascent of Jura Knob.

For those who would like to climb North Twilight Peak, the challenge has just begun, for the next mile brings steep climbing and one and a half times as much altitude gain as has already been made in five and one-half miles. To begin the ascent, follow around the north side of the lake and start the climb on the lake's east end.

There is no fixed trail beyond this point, but you should have no difficulty finding your way because you are out of the timber by this time. A few hundred yards southeast and 150 feet higher is another little lake. At this point, turn southwest and ascend steeply toward the peak. The first top is a false one; from it you must climb down a little. Be careful here, for there is considerable exposure in this little dip. Climb out of the dip to the top (N 37 40.150, W 107 43.701) a quarter mile beyond.

198

The top itself is a smooth roll. From the top, you can see to the east the rugged Needles territory, where there are three 14,000-foot mountains as well as myriad other steep and rugged peaks. This is truly wild, roadless territory. Between Twilight and the Needles, steeply below, is the Animas River valley. If you are there at the right time of day, you might even hear the little Durango & Silverton Narrow Gauge Railroad whistle its loneliness up and out of the valley.

Options

North Twilight Peak is part of a massif called the West Needle Mountains; this includes Snowdon Peak to the northeast and Twilight, South Twilight, and West Needle mountains to the south. All of these peaks are in the 13,000-foot class. Hikers who have time and energy left after reaching North Twilight could take in Twilight and South Twilight in the next mile. Twilight (the middle of the Twilights) is actually the highest of the group, at 13,158 feet. The drop between North Twilight and Twilight is only 400 feet; however, the hike between them is not as simple as this sounds, for there is a deep gash on the west side of Twilight. The gash is a serious problem.

Descend farther south and west, cross a little gully, and move on ahead to where you begin to climb more easily toward the top of Twilight (N 37 39.775, W 107 43.624). After that summit, take another easy descent to the next saddle and then proceed on up to the top of South Twilight (N 37 39.552, W 107 43.424). This sounds easy enough, but there is a hazard. As soon as you cross the gully, you are on a place a few feet wide; it drops off sharply on the right with no handholds or footholds. There is the risk of a very serious fall at this gash. But there are more problems—the little area on which you are standing slopes down toward the drop-off and is made up of a lot of small, loose rocks. So what now? There is a rising ledge a few feet high on the left that offers some not-too-secure handholds. The tough part is only ten to twenty feet long. It can be done, but some may want ropes and pitons for security.

There is one other way to deal with the gash: Cross down and to the right of the highest part. Once you are at the bottom of the crevice, climb out the other side—it's steep but has good holds. This crossing spot is difficult to find, but it is there and is probably safer than the first method.

If you get past this point, you can climb both Twilight and South Twilight in an hour or more.

❖ Snowdon Peak ❖

Distance: 6 miles (round trip)
Starting elevation: 10,750 feet
Elevation gain: 2,327 feet
High point: 13,077 feet
Rating: Very difficult
Time allowed: 5 to 6 hours
Maps: 7.5′ Snowdon Peak; San Juan National Forest

Introduction

Snowdon is a twin-peaked mountain with each peak sloping gently toward the low point in between. The two are quite symmetrical and make a distinctive skyline view eastward from U.S. Highway 550 as you travel toward the top of Molas Pass from the south. The northern peak is thirty feet higher, and that's the climb described here. Although the two peaks slope gently toward each other in a north-south direction, the view you get from the west side makes the climb look impossible. It is a steep slab 800 feet down from the top. Although this is not the route suggested here, the climb should still be rated very difficult.

The Approach

The approach is the same as for Crater Lake–Twilight Peaks. Take the Andrews Lake road one mile south of Molas Pass. Park at the lake.

The Hike

Find the trail at the west end of the lake (N 37 43.690, W 107 42.649), and hike to the east along the south side of the lake. Turning south, you will find the trail zigzagging up a 400-foot rise; just beyond the top of this hill, you will find two little lakes below you on your left. Here you must leave the trail; the rest of the hike will require bushwhacking except for a few short pieces of trail.

Turn to the east between these two lakes. (At some times of the year they may be little more than swamps.) Cross a half mile of flats and a slowly rising area. There is a smaller peak to the north of the most northerly of the Snowdon peaks. Contour upward through the timber toward this peak, and hike above timberline a bit to the right to strike the 12,350-foot saddle (N 37 42.837, W 107 41.177) between this peak and the north Snowdon peak.

201

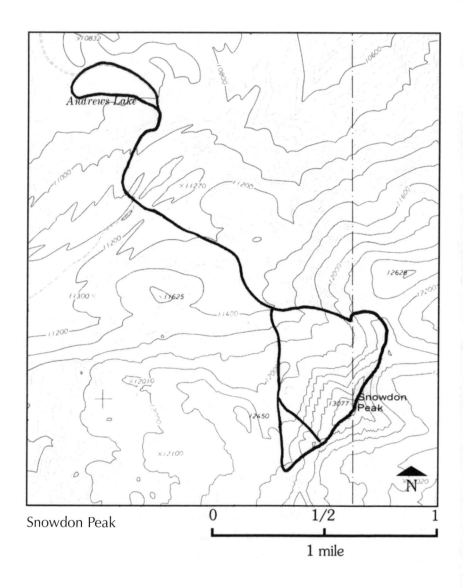

Snowdon Peak

0   1/2   1

1 mile

Snowdon Peak.

Continue up this ridge, now hiking south toward the top of Snowdon. Within a few hundred yards of the top, the rocks become too difficult on the face of the ridge. Here, you should move to the east side of the ridge and climb south, finishing up southwest of the summit. There is substantial exposure in this last section. Carefully test all handholds and footholds before trusting them. Climbers may need to stay close together to help one another through this area. Rope could be used here, but most experienced climbers do not rope up for this short distance.

The top itself (N 37 42.473, W 107 41.339) widens out to a broad roll of small rocks. It is fairly large. The views from the top include the Animas Valley steeply below to the east and the dramatic Grenadier Range straight to the east beyond. Mount Garfield is the first peak in the range.

The Grenadiers are a favorite place for technical climbers. Straight to the north is Grand Turk on the west side of the highway, with Sultan Mountain beyond. Just east of Sultan, on the right side of the valley, is Kendall Mountain, which is the peak that towers above Silverton. Beyond these is a grand panorama of many peaks.

Of the twin Snowdon peaks, the north one, which is the approach route described here, is the higher.

Options

The return may be varied from the approach. Go south toward the low point between the two peaks. There is a break in the rock here, and you will have to do some rock scrambling to get down. At the bottom of this scramble, you are faced with some interesting rock pylons. To the right is a steep couloir that can be used with great care. Sometimes there is enough snow here for a good glissade, but the slope is steep, and ice axes are needed for a possible arrest.

A more gradual route down can be found by keeping to the left. At the bottom of this steep area (now 1,000 feet below the north peak), continue north or a little northwest to get back to the flat, swampy area from which the approach was made. Westward across this will bring you back to the Crater Lake Trail. Turn right on it to go back to Andrews Lake.

❖ Molas Trail ❖

Distance: 7.6 miles (round trip)
Starting elevation: 10,600 feet
Elevation loss: 1,700 feet
Low point: 8,900 feet
Rating: Easy
Time allowed: 3.5 to 4.5 hours
Maps: 7.5′ Snowdon Peak; San Juan National Forest

Introduction

This is a good trail and offers a very fine half-day hike with excellent views of the Animas Canyon. Most hikes in this guide start at the low point and climb to a high point. This hike is the opposite; it starts at the high point and goes down to the low point at the river, which is at 8,900 feet. The elevation gain occurs on the return trip.

The Approach

Travel forty-one miles north from Durango on U.S. Highway 550—1.2 miles north of Molas Pass. This trail starts from the southeast side of the highway. There is a good turnout with a parking area. It's about six miles south of Silverton.

The Hike

Look for the trailhead (N 37 44.875, W 107 41.261) at the south end of the parking area; the trail begins fairly level,

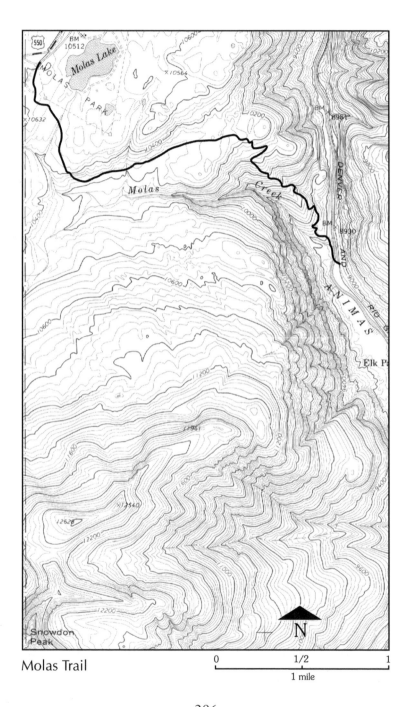

Molas Trail

but don't worry, it will drop soon. In 0.2 mile, you'll join the Colorado Trail (N 37 44.688, W 107 41.298), which comes down from the top of the pass. Go to the left (east) on the Colorado Trail.

The going gets steeper, and soon you'll hit a series of switchbacks that drops you down to within sight of Molas Creek (although you never come up next to it). The trail then heads downhill in a meadow on the north side of the Molas Creek valley. After crossing the flat meadow, you plunge into big spruce-fir timber. At 1.6 miles from the start, just before you begin the steep descent toward the Animas River, there's a good viewpoint off to the right.

The trail begins a series of switchbacks leading down to the river, 1,000 feet below. Here and there, a break in the trees affords a dramatic view of the canyon below. The river winds its way through the bottom, with the railroad tracks paralleling it on the east side.

Mount Garfield stands stalwart guard above the east side of the valley, while farther south, the Peak Fourteen massif seems to block off the whole canyon and reach all the way to the sky. In midafternoon, you have a good chance of seeing one of the tourist trains seeking its way south toward Durango. At the south end of the visible part of the valley, the train often stops to take on backpackers from Elk Creek.

At 3.7 miles from the start, you finally get to cross Molas Creek, and in another 0.1 mile, you emerge from the high vegetation to find a fine bridge across the Animas River (N 37 44.011, W 107 39.667). As far as this description is concerned, the hike ends here. The climb out of the canyon can be rated easy to moderate because none of the many switchbacks are steep.

Options

If you are backpacking or want to tack on a few more miles on a day trip, you can hike south 0.1 mile from the bridge, cross the railroad tracks, and head up the Elk Creek Trail. This trail follows Elk Creek to the top of the Continental Divide in another 8.2 miles.

You could also enter the trail from Molas Lake (not to be confused with Little Molas Lake, which is nearer the top of the pass). This is a recreational spot owned by the town of Silverton that offers camping, fishing, and supplies. From here, you reach the trail by going south-southwest from the lake until you strike the main trail going southeast.

The Molas Trail is an old trail that is now incorporated into the Colorado Trail, leading all the way from Durango to Denver—474 miles. You can also begin this hike from U.S. Highway 550 at the top of Molas Pass, where there is a nice overlook turnout and some parking. If you do park there, you have a steep climb up the Colorado Trail—another 300 feet in elevation gain—on the return trip.

❖ Sultan–Grand Turk ❖

Distance: 8.6 miles round trip
(9.8 miles if Grand Turk is included)
Starting elevation: 10,910 feet
Elevation gain: 2,458 feet
High point: 13,368 feet (Sultan summit)
Rating: Difficult
Time allowed: 5.5 to 6.5 hours
Maps: 7.5' Snowdon Peak; 7.5' Silverton;
San Juan National Forest

Introduction

This is a good climb, mostly above timberline; there are no really difficult spots. Most of it is on tundra and loose rock. You have to do a minimum amount of route-finding, as there is not a trail the entire way.

This trip can include either Grand Turk or Sultan or both. The 8.6-mile round trip takes Sultan only, but Grand Turk can easily be included.

The Approach

The hike starts near Little Molas Lake, which cannot be seen from the highway. To get there, take U.S. Highway 550 north from Durango forty miles; from the top of Molas Pass, go another 0.4 mile north and take a left-hand turn (west) onto a gravel road.

Follow this road about a mile to a point northwest of Little Molas, where it turns south. There is adequate parking just north of where the Colorado Trail crosses this road.

209

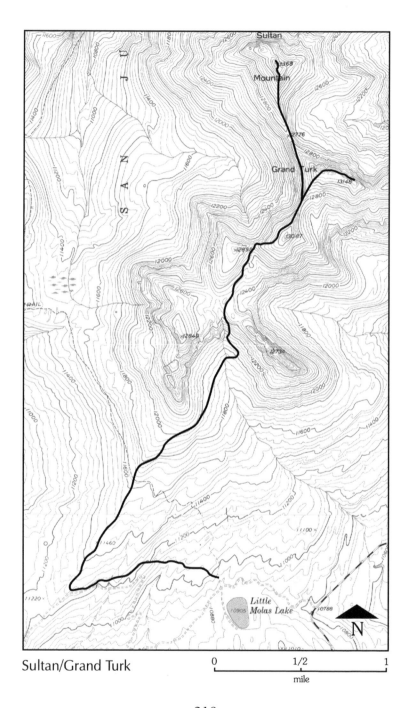

Sultan/Grand Turk

0   1/2   1

mile

The Hike

Find the Colorado Trail (there should be signs; N 37 44.694, W 107 42.611) and take it west through the forest. In a short time, you'll reach an open area created by an ancient burn. In one mile, the trail veers right (north-northeast) along a wide, open ridge. Enjoy the excellent views from here, including a look toward the Grenadiers and, farther in the distance, the Needles.

In another 0.7 mile, the Colorado Trail veers northwest (N 37 45.144, W 107 43.138), and you'll notice a trail coming up from your right (see option below). Ignore the maintained trails and head off-trail north-northeast along the top of the ridge toward the rocky bluffs straight ahead. Use your judgment, but at some point you'll want to veer right and contour under the bluffs, staying fairly high. There's a narrow path along here if you can find it.

As you swing around more toward the north, you'll drop into a valley. You should find a trail along here. Hike to the head of the valley, then hike on up, again following a fairly good trail. As the steep climb eases (N 37 45.995, W 107 42.572), veer northeast along a fairly gentle meadow. At this point, you're walking almost directly toward Grand Turk, and you should see it.

Traverse up the east side of a steep mountainside—again, you should find a trail, or maybe two. Follow it another quarter mile to a small saddle at 12,700 feet (N 37 46.299, W 107 42.364). Head northeast along the top of the ridge, climbing and then dropping down to the next saddle (still heading northeast). You lose about 300 feet on the drop. You are now at the base of Grand Turk. You should notice a trail heading almost due north from here (N 37 46.508, W 107 42.074), contouring over to a saddle below Sultan.

Grand Turk and Sultan mountains viewed across Silverton from the north.

To climb Grand Turk, which adds 1.2 miles round trip, just continue northeast up the ridge, and where it begins to spread out a bit, veer off to the right. Grand Turk has trouble deciding where to peak out. Actually, it has three peaks close together that are about the same height. The topographic map labels the one farthest east at 13,148 feet (N 37 46.590, W 107 41.749) and does not give heights for the others. Grand Turk also has twin peaks still a little farther east, but these are a hundred or more feet lower than the other three. These twin peaks are what you see as the distinctive split-topped mountain most frequently viewed from the highway and the train.

To continue on to Sultan, retrace the top of Grand Turk's ridge to the saddle where you saw the trail heading north toward Sultan. Head north along the mountainside to the next saddle, at 12,776 feet. Follow up the ridge north to the top of Sultan at 13,368 feet (N 37 47.153, W 107 42.236).

Sultan provides a fine view northeast down on Silverton, 4,000 feet below. North is Anvil Mountain, which connects with Red Mountain. In the valley, U.S. Highway 550 leads on up toward Ouray. To the west below is Bear Creek, and just beyond is Bear Mountain (12,987 feet). Beyond this is Ice Lakes country, with many rugged peaks and ridges.

The return can be made by the same route.

Option

There is a shortcut. From the trailhead near Little Molas Lake, instead of taking the Colorado Trail, go north from the parking area and find an unmaintained but obvious trail going almost due north. This trail is much steeper, but it will take three-quarters mile off your distance. It brings you to the "junction" below the bluffs where you left the Colorado Trail.

❖ South Mineral Creek– ❖
Cascade Valley

Distance: 12.9 miles (one way)
Starting elevation: 10,680 feet
Elevation gain: 1,670 feet
High point: 12,350 feet
Rating: Difficult, because of altitude and length
Time allowed: 6.5 to 9 hours
Maps: 7.5′ Ophir; 7.5′ Engineer Mountain;
  San Juan National Forest

Introduction

This hike is highly rewarding in beauty without requiring any difficult climbing. The beauty is in the natural scenery of nearby peaks and in a large expanse of wildflowers. Some people use this route for backpacking and an overnight stay, but it can be done in a day, including time to enjoy the scenery and take pictures.

That said, it would be very, very nice if someone— preferably with four-wheel-drive—dropped you off at the

South Mineral trailhead so that you didn't have to complete the shuttle. Buy them a twelve-pack or dinner or flowers—whatever seems appropriate.

The Approach

You'll want a car, or someone, at the southern end of this hike. To get there, take U.S. Highway 550 north from Thirty-Second Street and Main Avenue in Durango twenty-eight miles (0.9 mile past where the highway passes over Cascade Creek), and turn left onto a gravel road. It's about 200 yards down this road to the Engineer Mountain Trail trailhead. This is also the trailhead for the connector trail to Cascade Creek, on which you'll finish your hike.

Get in car number two and drive toward Silverton, another nineteen miles. From the Silverton Visitors' Center, drive 2.1 miles northwest on U.S. Highway 550 to a left-hand turn (west) on the gravel South Mineral Campground road. After 4.4 miles on that road, you'll come to the campground, which is just across the road from the Ice Lakes Basin trailhead.

From here, the road gets rougher; it's doable without four-wheel-drive, but a vehicle with some clearance is recommended. It can get pretty rough.

The road goes past the campground and turns southwest up a steep, rocky grade. It soon rises above timberline and continues on to the Bandora Mine. From the campground, it's 2.3 miles to the mine ruins. From the mine, the road swings downhill (south), crosses South Mineral Creek, and ends in another 0.5 mile. There's plenty of parking (N 37 46.880, W 107 48.197).

216

The Hike

Cross another fast-running branch of South Mineral Creek on a big log (slippery when wet), and head south into the forest on the Rico–Silverton Trail. It's 0.4 mile to another creek crossing, which can be tricky early in the summer. After the trail goes west briefly, it again heads south and climbs up to South Park in another one-tenth mile. The valley opens up, and soon you're walking through a gentle meadow, hugging the slopes of Rolling Mountain to your west.

The trail again begins to climb. In 1.8 miles from the start, you'll come to an interesting set of waterfalls carved into the rock.

At the 2.6-mile mark, you t-bone into the Colorado Trail at 12,350 feet (N 37 45.047, W 107 48.933). Your way is downhill to the left (east), but it's only a 0.2-mile side trip the other way up to Rolling Pass at 12,480 feet. This is highly recommended for the nice view down into Cascade Canyon. Also take time at some point to enjoy the views of Rolling Mountain (13,693 feet) to the northwest and the Twin Sisters (13,432 feet and 13,374 feet) to the northeast.

From the 2.6-mile junction, go east and then southeast 0.7 mile, just past a small tarn, to a junction with the Engineer Mountain Trail (N 37 44.787, W 107 48.318), and take it, heading south (the Colorado Trail goes northeast from here). The Engineer Mountain Trail climbs slightly, and soon you're rewarded with great views of Engineer Mountain itself, several miles away. You quickly reach a high point, then begin dropping down into the Engine Creek basin, with Jura Knob on your left. This is a very scenic spot.

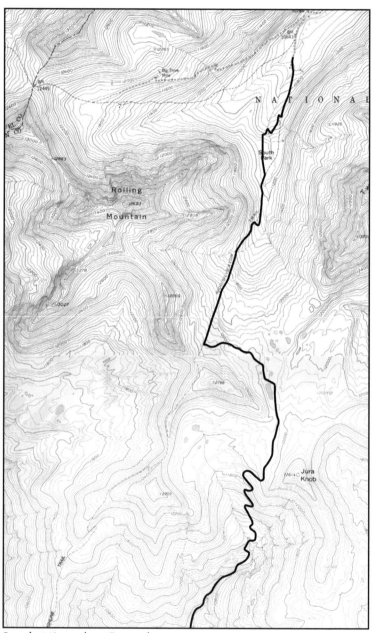

South Mineral to Cascade   (North segment)

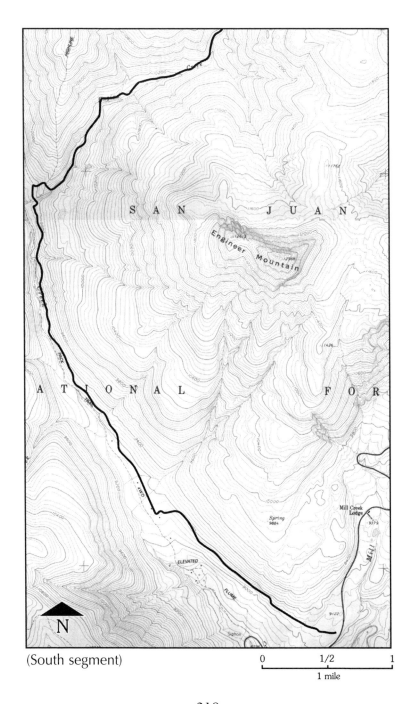

SAN JUAN

Engineer Mountain

ATIONAL

FOR

Mill Creek Lodge

Spring

ELEVATED

FLUME

Siphon

N

(South segment)

You'll head steeply downhill, quickly dropping about 700 feet. Just as the Engineer Mountain Trail ends its precipitous drop and begins to contour east along the mountainside, look for a four-way junction (N 37 44.043, W 107 48.596). This junction may or may not be marked. At this junction, White Creek Trail drops off to the west, and Engine Creek Trail drops off to the southeast through a campsite. To help as a guide, it's 1.4 miles on the Engineer Mountain Trail from the Colorado Trail to the Engine Creek Trail turnoff.

Take the Engine Creek Trail. It may not be obvious right away, but you should feel fairly comfortable that you've found it within one-tenth mile as it switchbacks downhill. The trail meets up with Engine Creek and follows along the creek, sometimes keeping above it at a dizzying height.

It's 3.4 miles along the Engine Creek Trail to a junction with the Cascade Creek Trail, which you reach at an open meadow at about 9,550 feet (N 37 42.415, W 107 50.526). Look back up the valley and enjoy the view of Grizzly Peak. Walk to the soothing sound of Cascade Creek; you've done the hard part, although you still have some miles ahead.

In just a short distance, you cross Engine Creek on a good forest service bridge. Just above the bridge, Engine Creek has a beautiful waterfall well worth exploring and photographing. In early June, before the snow has melted enough for this full hike, it is worth hiking up to the waterfall from the south end just to see the falls.

In 2.2 miles, Cascade Creek Trail becomes a road, and 0.7 mile after that, as you begin to pass a couple of cabins, a trail takes off to the left (east) from the road. You definitely must be on the lookout for this trail, but it is an obvious trail (N 37 40.361, W 107 49.574). It was built recently to connect the Cascade Trail with the U.S. Forest Service's Engineer Mountain Work Center, and to bypass the private cabins along the road. The road is public right-of-way, so if worse comes to worse and you miss the connection, you can hike to the highway at the bottom of Coal Bank Hill and hike (or hitchhike) back uphill on the highway to your car.

Assuming you find this trail, follow it as it contours above Cascade Creek 1.9 miles to the U.S. Forest Service Work Center and your car (N 37 39.601, W 107 48.025). In 1.9 miles, the trail loses about 100 feet overall.

Options

If you don't have a rugged vehicle to get all the way to the South Mineral Creek trailhead, you could walk the 2.6 miles from the campground to the trailhead. That means adding an extra hour of hiking and 800 feet of elevation gain.

You could park your southern car at the junction of U.S. Highway 550 and the Cascade Creek road, which leaves the highway just north of its crossing of Cascade Creek. This probably saves you about 0.3 mile of hiking but means hiking along a road for a mile and a half instead of on a trail.

❖ Hope Lake ❖

Distance: 5.2 miles (round trip from west side)
Starting elevation: 10,700 feet
Elevation gain: 1,150 feet (1,745 feet to the pass)
High point: 11,850 feet (12,445 feet at the pass)
Rating: Moderate
Time allowed: 2.5₂ to 4 hours
Maps: 7.5′ Ophir; 7.5′ Mount Wilson;
San Juan or Uncompahgre National Forests

Introduction

Hope Lake lies at the center of its own high basin a little above timberline. It is surrounded by dramatic sharp peaks well above 13,000 feet. There is a breathtaking ruggedness. Some of the peaks are very colorful, with a mixture of reds, oranges, and grays. The lake can at times provide good fishing. It is reachable by a well-maintained national forest trail. It is rated easy, although the last half mile is a bit steep.

An interesting aspect of this lake is that it is a part of the water supply for the Ames power plant. Hope Lake, at 11,850 feet, is at the headwaters of the Lake Fork of the San Miguel River. Its water flows into Trout Lake. The varying demands of water for power can make Hope Lake beautiful when full and less attractive when drained down. This can also affect the fishing.

From Trout Lake, the water passes through a flume to the power plant. Ames is where the first commercial alternating current in the United States was generated. The motivation here was to get power more conveniently to the high-altitude mines in the area. There were many doubters, but the Ames plant was put into operation in 1892 and ran successfully for thirty days without a shutdown.

One other tidbit: The USGS map calls it Lake Hope, but a forest service district ranger swears it should be Hope Lake. You decide if it makes a difference.

The Approach

The route to Hope Lake from the west side is via Colorado Highway 145. Trout Lake is on the east side of the highway two miles north of Lizard Head Pass between Telluride and Rico. This is about twelve miles south of the Telluride turnoff from Colorado Highway 145. At Trout Lake there is a good gravel road (Forest Service Road 626) along the north side of the lake. Take it 1.8 miles from the highway, then watch for a turn to the left, going uphill on Forest Service Road 627. This climbs steeply at times but is quite satisfactory for ordinary cars, at least when it is dry. After 2.6 miles, the road switches back sharply to the left, but there is good parking here for several cars. The trailhead (N 37 48.298, W 107 51.101) is well marked.

The Hike

The hike is a spectacular one. It crosses tiny tributaries and larger creeks, with great views looking back toward Trout Lake and the Wilson range beyond (Lizard Head, Mount

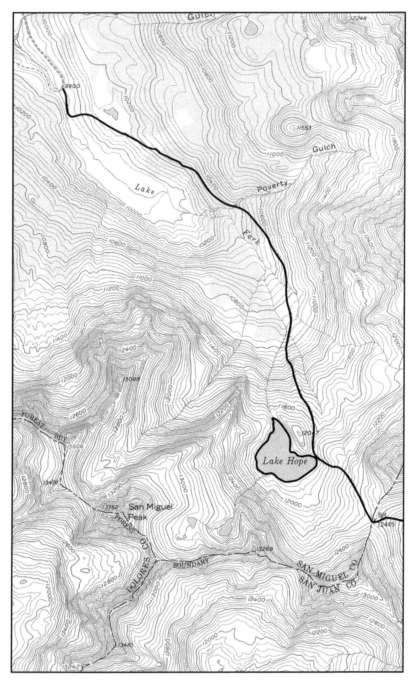

Hope Lake

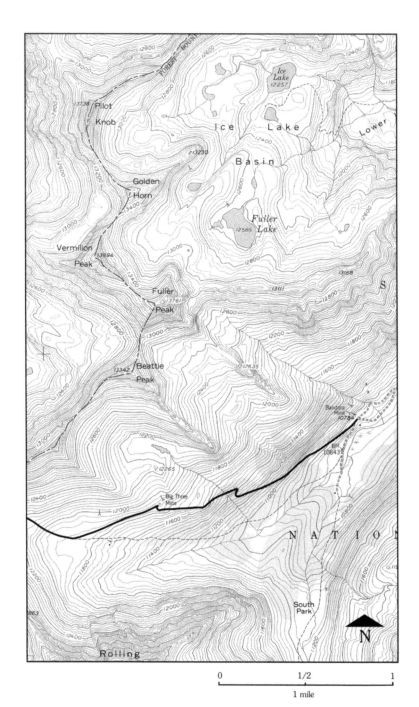

0   1/2   1

1 mile

Wilson, Wilson Peak). The first mile is fairly flat but then switchbacks steeply uphill. At 2.6 miles, you reach the lake (N 37 47.033, W 107 50.713). The trail continues on above the lake another 0.7 mile to a pass at 12,445 feet (N 37 46.705, W 107 50.373). From here, you can look down into the South Mineral Creek valley.

Option

The hike to get to Hope Lake from the east (Silverton) side means about the same distance (3.3 miles each way), but the drive is rougher and there is a 600-foot elevation gain back out from the lake.

From the Silverton Visitors' Center, drive 2.1 miles northwest on U.S. Highway 550 to a left-hand turn (west) on the gravel South Mineral Campground Road. In 4.4 miles on that road, you'll come to the campground. From here, the road gets rougher; it's doable without four-wheel-drive, but a vehicle with some clearance is recommended. It can get pretty rough.

From the campground, it's 2.3 miles to the Bandora Mine ruins at 10,750 feet (N 37 47.182, W 107 48.076). Although the road continues from here a short way, park near the mine ruins and look for a narrow, abandoned road heading southwest uphill. This route is not maintained and is rocky in places, but it is easy to follow and not too steep. Make sure that in 0.8 mile you take the switchback uphill to the right (N 37 46.813, W 107 48.828); soon the road switches back again to the west.

In 2.3 miles from the start, begin snaking your way on a trail up toward the pass (it might be tempting to continue left on the level road, but don't). In another 0.3 mile of steep climbing, you'll hit the top of the pass at 12,445 feet. The view at the top of the pass is dramatic as you first glimpse the sharp peaks, Hope Lake below, and Trout Lake still farther down. From here, it's 0.7 mile and 595 feet in elevation down to Hope Lake.

Total elevation gain, including the hike up to the pass from the Bandora Mine and the hike back up to the pass from the lake: 2,290 feet.

❖ Ice Lakes ❖

Distance: 7 miles (round trip)
Starting elevation: 9,850 feet
Elevation gain: 2,407 feet
High point: 12,257 feet
Rating: Moderate
Time allowed: 4 to 5 hours
Maps: 7.5′ Ophir; San Juan National Forest

Introduction

There are two Ice Lake basins—upper and lower. The upper (main) basin is far more interesting. The lower basin is on the way to the upper basin; its lake is small and shallow. The main basin lies above 12,000 feet and is one of the most interesting high-altitude basins in the San Juans. There are two rather large lakes (several acres each) and several small ones. Ice Lake is at 12,257 feet. Three-quarters mile south of it, at 12,585 feet, is Fuller Lake. About the

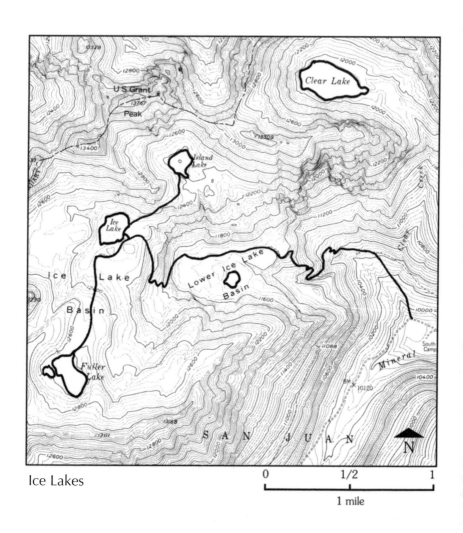

Ice Lakes

same distance northeast of Ice Lake, on a traverse around the end of a ridge in its own basin, is Island Lake. This whole basin area is surrounded by sharp and colorful peaks, all well above 13,000 feet but none quite reaching 14,000 feet.

The peaks all make interesting climbs. They are, in order from the south around west to the north: Fuller Peak (13,761 feet), Vermilion Peak (13,894 feet), Golden Horn (13,780 feet), Pilot Knob (13,738 feet), and U.S. Grant Peak (13,767 feet). Clear Lake, which is larger than the Ice Lakes, is only a mile northeast of Island Lake and at a slightly lower altitude, but a high ridge separates it off. Therefore, it will be reached by a different route.

The Approach

From the Silverton Visitors' Center, drive 2.1 miles north-west on U.S. Highway 550 to a left-hand turn (west) on the gravel South Mineral Campground Road. In 4.4 miles on that road, you'll come to the campground; just across the road is a large parking area for the Ice Lakes Basin Trail (N 37 48.394, W 107 46.428).

The Hike

The Ice Lakes Basin Trail climbs steeply uphill to the north and west. After it gains a few hundred feet, it moves more westerly, climbing steadily through both straight stretches and switchbacks up to the lower basin. The trail gains little altitude as it moves through the lower basin; lower Ice Lake is off to your left (south).

At the far end of the basin, after crossing the streams coming down from both Island Lake and upper Ice Lake (this one can be a little tricky if you don't want to get your feet wet), the trail begins to climb again. The first 200 yards are rocky and furnish the only difficulty on the entire trail, but it is bad in only one short spot. Another mile brings you to beautiful Ice Lake (N 37 48.778, W 107 48.470).

This is an easy trail to follow into the large upper basin. The surrounding peaks and the lakes make the hike well worthwhile. These lakes are high but are large enough for good fishing. There are many beautiful wildflowers along the route and small tundra flowers in the basin itself.

The return is to be made by the same route as the approach.

Option

Moving around to the south end of Ice Lake, you should be able to find a trail heading south toward Fuller Lake. This makes a nice side trip, with 230 feet more of climbing to the lake at 12,585 feet. Near the lake is an abandoned building.

As stated before, there are several climbable peaks in the vicinity. Any of them could conceivably be climbed, making for a fairly long day.

❖ Island Lake ❖

A short and worthwhile extension of the Ice Lake trip is Island Lake. Fuller Lake is in the same basin as Ice Lake, but Island Lake is separated off in its own basin and needs some additional explanation. It is three-fourths mile farther and, at 12,400 feet, is 143 feet higher than Ice Lake. It is located in a tight glacial pocket surrounded by U.S. Grant Peak and its shoulder ridges. There is a single, large, flat-topped rock island rising out of the middle of it.

To get to Island Lake, hike northeast from Ice Lake, starting on the north side of the stream that drains Ice Lake. At first there is no trail, but looking ahead a little in the tundra, you can see several sheep trails converging. From this point on, there is a well-defined trail the rest of the way around an east-west ridge to the lake (N 37 49.106, W 107 48.133). The trail has a couple of rocky spots, but the hike can be completed in twenty minutes. Ice Lake is frequented by many hikers on nice weekend summer days, but Island Lake is more isolated and is seen by a much smaller number of people. It is beautiful and well worth the extra time.

❖ U.S. Grant Peak ❖

U.S. Grant Peak (13,767 feet) is not for beginners. There is some exposure. But anyone with decent climbing skills will find a route with firm holds to the top. It is not technical.

The best way to climb U.S. Grant is from Island Lake. Go up from the lake to a saddle (N 37 49.344, W 107 48.603) between U.S. Grant and an unnamed peak to the south. At the saddle, turn right up the ridge. It has a few difficult spots, the most difficult being where it joins the main part of the mountain. Here, there is a straight-up spot about

Ascending the steep, small ledges of U.S. Grant above the saddle.

five feet high, but the holds are adequate for you to make it up. At the top is a narrow ledge. The ledge appears to be blocked off, but a close squeeze next to it, going right around the corner, opens up to easier going and a scramble up to the summit (N 37 49.470, W 107 48.435). All the tops in this area are very rugged. U.S. Grant rises 1,367 feet above the lake.

❖ Clear Lake ❖

Distance: 7.5 miles (round trip)
Starting elevation: 9,850 feet
Elevation gain: 2,110 feet
High point: 11,960 feet
Rating: Moderate
Time allowed: 4.5 to 5.5 hours
Maps: 7.5' Ophir; San Juan National Forest

Introduction

Clear Lake also lies above South Mineral Campground in a high-walled, tightly shaped glacial cirque. The peaks rise abruptly to more than 13,000 feet right out of the lake on two sides. The north and east sides leave enough room for camping and picnicking, but the total effect is of being in a big, rocky pocket.

The lake itself is four-tenths mile long and about half that wide. It is a good fishing spot, but, being well above timberline, its surroundings show a harsh and rugged beauty.

The Approach

From the Silverton Visitors' Center, drive 2.1 miles northwest on U.S. Highway 550 to a left-hand turn (west) on the gravel South Mineral Campground Road. In 3.7 miles on that road, you'll see a road going uphill to the right off of the main road. You could drive all the way to the lake on this well-maintained four-wheel-drive road, which is

233

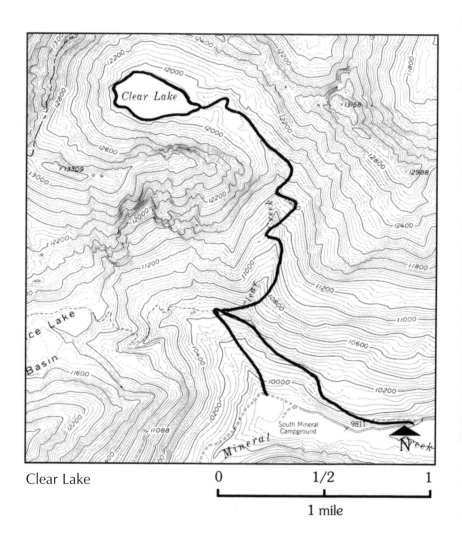

Clear Lake

0   1/2   1

1 mile

good enough for two-wheel-drive vehicles with high clearance when it is dry.

For the hike, go another 0.7 mile to the Ice Lakes Basin trailhead across from the entrance to South Mineral Campground.

The Hike

The Ice Lake Basin and Clear Lake trails are one and the same for seven-tenths mile, where the Ice Lake Basin Trail switches back to the left. The Clear Lake Trail goes straight on, crossing Clear Creek at a very nice falls. A couple of hundred yards farther, the trail joins the road and uses it the rest of the way to the top, two and three-fourths miles.

South Mineral Creek valley is surrounded by steep walls and rugged, jagged peaks. Many breathtaking views appear along this route; it is well worth hiking in spite of the road.

❖ Kendall Mountain ❖

Distance: 12 miles (round trip)
Starting elevation: 9,300 feet
Elevation gain: 3,766 feet
High point: 13,066 feet
Rating: Moderate
Time allowed: 6 to 7 hours
Maps: 7.5′ Silverton; San Juan National Forest

Introduction

Kendall Mountain is just over 13,000 feet high and can be seen rising up southeast of Silverton. The hike described here is up a steep, rocky road, with a trail scramble up the last part to the top. Four-wheel-drive vehicles can go most of the way. Two-wheel-drives with good clearance can go halfway or more, so the total length of the hike can be reduced substantially.

Kendall Mountain, over this same route, is the site of an annual footrace each summer. If you hike it, you will see that it has to be grueling for a race. The best runners make the round trip in less than two hours.

The Approach

Take the main drag, Greene Street, through downtown Silverton, and turn right onto Fourteenth Street. This street crosses the Animas River on a bridge, and not long after you reach the other side, it splits; go right onto County Road 33, and park in the vicinity. (Going left at the split takes you to the Kendall Mountain Recreation Area.)

The Hike

Start hiking the road south-southwest along the base of the mountain. After briefly staying near river level, the road begins heading up the mountainside, climbing steadily. The road spirals around and up the mountain, at first south, then southeast and east. Most of the route is open so that many fine views are accessible; you'll see and hear cars chugging up Molas Pass.

236

Kendall Mountain from the north end of Silverton.

At 3.0 miles, you'll reach an intersection, where the Deer Park Road (probably unsigned) takes off to the right (south) downhill (N 37 46.984, W 107 39.043). You want to stay to the left and keep going uphill another 1.8 miles more, where a side road (N 37 47.327, W 107 37.824) makes a sharp turn to the left (northwest) uphill toward Kendall Mountain #2 (as it's labeled on the topo maps). (The main road goes on up Kendall Gulch to several old mines.)

The side road goes steeply uphill bearing west-north-west. Where it ends, you have to scramble up a steep chute (not technical and not exposed), then make your way up a rocky slope to the top. It's about 1.2 miles from the sharp left-hand turn to the top (N 37 47.637, W 107 38.519).

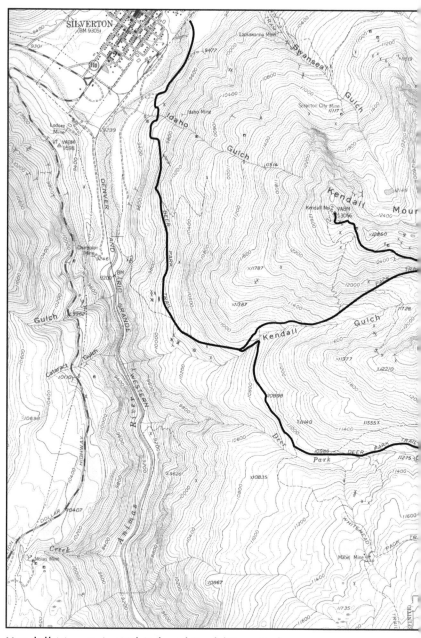

Kendall Mountain, Whitehead Peak/Deer Park

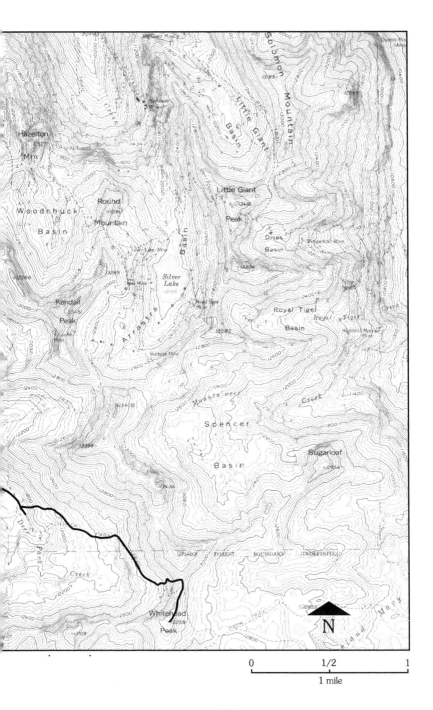

0   1/2   1

1 mile

Enjoy the views back toward town to the north, of the Animas River valley to the south, and of Grand Turk and Sultan mountains to the west.

The return should be over the same route.

Option

Drive 3.0 miles up the road to the junction with Deer Park Road. Park around here to begin the hike. If you do the easy math, this takes 6.0 miles off the hike and makes it more of a half-day than a full-day trip. It also takes off 1,500 feet of elevation gain.

❖ Deer Park Trail– ❖ Whitehead Peak

Distance: 13.8 miles (round trip)
Starting elevation: 9,300 feet
Elevation gain: 3,959 feet
High point: 13,259 feet
Rating: Difficult (due to length and steepness)
Time allowed: 6 to 8 hours
Maps: 7.5' Silverton; 7.5' Howardsville;
San Juan National Forest

Introduction

This hike includes a beautiful high-altitude basin at timberline and a peak with good views, particularly of the spectacular Grenadiers. It lies southeast of Silverton off of the Kendall Mountain Road. The hike distance and elevation gain are calculated from the bridge over the Animas River at Silverton. This can be shortened a great deal by those who want to drive partway.

The Approach

Take Greene Street through downtown Silverton, and turn right onto Fourteenth Street. This street crosses the Animas River on a bridge, and on the other side it splits; go right onto County Road 33, and park. (Going left at the split takes you to the Kendall Mountain Recreation Area.)

The Hike

Take the Kendall Mountain road up 3.0 miles from the river bridge, where there's a split (N 37 46.984, W 107 39.043) and a road goes to the right downhill to the south. This intersection may not be signed but should be fairly obvious. The road to the right quickly crosses Kendall Gulch.

This often rough road goes south and southeast for 0.9 mile to an open meadow, where it veers left (east). Deer Park Creek runs down the far (south) side of this meadow. It's 0.4 mile through this meadow, and then the road begins climbing steadily again. In another 0.7 mile, the road levels out at a large plateau. From here, you can see east up to the head of the basin to a saddle between two high points. (It's 1.6 miles from the west end of this large plateau to the saddle. The high point to the right is Whitehead Peak.) A meadow covers this plateau, and there are camping spots available up here. The main road stays to the north of the meadow, and here it gets a little tricky.

241

When the road begins to swing back to the right (south), you need to scamper up the mountainside where there is little or no semblance of a trail (somewhere around N 37 46.209, W 107 37.450). The problem is, if you stay on the road, you'll reach a dead end: private property and a "no trespassing" sign. The old cabins you'll see are on private property.

So, scramble steeply uphill and after getting through the willows and thick brush, look for a narrow, vague trail that heads gently uphill basically to the east. If you scramble uphill at the point described above, you should be able to head almost due east and find the vague trail at about the 12,000-foot level. As best as you can, follow this trail, keeping well above and to the north of a high meadow at 12,200 feet. You'll veer southeast, then have to make your way east up a steep, loose slope with no well-defined trail to a pass at 13,150 feet (N 37 45.801, W 107 36.306). (If you do end up at the 12,200-foot meadow, just head almost due east toward the pass. This just means a steeper approach.)

From the pass, go right (south) up the ridge 0.3 mile to the summit of Whitehead Peak (N 37 45.584, W 107 36.403). From the top, there is a good view south to the Grenadiers. The view to the east down across the tundra includes the Highland Mary Lakes.

The return can be made by the approach route. The 13.2-mile round trip in the heading is based on this.

Options

A trail leads on across the saddle down to the Highland Mary Lakes in open tundra in just over two miles. You could go there and north down the Highland Mary Trail to the head of Cunningham Gulch as an alternate way out, assuming you have a way of being picked up there. From the saddle next to Whitehead Peak, to Cunningham Gulch via the lakes, is five miles, all downhill. (See the Highland Mary Lakes hike for details of that route.)

Four-wheel-drive vehicles can do much of this "hike," cutting the round trip by as many as ten miles and 2,300 feet of elevation. Two-wheel-drives can probably drive the first three miles on the Kendall Mountain Road, if it's in good condition.

❖ Silver Lake ❖

Distance: 4.0 miles (round trip)
Starting elevation: 10,600 feet
Elevation gain: 1,586 feet
High point: 12,186 feet
Rating: Moderate
Time allowed: 2 to 4 hours
Maps: 7.5' Howardsville; San Juan National Forest

Introduction

Silver Lake is surrounded by many old mines. It is not good for fishing because the water is highly mineralized from the mines. It is a great place for mining buffs. It used to be a great place for bottle hunters, but within the last decade or two, most old trophies have disappeared.

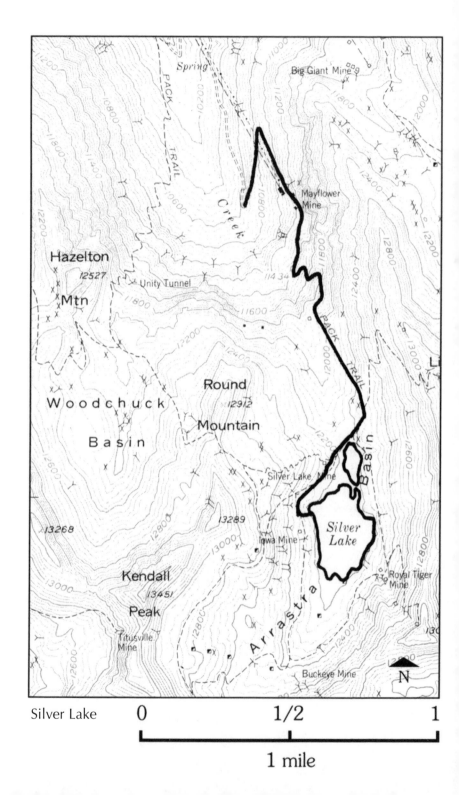

Silver Lake

0   1/2   1

1 mile

The Mayflower Mine on the steep mountainside on the approach to Silver Lake.

There is no road up to the lake and never has been. However, quite an operation took place there. Several buildings were constructed for mining and milling the ore. By milling it there, only the concentrate had to be carried down—over the steep trail, on the backs of mules. Some buildings are still in fairly good shape, although most have collapsed under the heavy snow, spilling their load of machinery. As a result, rollers and other equipment have mixed in with piles of building materials and a few old shoes, clothes, bedsprings, and other junk. It is interesting to study the heaps to try to understand the way of life and work of these miners. The lake and the buildings are above timberline but are surrounded by still higher peaks except on the north side—your ascent route.

The Approach

Take Colorado Route 110 northeast out of Silverton 2.4 miles to where, just after the pavement ends, there's a turnoff going to the right downhill and across the Animas River. This brings you into Arrastra Gulch. From where you turned off Colorado Route 110, it is about two miles to where there's a major left-hand switchback above timberline (N 37 48.309, W 107 36.747). From here, the road is really too rough to drive, so park here, well below the Mayflower Mine.

There are several side roads where you can get lost on this approach road. The correct road basically parallels an old mining tramway and eventually crosses back (below) to the right side of it. During the time you're above the tramway, one road veers off to the left; skip this one—it goes up to Little Giant Basin.

The Hike

Start northeast uphill up the old road, making one switchback and then coming to the fairly elaborate buildings of the Mayflower Mine high on the east side of the canyon. From the mine, a good trail leads south and a little east on up to the lake in a mile and a quarter, some of which is fairly steep.

Not long after you leave the mine, you may run into snowfields, and they could cause a problem, particularly earlier in the summer. The snow is from an avalanche path and is likely to be of a very hard consistency. It might be possible to kick steps into the snow, but the path is fairly steep, so this is risky. Another option might avail itself.

Where the snow goes over the trail, there is some vertical, solid rock on the uphill side. When warm weather arrives, the rocks warm up faster than the snow. The warm rocks melt a tunnel under the deep part of the snow next to the rocks. Sometimes it's possible to squeeze through this gap for ten or twenty yards and find the trail on the other side.

You approach the lake from the north (N 37 47.532, W 107 36.418). To get around on the west side of the lake, you have to wade through the old debris. It's nice to have hiking boots around here to avoid accidentally cutting your feet on the old junk.

The views are of surrounding hills—not spectacular, but still a great lunch spot.

❖ Highland Mary Lakes ❖

Distance: 4.0 miles
  (round trip to larger Highland Mary Lake)
Starting elevation: 10,770 feet
Elevation gain: 1,320 feet
High point: 12,090 feet
Rating: Moderate
Time allowed: 2 to 3 hours
Maps: 7.5′ Howardsville; San Juan National Forest

Introduction

Highland Mary Lakes is a favorite high-altitude area for fishing and for just being around water above timberline. It's quick, easy to get to, and beautiful. This has made it a popular hike. The area has one large lake and several smaller ones. They are in a big tundra basin with a number of peaks visible around them.

The Approach

Go to the northeast end of Greene Street (the main street in Silverton) and turn right on Colorado Route 110; follow this road along the Animas River 4.4 miles to a right turn (south) up Cunningham Gulch. Along this route, other roads turn off up the mountainside, including the road up to Stony Pass, but the main road stays near the bottom of the canyon near Cunningham Creek.

248

From the turn onto Cunningham Gulch road, go south 4.8 miles. At 3.7 miles, you'll near the head of the valley; veer right at a "Y" and cross Cunningham Gulch over a culvert. If you don't have four-wheel-drive or good clearance, you'll probably want to park here.

If you keep driving, you'll wind around a switchback and eventually head south. At 4.6 miles, turn off to the left and go down toward the gulch. The crossing here is a little tricky but should be doable. After the crossing, the road heads back to the south, and at 4.8 miles there's a nice parking area at road's end (N 37 46.867, W 107 34.789).

The Hike

Start south on the trail, climbing steadily on the east side of Cunningham Gulch, which provides loud rushing water and beautiful falls.

In 1.0 mile (N 37 46.199, W 107 34.552), make sure to cross the gulch toward the west. It's easy to keep going south along the gulch, and there's a misleading blaze on a tree. So keep an eye open for the crossing. There should be logs on which you can carefully make your way across a couple of braids of the gulch.

After this crossing, you will be going uphill to the west, and you will reach timberline quickly. The route twists around quite a bit, then bears to the south, going uphill steeply.

In another 0.8 mile, you'll come to the first lake, on your right (N 37 45.883, W 107 34.787). The trail continues southeast another 0.2 mile to the second, larger, lake, then goes south toward the Verde Lakes.

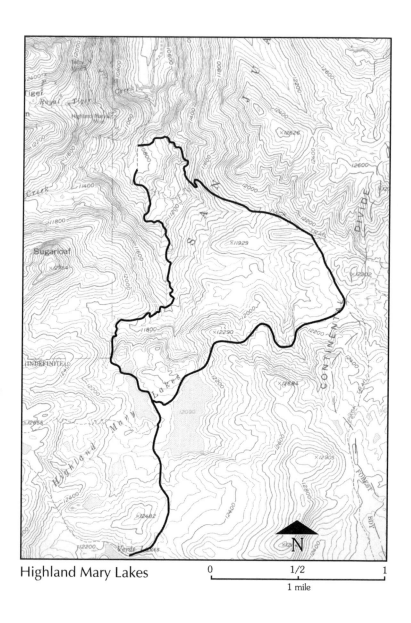

Highland Mary Lakes

0   1/2   1

1 mile

N

Options

The Verde Lakes are also worth visiting and lie one-half mile south of the southwest corner of the largest of the Highland Mary Lakes. There is a trail, but the Verde Lakes are easy to find anyway, since all this territory is open tundra above timberline. The Verde Lakes are only 100 feet higher. A quarter mile south of Verde Lakes and a half mile west is still another accessible lake called Lost Lake. It is at about the same altitude.

Highland Mary Lakes can also be approached from another route via Spencer Basin. For this route, go to the head of Cunningham Gulch as before, but instead of turning downhill to the left at the 4.6-mile mark, follow the old mining road west up out of the gulch. Four-wheel-drive vehicles can take this road up into Spencer Basin about two miles up a series of switchbacks and across Mountaineer Creek to the south side of the basin. Out of the basin, hike south up 400 feet to a saddle. Over the saddle a little way, you can look eastward down onto the Highland Mary Lakes. It is just over a one-mile hike to them; most of the way there is no trail, but this offers no problem except for short patches of brush.

Back at the Highland Mary Lakes, there is another route for returning. Go around the north end of the biggest lake and hike uphill to the northeast around the end of a ridge, about 500 feet above the lake. Turning more to the east after rounding the end of the hill, you soon cross another higher stream and then come to a north-south trail running along the top of the Continental Divide. In this area, the steepness gives way to smaller undulating hills—all above timberline. In July, this can be one vast flower garden as far as the eye can see.

To continue the journey back, follow the Divide Trail to the left; the Divide Trail will descend gently to an intersection with another trail. Take this one to the left; it descends more rapidly now and will bring you back to Cunningham Creek, close to your parking spot. Shortly before you get all the way down to complete the hike, the trail splits. Both routes go down to the creek, but the left one should be closer to where you want to be.

❖ Continental Divide ❖

Distance: 15 miles (round trip)
Starting elevation: 10,750 feet
Elevation gain: 2,090 feet
High point: 12,840 feet
Rating: Difficult
Time allowed: 10 to 13 hours
Maps: 7.5′ Howardsville; 7.5′ Storm King;
San Juan National Forest

Introduction

This is rather ambitious for a one-day hike, but strong hikers can make it with no problem. The trip is well worthwhile, for it is one of the highest and most beautiful hikes in the state of Colorado. The Continental Divide raises its spiny back across the entire width of the state north to south; a trail follows along most of that distance. This particular chunk is east of Silverton, where much of the best in the San Juan Mountains can be seen. Fortunately, most of the ascent is made in the first three miles. After that, it rises only gradually.

Along the Continental Divide, the east side looks down into the headwaters of the Rio Grande River and into the Rio Grande National Forest. The west side looks into the Highland Mary Lakes basin and, near the end of the hike, into the deep Elk Creek canyon. But the most dramatic scenery is to the south and southwest, where the Grenadiers rise in many sharp and jagged peaks, their sheer cliffs plunging straight down along the north sides. Beyond the Grenadiers are the Needles. This is truly wild country!

The Approach

Follow the route described for the Highland Mary Lakes hike, but just after you ford Cunningham Gulch in your vehicle, look for the Continental Divide trailhead on your left. If you reach the Highland Mary Lakes trailhead, retrace your route to find the Continental Divide trailhead. It should be marked with a small wooden sign.

The Hike

Take this trail east and southeast up to the Continental Divide Trail (about 1,500 feet in elevation gain), and turn right. The projected hike goes five miles south on the Divide Trail. At three and one-half miles, the trail splits (N 37 43.476, W 107 32.495). You want to go left. (The right side starts to the west and soon swings south and descends several hundred feet, joining the Elk Creek Trail and heading west toward the Animas River.)

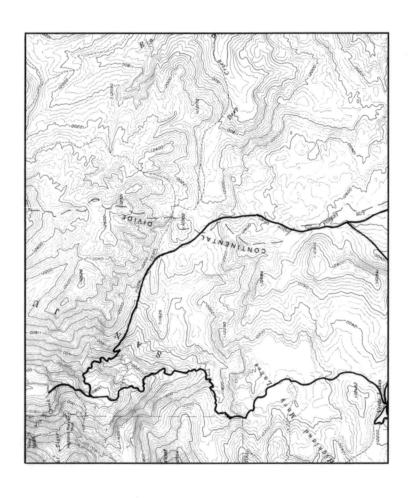

254

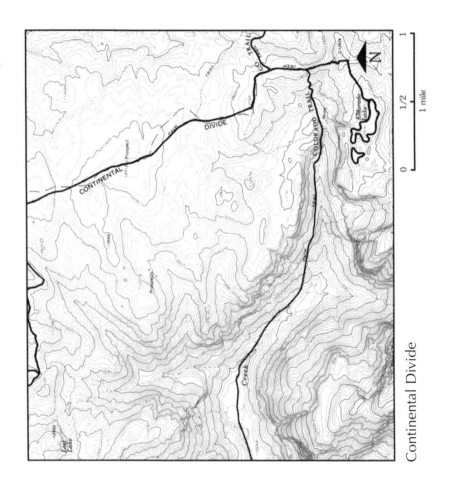

Continental Divide

Elk portrait.

So go left, moving eastward for a quarter of a mile. The route rises gently, then swings to the south. Soon you will join the Colorado Trail; it swings off to the left and goes down the east side of the Continental Divide. Do not take this, but continue on south; this will be the Colorado Trail for a quarter of a mile until you reach the point where it comes up Elk Creek from the west. You should keep going south on the Continental Divide Trail for another quarter mile to where a small trail (N 37 42.834, W 107 32.092) goes right to Eldorado Lake, 300 feet below, in about a half mile. The lake is at 12,504 feet.

This is a long hike and is beautiful all the way, but you can shorten it to just before Eldorado Lake.

Options

The return trip can be made by the same route, but some of it can be varied. For this, go back along the same route about four miles, where there is a trail going to the west one and one-half miles to Verde Lakes. The start of this trail is not always obvious because it starts out over grass, which may or may not be worn down. There should, however, be a cairn at the right point; also, looking southwest from the right point, you have one of the best views down through the beginning of a canyon to the Grenadier Range of stunning, sharp peaks—some of the best in the San Juans. Start out by going southwest toward this canyon; the trail should become more distinct in a few hundred yards and be all right the rest of the way to the lakes. The trail actually enters the upper end of the canyon and then swings around a point out of it, soon heading quite westerly. From these lakes, you can follow another trail north two-thirds mile to Highland Mary Lakes and pick up the trail that goes on down between the two largest lakes. Follow it three miles as it winds around, sometimes steeply, generally going north, back to your parking spot at the head of Cunningham Gulch.

If you are interested in backpacking, you could spend the night at Eldorado Lake and then go back to the Colorado Trail, taking it west down Elk Creek to the Animas River and then out the Molas Trail to U.S. Highway 550. For this kind of hike, you might want to spend a second night at or near the river, because the hike out involves a steep climb of close to 2,000 feet—on a very good trail, however. Consult the Molas Trail description for more details.

Tired but happy campers waiting for the Durango train at
Needleton after climbing Fourteeners around Chicago Basin,
northeast of Durango.

The train arriving at Needleton.

THE AREA FOURTEENERS

Most people with some experience climbing in Colorado sooner or later get bitten by the Fourteener bug. By last official count, there are fifty-four mountains in the state above 14,000 feet. Sunshine Peak is the lowest at 14,001 feet, and Mount Elbert is the highest at 14,433 feet. Only Mount Whitney in California, of the other peaks in the contiguous states, is taller—and that is only by sixty-five feet.

Being a Fourteener is a blessing and a curse. These majestic peaks are being loved to death, in many people's minds, and are visited 500,000 times a year according to the Colorado Fourteeners Initiative (www.14ers.org).

Fourteeners present a unique challenge to the Colorado hiker; some of them are very difficult and are only for the experienced climber. Others are not difficult at all; they are no more difficult than some lower climbs except that they present the problem of thin air. People with a history of heart trouble or high blood pressure should not attempt any Fourteeners without prior medical approval. For anyone else, a period of a few days of acclimatization at altitudes above 6,000 feet will be helpful. A person who has done some aerobic training, such as jogging or vigorous hiking at low altitude, will likely be all right. Everyone at these higher elevations experiences some shortness of breath. For the well trained, it only means slowing down

Climbers on Sunlight.

some and taking frequent short rests. Drinking water periodically goes a long way in helping to avoid altitude sickness.

Older people in good physical shape are not to be discouraged. People in their seventies and eighties have been known to summit Fourteeners.

Twelve of the fifty-four Fourteeners are located in southwestern Colorado. They are: Handies, Redcloud, Sunshine, Wilson Peak, Mount Wilson, El Diente, Sunlight, Windom, Eolus, Sneffels, Wetterhorn, and Uncompahgre. I will describe the seven of these that fit into the other limits set for this work: no technical climbing and no overnight backpacking. The other five involve more difficulty in climbing or overnight stays on the trail. Of the seven described, some hikers may prefer to car camp for a night if they have had to drive some distance to the trailhead, but none require the extra weight of sleeping equipment to be carried on the trail; day packs and canteens are adequate.

For those who want to branch out and climb other Fourteeners, two guidebooks are recommended. The first is published by the Colorado Mountain Club and is written by Robert M. Ormes and Randy Jacobs. It is *Guide to the Colorado Mountains* (fully revised tenth edition, 2000). The second book is by Walter R. Borneman and Lyndon J. Lampert. It is *A Climbing Guide to Colorado's Fourteeners* (second edition, 1990), published by Pruett Publishing Company. Several other good books are also in bookstores, mountaineering shops, online, or elsewhere.

There is one other caution for climbing the Fourteeners: the snow problem. Unless you enjoy snow climbing and like to use crampons and ice axes, climbing in these mountains should be restricted to July through early September. Some years, snow conditions permit a little earlier and/or a little later climb. Even during the prime time, you may be called upon to cross some small snowfields. This requires extra care if they are steep. The extra care means kicking good, solid steps or using an ice axe if the snow is too hard for steps. If you don't have an ice axe, you may be able to go around the snow above or below.

❖ Mount Sneffels ❖

Distance: 3 miles (round trip)
Starting elevation: 12,400 feet
Elevation gain: 1,750 feet
High point: 14,150 feet
Rating: Moderate
Time allowed: 3 to 5 hours
Maps: 7.5′ Mount Sneffels; 7.5′ Telluride;
Uncompahgre National Forest

Introduction

Mount Sneffels is fairly easy to climb by the route described here. The north face, however, is a challenge even for technical climbers. Since it is the highest point in the area, it commands tremendous views. The climb is especially rewarding in late September (if the snows have held off) during the season of aspen foliage color. The north and west sides of the mountain and the lower country to the south are mottled with gold mixed with the dark green of the high-altitude conifers. There is a long, wide valley to the north toward Ridgway and Montrose, with Grand Mesa in the dim distance. Immediately to the south is St. Sophia Ridge, containing a half dozen or more peaks above 13,000 feet. Beyond that is lower timbered land, and still farther are the San Miguels, with three Fourteeners, and the unique shaft pointing skyward known as Lizard Head. The Fourteeners here are Mount Wilson, Wilson Peak, and El Diente. To the east are the many, many high peaks of the San Juans.

Just so you know: In the last couple of decades, this has become a popular area for all kinds of people and vehicles: four-wheel-drives, all-terrain vehicles, motorbikes, hikers, etc. So it can become fairly crowded, especially on weekends.

The mileage and altitude gain given above depend upon four-wheel-drive transportation. Two-wheel-drives will usually have to stop two miles and 1,700 feet farther down near the old mining town of Sneffels. The hiking in these two miles is easy on the road.

The highway itself between Durango and Ouray is one of the most scenic in the state. It takes you over three passes that are 10,000 to 11,000 feet high. The stretch just before Ouray is called the Million-Dollar Highway, and even historians aren't sure exactly why. One legend is that mine-dump tailings were used as the base of the road in the 1880s, and there's a million dollars of gold in that base. Another hypothesis is that road renovations in the 1920s cost a million dollars a mile. Maybe, another theory goes, the road gives you a million dollars' worth of thrills. It is exciting. Sometimes along this stretch you are riding on the edge of a sheer canyon wall. Lowlanders are known to freak out and drive agonizingly slowly; if one is driving in front of you and you're nice, you won't tail him or her too closely.

The twenty-five miles between Silverton and Ouray are some of the most avalanche-prone stretches of highway in Colorado. Many avalanche paths run regularly each winter. There is an institute in Silverton for avalanche studies. Much is yet to be learned about what causes avalanches to run at certain times and not at other times. When they do run, they have tremendous force. The East Riverside slide

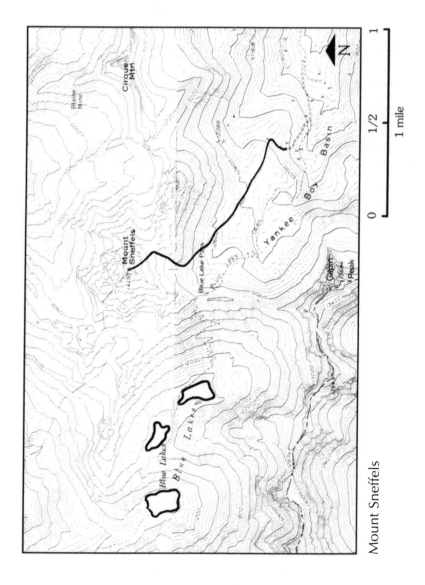

Mount Sneffels

Falls on Sneffels Creek in Yankee Boy Basin, below the climbing.

falls several thousand feet; in recent years, it has swept off the road and demolished both a bulldozer and a heavy snowplow truck, taking their operators to death in the process. Its fury was tamed in the summer of 1986, when the highway department built a snowshed over the road to take the sliding snow harmlessly across to the canyon below. The avalanche paths can be recognized in the summer by the treeless strips down a mountain that are surrounded on either side by heavy timber. Early in the summer, there will be large, hard piles of snow, often containing tree branches, at the bottoms of these chutes.

The Approach

To reach Mount Sneffels, head toward Ouray on U.S. Highway 550, seventy-five miles north of Durango. Just before the last switchback down into Ouray, a picturesque little town nestled in a small valley with high cliffs rising all around it, turn left onto the Camp Bird Mine road. This is a good gravel road going southwest to the Camp Bird entrance.

Beyond Camp Bird the road gets rougher. Near a split in the road where Imogene Pass Road takes off toward the south is a flat spot and the ghost town of Sneffels, about seven miles from the highway. Here you will find ruins of its large ore-processing mill. Just past the ghost town, you come to a side road that takes off to the left. This is a good place to park two-wheel-drives (N 37 58.664, W 107 45.431).

The road continues, and after a fairly level spot just above timberline, the road climbs very steeply and ends up moving to the north on the north side of Yankee Boy Basin—a beautiful valley with many wildflowers and a lovely waterfall. There is adequate parking here (N 37 59.376, W 107 46.276), but you should not move out onto the tundra with a vehicle because the tundra is very fragile and scars can last many years.

The Hike

From the parking place, start off on the Blue Lakes Pass Trail, then branch off to the right onto a trail that heads up toward Mount Sneffels. Hike west across talus through a relatively flat area for three-quarters mile. There is a fairly good trail most of this way. At this point, you will come to a wide couloir or chute. Follow it north up a steep slope to a saddle (N 38 00.103, W 107 47.402). This will be fairly difficult climbing, because the scree on the slope is loose.

A well-deserved lunch break on top of Mount Sneffels.

Often it is easier to step out of the main path and climb on rocks that are a little larger. The scree is great for a rapid, shuffling descent.

At the saddle, turn west (left), and ascend another steep couloir; this one is filled with big rocks that you have to climb over and around. Just below the top of this, climb out the south side of the couloir and continue on up the cone to the summit. There is a fairly well-worn route that you can follow easily. There is some exposure here, but it is not really dangerous if you move with care. The top (N 38 00.224, W 107 47.539) is very small and can only accommodate a few people at a time.

The descent is made by the same route as the climb. The scree becomes fun on the way down.

Option

On the south side of the mountain is a small north-south ridge that is substantially below the summit separating Yankee Boy Basin from the Blue Lakes area. You can return this way, or climb up this way, if you wish to vary the route, but it's fairly slow going—and be careful of the route you pick. A trail at Blue Lakes Pass will take you back down to the basin.

❖ Wilson Peak ❖

In hopes that this peak will again be easily accessible, we'll leave in a semblance of a description. But here's the deal as it stood in the fall of 2005:

A landowner has cut off access from the traditional Silver Pick route from the north. In fact, this man owns two mining patents along the top of the southwest ridge—the only relatively easy way to the top from any direction. (This includes the entire Rock of Ages saddle on both sides, which the Silver Pick approach ultimately uses.) There is no easy way to skirt these private patents. The Colorado Fourteeners Initiative spent a week and a half in the summer of 2004 trying to figure out a nontechnical route but was unsuccessful. So, at this point, there is no nontechnical route that does not trespass on private property.

Keep checking the Fourteeners Initiative's website (www.14ers.org) for a possible update.

The forest service has denied several of the landowner's proposals for land exchanges, finding them exhorbitant.

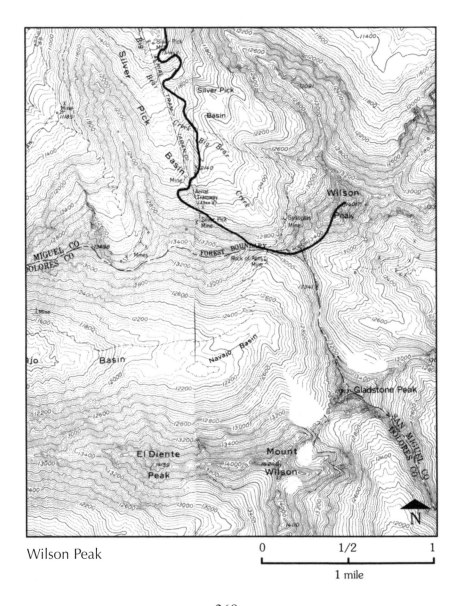

Wilson Peak

The forest service has taken down trailhead signs and considers the Silver Pick Trail as nonexistent at this point. Some guides are leading technical routes up the peak on public land.

Wilson Peak is one of three Fourteeners in the San Miguel Mountains. The other two in the group are Mount Wilson and El Diente ("the tooth" in Spanish); because they require a backpack for the average climber, and are quite hard at the top, they will not be discussed in this guide. The ridge between them is known as one of the toughest in the state.

The Approach

The Silver Pick approach to Wilson Peak is made from Colorado Highway 145 between Placerville and Telluride. About seven miles southeast of Placerville, or ten miles west of Telluride, are the remnants of the town of Vanadium. A dirt road turns south off of the highway here, crosses the San Miguel River, and follows up Bear Creek. (Don't make the mistake of turning off farther west at the Fall Creek turnoff.)

Keep heading toward Silver Pick. The distance from the highway to the Wilson Mountains Primitive Area barrier is about seven and one-half miles. There is a good parking and small camping area to the left of the road just before the barrier. You can park or car camp here. The last three to four miles of road are all right for two-wheel-drive vehicles when the road is dry, but you will need four-wheel-drive when the road is wet. The rest of the road is good gravel.

Hiking starts up the same road beyond the barrier. It's about a mile to the private land, at which point you'll have to turn around, unless a deal has been worked out with the landowner. The route in the past has gone south to the Rock of Ages saddle at 13,000 feet, then east and northeast to the summit.

Options

Both of these options also use the southwest ridge for the final ascent and therefore involve trespassing. They are listed here, again, in hopes that a deal will be worked out with the private landowner.

One route starts off of a little dirt road that turns west off of Colorado Highway 145 about one and one-half miles south of the top of Lizard Head Pass. This route passes by the base of the Lizard Head shaft and into Bilk Basin for the ascent of Wilson Peak. This route is long and requires backpacking.

A second route involves going into Navajo Basin—an overnight backpack for most of us humans. Six miles southwest of Lizard Head Pass, take Dunton Road about seven miles to the Navajo Basin trailhead. It's about six miles to Navajo Lake, from where you could begin a climb of Wilson Peak, as well as Mount Wilson and El Diente.

Note: Mount Wilson and El Diente are **not** on private land, and there are no private-land issues when climbing them from Navajo Basin.

❖ Handies Peak ❖

Distance: 5 miles (round trip)
Starting elevation: 11,600 feet
Elevation gain: 2,448 feet
High point: 14,048 feet
Rating: Moderate
Time allowed: 4 to 5.5 hours
Maps: 7.5′ Handies Peak; 7.5′ Redcloud Peak;
Uncompahgre National Forest

Introduction

As Fourteeners go, Handies is an easy one; it is rated a moderate hike only because of the altitude. But it is rewarding, because its summit provides an unrestricted view in all directions. The skylines here are tremendous, better than those of any city in the world, for there are hundreds of high peaks visible on a clear day, typical of the summer forenoons.

Handies is in a remote area. From Durango, it means driving to Silverton, then over Cinnamon Pass on a four-wheel-drive road to the start of the climb. Hikers with only two-wheel-drive vehicles will need to use the Grizzly Gulch Trail, which is accessed from the east via Colorado State Highway 149 through Lake City. The Silverton route is described here as the main route.

The Approach

At the northeast end of Silverton's Greene Street (the main street of the town), turn right and follow Colorado Route

110. This starts as pavement but turns to gravel a mile later. Follow this road twelve miles to a division, where the left side leads down along the river to the ghost town of Animas Forks. Take the right fork uphill (toward Engineer and Cinnamon passes), and shift into four-wheel-drive.

In 0.7 mile, the Cinnamon Pass Road turns off very sharply and steeply uphill to the right; it is so sharp that vehicles with longer wheelbases have to go past the turn, turn around in the road, and come back to it. This is a picturesque road above timberline, with high peaks and deep canyons to impress you with nature's ability in sculpturing. It's 2.2 miles up this road to the top of Cinnamon Pass at 12,600 feet.

Being careful on a couple of nasty switchbacks, go down the other side 2.3 miles; shortly after entering timber again, as you are rounding a left-turn switchback, a road turns off sharply to the right, going downhill. There should be a sign indicating "American Basin." Take this road. About 0.8 mile up this rough road brings you to a roadblock, where good parking is available (N 37 55.180, W 107 30.997). As you face south to the head of American Basin, you will see it walled off with high, broken cliffs—awesome bastions protecting the valley.

The Hike

The trail heads uphill to the south, climbing up through talus in about a mile to Sloan Lake, a nice little gem in a rocky setting that is totally lacking in vegetation. The trail does not go directly to the lake, but a short side trail does; it is well worth taking. Rumor is that it has some hungry trout in it.

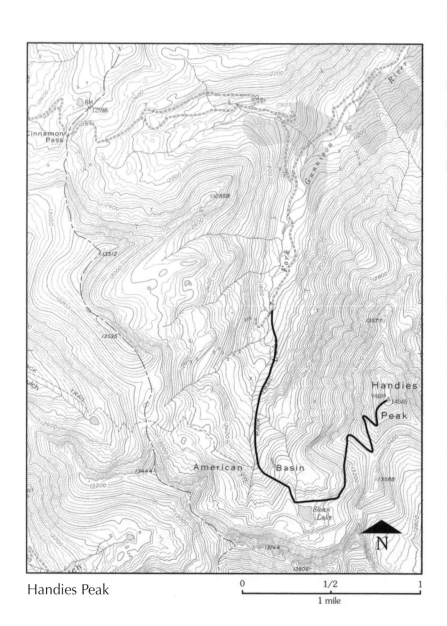

Handies Peak

A fine columbine specimen with other wildflowers above timberline.

The main trail swings back to the northeast over talus and in a quarter mile begins the final ascent, going north over tundra to the summit in about a mile of distance and a thousand feet of elevation gain. Switchbacks at appropriate places make this one of the easiest final ascents of any of the Fourteeners. The top (N 37 54.778, W 107 30.261) is broad and relatively smooth.

There is a steep drop-off northeastward into Grizzly Gulch. Looking across this into and up the other side of the Lake Fork of the Gunnison River, you will see Redcloud and Sunshine, both Fourteeners. Farther north on the horizon, you can see two more Fourteeners—Wetterhorn (14,015 feet) and Uncompahgre (14,309 feet). To the west and a bit north, Sneffels (14,150 feet) should be the highest point on the skyline. To the south is a great host of other San Juan peaks.

The return trip is by the same route.

Options

An alternate route up Handies is up Grizzly Gulch. To reach this, take the Lake Fork of the Gunnison road (paved at first), which begins about three miles south of Lake City off of Colorado Highway 149. This soon brings you alongside beautiful Lake San Cristobal. It's 16.5 miles from the highway to the trailhead. This is a busy area, because the trail for Redcloud and Sunshine goes northeast from here, while the Handies trailhead goes southwest, crossing the Lake Fork on a nice bridge.

The Grizzly Gulch Trail is a good trail four miles to the top of Handies, starting at 10,400 feet and producing a total gain of 3,648 feet. This route is steeper and has more total altitude gain than the American Basin route.

You can also reach the American Basin route from the Lake Fork of the Gunnison road. Continue past the Grizzly Gulch trailhead 3.6 miles to the left-hand turn into American Basin. The road gets a bit rougher past the Grizzly Gulch trailhead but should be doable for most vehicles. It's nice to have good clearance.

❖ Redcloud and ❖ Sunshine Peaks

Distance: 12 miles (round trip)
Starting elevation: 11,600 feet
Elevation gain: 4,634 feet (this includes 1,000 feet that are lost and regained between the two peaks)
High point: 14,034 feet
Rating: Difficult
Time allowed: 7 to 8.5 hours
Maps: 7.5' Redcloud Peak; Uncompahgre National Forest

Introduction

Redcloud and Sunshine are two Fourteeners that are usually climbed together. There is a 500-foot drop to the saddle between the two peaks, which is all that has to be regained to reach the second peak on the same trip. So here is a fairly easy way to bag two Fourteeners in one day. In fact, they are close enough to Handies that very strong parties, bent on making fast time, could potentially do all three in one day. It would be a long and grueling day for most people. The rating of difficult is given because of the distance and total altitude gain, which are enough to tire even practiced climbers. However, there is no really difficult spot anywhere along this route.

The Approach

To reach the trailhead, follow the same directions from Silverton given for Handies Peak, going 3.6 miles past

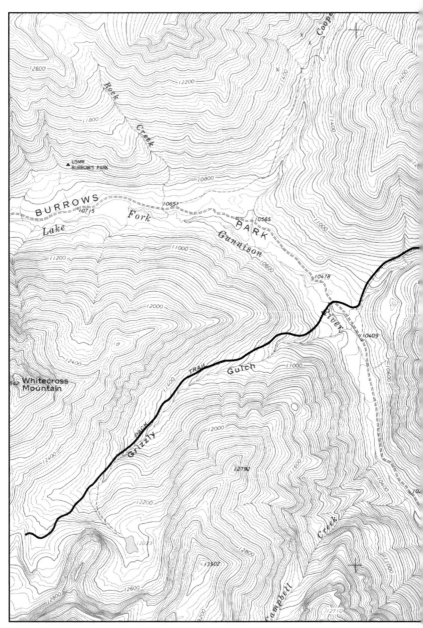

Redcloud and Sunshine

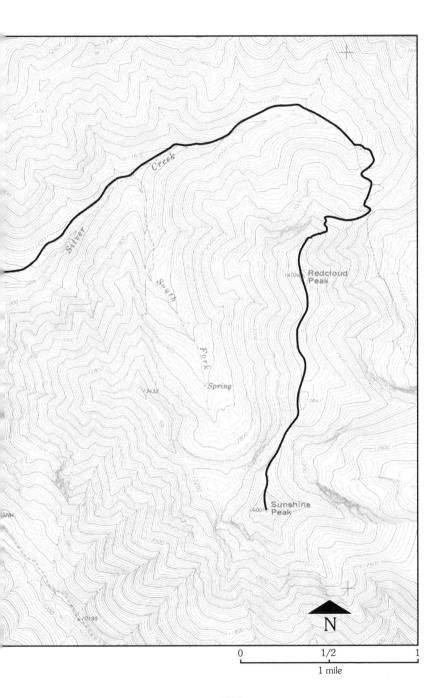

American Basin to the trailhead; it is where Grizzly Creek and Silver Creek both come into Lake Fork.

From Lake City, take the Lake Fork of the Gunnison road that begins about three miles south of Lake City off of Colorado Highway 149. It's 16.5 miles from the highway to the trailhead.

On both sides of the road at the trailhead there is plenty of parking space (N 37 56.218, W 107 27.642). Although it is not the quietest spot, this area is used by some people for camping, presumably so they can get an early-morning start. There's an outhouse and a couple of restabilized historic buildings from the 1800s. Between American Basin and this trailhead is a lot of private land, making it difficult to find a good camping spot along that stretch.

The Hike

The trail follows an old road uphill. In 1.0 mile, you'll exit the forest and be welcomed by great views of the valley up ahead and Silver Creek rushing by below. In another 1.1 miles, you leave the proximity of the creek and head steeply uphill to the left; in 0.1 mile, the trail levels out again and you can see the valley ahead, curving around to the right (east and southeast).

At 3.0 miles from the trailhead, the climbing begins in earnest as you hike up to a saddle 0.7 mile beyond at 13,000 feet (N 37 56.766, W 107 24.880). From the saddle, go southwest along the ridge until the ridge steepens; then follow the trail as it contours more gently and switchbacks up the mountain. You shouldn't get too far from the ridge.

Keep climbing, and when the ridge tops out, turn south and have a relatively easy 0.2 mile to the summit (N 37

Many marmots can be seen above timberline and sometimes may even be approached, carefully.

56.456, W 107 25.305). Standing on the top, feast your eyes on peaks and valleys galore. To the north are the unmistakable summits of Wetterhorn and Uncompahgre. To the southwest are the Grenadiers and more, and, of course, Sunshine looms large to the south.

Marmots inhabit much of the backcountry's high altitudes (9,000 feet or less and up). They are furry rodents with bushy tails and weigh about eight pounds. Because of their whistlelike call, they are nicknamed "whistle pigs." They like to sit up on their hind legs and stare at you or peek from behind a rock. Sometimes you can get within a few feet of them, but usually they quickly duck into a nearby hole that they have kept conveniently close to.

From Redcloud, it is an easy mile and a half southward down into a saddle (N 37 55.710, W 107 25.420) and out again up to the top of Sunshine (N 37 55.364, W 107 25.531).

For the return trip, it is possible to shorten the distance by going back to the saddle north below Sunshine and down into South Fork. Don't do this for two reasons. First, it causes erosion. Second, it's not that easy, and you can end up launching rocks on your climbing partners. The Colorado Mountain Club has called upon its members and hike leaders to stop using the saddle return. It also doesn't save all that much time, because the going is slower and the trail is much rougher.

Instead, go back over Redcloud and go down the same trail you came all the way up.

❖ Uncompahgre Peak ❖

Distance: 8 miles (round trip)
Starting elevation: 11,400 feet
Elevation gain: 2,900
High point: 14,309 feet
Rating: Moderate
Time allowed: 4 to 5 hours
Maps: 7.5′ Uncompahgre Peak;
   Uncompahgre National Forest

Introduction

Uncompahgre Peak is one of the easiest Fourteeners in the state to climb. As with all the Fourteeners, it stands out above most of its surroundings, so the view from the top is certainly rewarding. Actually, it is the highest point in southwestern Colorado and is the sixth highest peak in the state. The rating is moderate, not because there are any difficulties, but only because of the altitude.

Uncompahgre has a very distinctive top that can be recognized easily from the east, the west, and the south. The top is very large and relatively smooth compared to most high peaks, being something close to 300 yards long and 100 yards wide with a gentle slope to the southeast. This is the approach for the climb. The north face is, however, a complete contrast, plunging straight down nearly 1,000 feet. It is awesome!

The Approach

There are two methods, depending on whether you'd rather take the rough, four-wheel-drive way (approximately four hours to drive from Durango) or the smooth, mostly paved way (approximately five hours to drive from Durango).

If you drive on paved highways to Lake City, go west from town about five miles on the Henson Creek Road to the Nellie Creek turnoff, heading north up alongside Nellie Creek.

For the four-wheel-drive method, go twelve miles from Silverton to a division just before you reach Animas Forks. Where there's a split, go uphill to the right (toward Engineer and Cinnamon passes), and shift into four-wheel-drive. At a junction in 0.7 mile, continue straight toward Engineer Pass. It's another 4.4 miles to the high point, where the road veers right (northeast) and actually drops down to Engineer Pass 0.4 mile beyond.

Uncompahgre Peak.

There are a few slow spots, but generally this road provides for easy going, particularly when you get a mile or two down from the pass. It's 9.3 miles from the top of the pass to the old site of Capitol City, then another 4.0 miles from there to the Nellie Creek turnoff (Forest Service Road 877).

Once you are on the Nellie Creek Road, it's four miles of four-wheel-driving to the end of the road at the Big Blue Wilderness boundary at about 11,400 feet. Park here (N 38 03.790, W 107 25.335).

The Hike

The route begins to the northwest, following Nellie Creek. It eventually bears west toward the peak, then goes south to reach a ridgeline at 12,900 feet (N 38 03.769, W 107 27.032).

284

The trail swings around again, this time toward the northwest, and joins a more distinct ridge. The ridge drops off steeply to your left, although there are possible routes up and down this way.

Continue the easy, gradual climb (easy if you can find any oxygen) for a mile along this final distinct ridgeline to the top (N 38 04.303, W 107 27.732).

Once you are on top, you are king or queen of the mountain, for this is the highest point in the area, and you can see many miles in all directions on a good day, and vast stretches of peaks and big valleys. The nearest peaks, of course, are Matterhorn, which you can now look down on, and Wetterhorn. To the north of Wetterhorn is Coxcomb, so named because of the appearance of its unique top.

The descent is best made by the approach route.

Options

You could add Wetterhorn and/or Matterhorn to your day by using the North Henson Creek approach. (See the approach for Wetterhorn.)

Head up the Matterhorn Creek Trail; at a junction at 1.7 miles from the road's end, veer to the right. As you reach higher ground in the openness of the tundra, you can begin to see the three high peaks of the area. Wetterhorn (14,015 feet) is to the left; Matterhorn (13,590 feet) is almost straight ahead; Uncompahgre, your objective, is off to the right.

Follow the trail to a saddle between Matterhorn and Uncompahgre, taking the right-hand side where the trails come in from the north. The Uncompahgre Trail swings

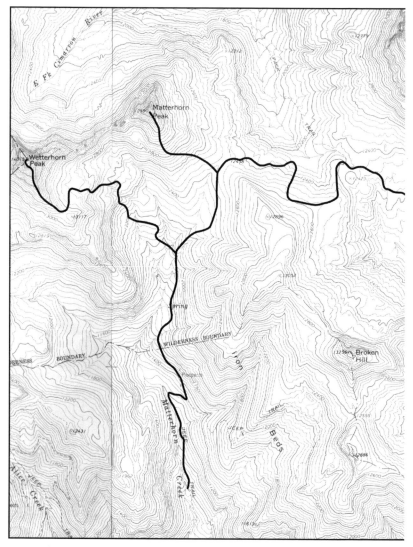

Wetterhorn and Uncompahgre

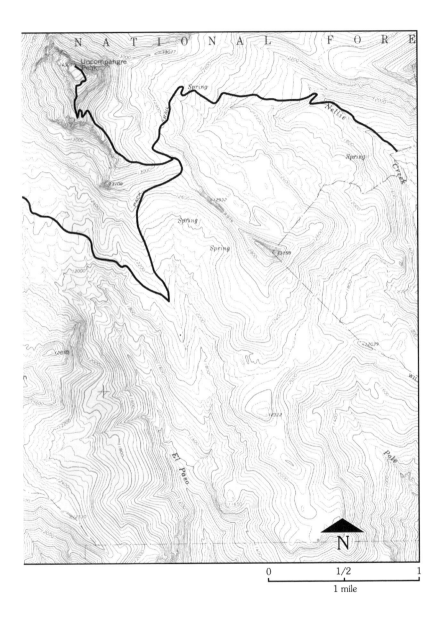

back southeast for one and one-half miles beyond the saddle, joins a trail there going north another mile, and joins still another trail that ascends the southeast ridge, at first westerly and then northwesterly, another mile to the top. This is a long, gradual, easy route.

An alternative route can cut off as much as two miles but is much steeper. It is worth it to many hikers for the time saved. At the Matterhorn–Uncompahgre saddle where the trail starts southeast, abandon it and strike out to the northeast toward the mountain itself. There are two ways it can be climbed from the west side, neither of which is a trail. There is a large notch one-half mile south of the summit filled with steep talus. The route works well, although some of the rocks near the top are loose enough to require some care. Once you are over the top of this, on the solid again, you will find the trail ascending from the southeast. Join it for an easy half mile to the top—not *too* easy, though, for it includes another 900 feet of altitude gain.

Matterhorn also is no problem. It can be climbed by bushwhacking up the southeast side on the way back from Uncompahgre. It is steep tundra at first; this gives way to large rocks—some loose, some fixed—as you get within 500 or 600 feet from the top. In some locations, Matterhorn would be an impressive peak, but here it is subdued by its two higher neighbors. The most impressive view here is the ridge on the west side connecting to Wetterhorn. This is a jagged knife edge a mile long. Just looking at it is scary.

If you're climbing Matterhorn from Wetterhorn, try to stay as high as you reasonably can, then take the south-southeast ridge to the summit.

❖ **Wetterhorn Peak** ❖

Distance: 7.2 miles (round trip)
Starting elevation: 10,850 feet
Elevation gain: 3,165 feet
High point: 14,015 feet
Rating: Difficult
Time allowed: 4 to 6 hours
Maps: 7.5′ Uncompahgre Peak; 7.5′ Wetterhorn Peak;
　Uncompahgre National Forest

Introduction

This is a fun climb with just enough exposure and scrambling to make it interesting. It's probably not good for a Fourteener first-timer, but it's a good one to get some experience on before attempting the harder ones.

The Approach

At the northeast end of Silverton's Greene Street (the main street of the town), turn right and follow Colorado Route 110. This starts as pavement but turns to gravel a mile later. Follow this road twelve miles to a division, where the left side leads down along the river to the ghost town of Animas Forks. Take the right fork uphill (toward Engineer and Cinnamon passes), and shift into four-wheel-drive.

At a junction in 0.7 mile, continue straight toward Engineer Pass; the Cinnamon Pass Road turns off steeply uphill to the right. It's another 4.4 miles from this junction to the high point, where the road veers to the right (northeast) and actually drops down to Engineer Pass 0.4 mile beyond.

There are a few slow spots, but generally this road is easy to drive, particularly when you get a mile or two down from the pass. It's 9.3 miles from the top of the pass to the old site of Capitol City, where you make a left turn onto North Henson Road.

Capitol City is a ghost town with a few old buildings still standing in the largest flat spot in Henson Creek valley (several new houses have been built recently). Its mining founders of a hundred years ago were ambitious and dreamed of replacing Denver as the state capital.

There are several camping spots along North Henson Road, which follows the north fork of Henson Creek. In 2.0 miles, take a right-hand turn (N 38 01.394, W 107 29.566) off of this road onto a four-wheel-drive road that heads up north along Matterhorn Creek to the Wetterhorn/Matterhorn trailhead. This is a very rough road, and it's only 0.7 mile to the trailhead from here; you could hoof this part, but it would mean an extra 450 feet of climbing. There's room for a few cars at the trailhead (N 38 01.839, W 107 29.475).

The Hike

Begin hiking north up the closed-off old road. It switches back twice, going to the east momentarily, then heading back north. In 1.7 miles from the start, at 12,000 feet, you'll reach an intersection (N 38 03.105, W 107 29.577) of the Wetterhorn Trail with the Ridgestock Driveway (now closed to stock use, as the sign there says). Go left on the Wetterhorn Trail; the next mile-plus of this trail was reconstructed in a joint effort in 2004 of the Colorado Fourteeners Initiative with help from AmeriCorps.

From the intersection, you get a nice view northwest toward the Wetterhorn summit. Go a little farther and soon you'll see Uncompahgre off to the northeast. The trail is well cairned as it weaves up through a rock field and gets to a point almost due east of the summit. Undoubtedly you'll notice marmots (the porcupine-sized furry animals) and picas (the tiny mouselike ones) moving in the rock field.

The trail heads southwest and then west to reach Wetterhorn's southeast ridge, 1.3 miles from the intersection mentioned previously. When you reach the ridge, you're at 13,100 feet (N 38 03.345, W 107 30.400). It's another 0.3 mile along the ridge to about 13,600 feet, where you'll need to start doing some serious route finding up the steep rocks. Pick the best way up and don't kick rocks on the person below you. We started up one gully, then crossed over to the next one, by going up a short, steep set of rocks and down the other side on an obvious, smooth ramp. At some point you should begin seeing yellow and orange frayed-plastic ribbons sticking up from the ground. Following these, as well as cairns, helps lead you to the summit (N 38 03.642, W 107 30.653).

Options

You could make a big day of this by climbing Matterhorn and/or Uncompahgre. See options for Uncompahgre.

THE COLORADO TRAIL

If you hike much around these parts, it won't be too long before you bump into the Colorado Trail, a 474-mile-long tread that connects southwestern Denver and the Durango environs. There have been pushes to lengthen the trail into downtown Durango, but for now it's about four miles by paved road from the town to the trailhead.

Southwest Colorado is fortunate in having a high percentage of these 474 miles, because the trail must do a lot of winding to get through the rugged San Juan Mountains. There are seventy-eight miles of the trail in the Animas District (where Durango is located) of the San Juan National Forest alone.

This section of the book gives you several options for using the Colorado Trail for day hikes. Another option is to take five to seven weeks and backpack the whole darned thing—Denver to Durango, or vice versa—but that's not what this book is about.

History

The Colorado Trail was conceived and actually started in the mid-1970s but soon languished, and the original organization developing it fell apart. The idea nearly died until three groups got together and combined sponsorship:

Natives surveying the neighborhood's visitors.

the U.S. Forest Service, one of the originators of the concept and an enthusiastic booster from the first; the Friends of the Colorado Trail, a group organized specifically for planning and promoting construction of the trail; and the Colorado Mountain Club (CMC).

Gudy Gaskill was appointed chairperson of the CMC's Trail and Huts Committee. She began work on the trail, using all-volunteer labor. The plan was to use existing trails as much as possible and to work out new connections between them. For special reasons, existing trails might be bypassed, and were, in a few cases. Progress was still slow, but moving; some people were pessimistic, expressing doubt that the trail would ever be completed. Eventually the project came to the attention of Richard Lamm, then governor of Colorado and an avid hiker and jogger. He and Gudy Gaskill got together and planned to complete the trail within two years with all-volunteer labor. Gaskill put a prodigious amount of effort into organizing work teams and putting them on their assignments. In the last full summer, nearly a thousand volunteers were at work. Those volunteers included old-timers such as Donald Peel (father of this book's co-author), a long-time CMC member and president in 1955. The U.S. Forest Service, too, gave excellent support.

The trail was completed in time for ceremonies marking the event in Durango and Denver in September 1987. It was completed only in the sense that all trails used were connected at that time. But work has continued since then, on a smaller scale, to improve some sections that were hardly recognizable as trail in 1987, and to make spur trails that would provide many good access points throughout the state.

Using the Trail

This book discusses out-and-back hikes on the Colorado Trail, loop hikes using other trails, and point-to-point hikes that are possible by leaving a car at each end.

If you want to backpack longer sections of the trail, get the official guidebook, titled simply *The Colorado Trail*, and written and published by the Colorado Trail Foundation (www.coloradotrail.org). The seventh edition was scheduled for release in April 2006. The Colorado Trail Foundation has also released a complete set of GPS reference maps on CD-ROM. One small disadvantage for the Durango hiker is that Denver is taken as the starting point. Therefore, if you're going the opposite way, the book and maps have to be read backward. It is helpful that mileages are given by sections. The latest issue of the San Juan

National Forest map also has the trail on it as a tiny dashed red line—hard to see but usable.

Here's a rundown of the most used access points. The ones in bold are covered in this section:

1. **The Durango Trailhead**
2. Hoffheins and Dry Fork trails (covered in "Hikes In and Near Durango," Dry Fork Loop)
3. Sliderock Trail (covered in "La Plata Mountain Climbs," Kennebec Pass–Taylor Lake)
4. **La Plata Canyon**
5. Sharkstooth Trail (covered in "La Plata Mountain Climbs," Centennial and Sharkstooth Peaks)
6. **Scotch Creek**
7. **Hotel Draw and Bolam Pass**
8. Cascade Divide Road (covered in "Hikes Between Durango and Silverton," Grizzly Peak)
9. South Mineral Creek (covered in "Hikes Out of Silverton," South Mineral Creek–Cascade Valley)
10. **Molas Pass**

❖ The Durango Trailhead ❖

Distance: 8 miles (round trip to Gudy's Rest)
Starting elevation: 6,960 feet
Elevation gain: 1,040 feet
High point: 8,000 feet
Rating: Easy
Time allowed: 5 hours (round trip)
Maps: 7.5′ Durango West; 7.5 Monument Hill;
San Juan National Forest

Introduction

This popular stretch of trail is used almost year-round. Often in the winter, the snow isn't deep enough to keep hikers or snowshoers off of it. Like any trail, it does get a bit muddy when the snow melts.

You'll find a lot of company, including mountain bikers, but it's still a great, close-to-town trail. It's hard not to be in a good mood as you follow along Junction Creek, sometimes right next to it, sometimes well above it. The hike follows the Junction Creek canyon until it crosses Junction Creek and heads uphill toward Gudy's Rest.

The Approach

Take Main Avenue to Twenty-Fifth Street and turn left (west). At the edge of town it becomes Junction Creek Road. Follow it from Main Avenue three and one-half miles to the national forest. Just as you cross the cattle

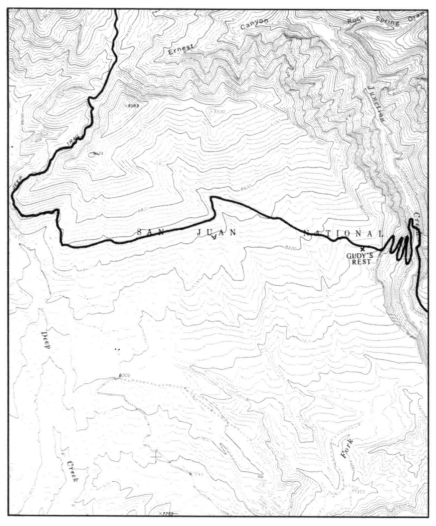

Colorado Trail—The Durango Trailhead

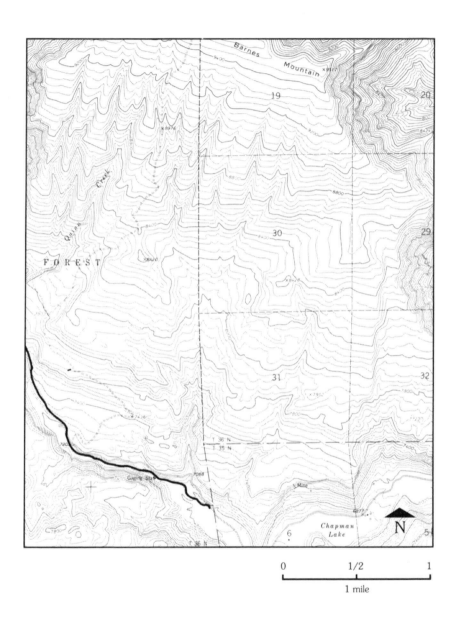

guard that marks the forest boundary, and just as the road turns from pavement to gravel, there's a parking area and outhouse, and the trail begins (N 37 19.881, W 107 54.165).

(To shorten the trip to Gudy's Rest, continue on the gravel Junction Creek Road for a mile and a quarter, where there is a sharp switchback to the northeast; not too far beyond this is the Junction Creek Campground. You can begin hiking west here at this switchback, and in a hundred yards [N 37 20.267, W 107 55.194] you will strike the Colorado Trail.)

The Hike

The trail goes 2.6 miles, rising gradually, before crossing the stream over a good forest service bridge (N 37 21.291, W 107 55.668). It then begins a series of switchbacks up the steep canyon side. From the bridge, it's 1.4 miles until the trail tops out at a nice rest area with a bench, called "Gudy's Rest" (N 37 21.185, W 107 55.900), for viewing down the valley toward Durango.

Options

The trail above here climbs gradually for several miles before descending back into Junction Creek canyon and crossing Junction Creek at a nice bridge that looks out of place in what is basically backcountry. From here on, there is quite a bit of up and down, mostly up, until you arrive—in eighteen miles from the trailhead—at the next possible road access. This is the beginning of the Sliderock Trail, covered earlier in the description for Kennebec Pass–Taylor Lake. This is more than most people want to do in a day hike, especially since the trail starts at 6,960 feet; the Sliderock trailhead is at 10,340 feet for a net gain of 3,380 feet, and more than that counting the downhill distances that have to be regained. This is beautiful big-timber and mountain country.

For the return, most people elect to go back from Gudy's Rest by the way they came, but there are a couple more options. The Hoffheins Connection Trail comes up to the Colorado Trail just beyond Gudy's Rest. You can take it down to the Dry Creek Road in 2.1 miles. The other option is to go up the Colorado Trail another 2.6 miles to where the Dry Fork Trail comes up. It will take you back down to the Dry Creek Road at the same place as Hoffheins Connection in 4.0 miles. These are point-to-point hikes, necessitating a car at both ends. For a full explanation of these trails, see the Dry Fork Loop.

❖ La Plata Canyon ❖

Distance: 2.5 miles (round trip to Taylor Lake)
Starting elevation: 11,600 feet
Elevation gain: 20 feet
High point: 11,620 feet
Rating: Easy
Time allowed: 1.5 to 2 hours (round trip)
Maps: 7.5′ La Plata; San Juan National Forest

Introduction

This is basically a long four-wheel-drive road to a short but rewarding hike to a high-altitude lake. It's a great family hike. The trail from the starting point to the lake is relatively flat, but summertime flowers put on quite a display. And there are plenty of options (hopefully not so many they confuse you—see below) for increasing the mileage.

The Approach

Go north of Durango about 10.5 miles, just past the Hesperus post office, and take a right onto County Road 124, which is the La Plata Canyon Road. Past the little town of Mayday, the road becomes gravel, but it is still smooth enough for all cars. At about 9.4 miles from the highway, just past an old, tall chimney and just past the turnoff up Lewis Creek, the road becomes rougher and may be unsuitable for some vehicles.

It's another 2.9 miles past Lewis Creek to a split in the road; go left up toward Kennebec Pass (the road to the right takes you up toward Columbus Basin). In 0.6 mile past the split, the road makes a switchback and crosses La Plata River. You'll almost certainly need four-wheel-drive from here, as the road gets steep and rocky as it winds up toward Kennebec Pass.

In 1.5 miles from the crossing, you'll come to a saddle at the top of a steep climb. There will be a trailhead on the left (N 37 27.083, W 108 00.727); that's the one you want to take to Taylor Lake. It's both the Colorado Trail and the old Highline Trail. There's plenty of parking and a great panoramic view of San Juan peaks. Not only that—there's an outhouse.

The road actually keeps going southeast toward "The Notch" in about a mile. If you want to take the Colorado Trail east, toward Kennebec Pass and town, you'll find it as a single-track trail leaving the road about twenty yards up from the Taylor Lake parking area.

The Hike

Start west from the saddle parking spot, and in a little more than a mile you'll come to Taylor Lake, a lovely spot in a mountain cirque. The lake is stocked for fishing. Just before reaching the lake, the trail splits. The right fork is the Highline Trail, which is one and the same as the Colorado Trail. It soon begins to climb steeply, reaching the ridge 500 feet above the lake in a half mile. Here the trail swings north and follows the ridge for many miles, passing over or just below several ridge points before reaching the Roaring Fork Road that comes up from the Dolores River valley on the west. This point is already well beyond day-hike range, so you will want to turn around somewhere earlier on the ridge. The first several miles of the ridge are above 12,000 feet.

If you're brave, you could continue along the high ridge, going north, and make a twenty-mile hike (one way) from the parking area to Hotel Draw.

Options

Another optional route is at the split just before Taylor Lake. The left fork here becomes the Sharkstooth Trail and soon brings you to the lake, but it goes on south for a half mile and then west another half mile, where it crosses the

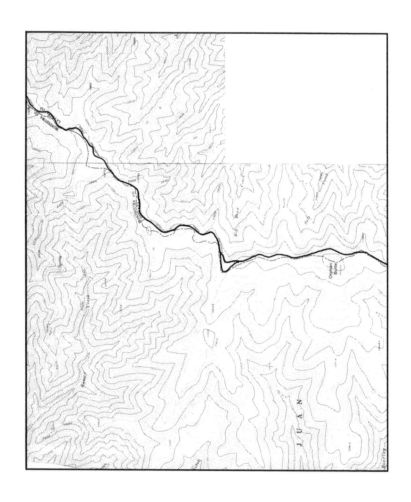

304

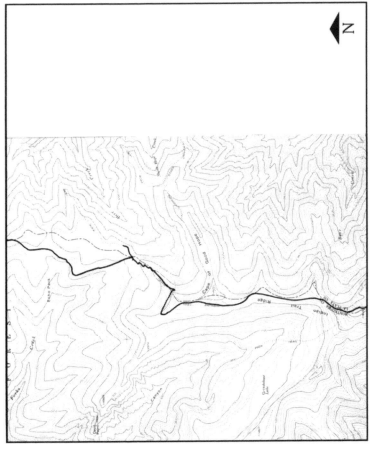

Colorado Trail—La Plata Canyon

The road over to the Notch from the Colorado Trail at the top of La Plata Canyon.

ridge below 12,000 feet and enters the head of Bear Creek Canyon. On around farther, the trail splits again; the right-hand side drops into the canyon and follows Bear Creek many miles through rugged territory to the Dolores River—definitely backpacking distance. At the split where Bear Creek Trail goes down and to the right, Sharkstooth Trail continues straight, crossing the head of the canyon below Diorite Peak and going on over to the pass between Sharkstooth Peak and Centennial Peak. At this point, you are approximately five miles from your car; you may want to turn back, but you could go on down the other side for a mile and a half to the Sharkstooth trailhead, where you might want to have another car waiting. See the Centennial Peak and Sharkstooth description for this access.

Another option is toward the "Notch." This can be taken in a four-wheel-drive or hiked. At the Notch, there is only room to park two cars, but it is a side trip well worth doing. Down the other side of the Notch the view is dramatic. You can look down into the diverse drainages that come together to make Junction Creek and on over a vast forested area into the Animas Valley and the city of Durango in the distance far below; Fort Lewis College is located on a shelf just beyond and above the city.

It's not too far—about one-half mile—from the parking area along the Colorado Trail to Kennebec Pass.

Still another option is to head up the fairly gentle slope just north of the road to the Notch, and climb to the top of Cumberland Mountain, whose summit is 12,388 feet. That's less than an 800-foot gain from the parking area. And if you get to the top of Cumberland and aren't satisfied, go southwest off Cumberland, cross the Notch, and make your way up southwest (where it isn't too steep) to the top of Snowstorm Peak, at 12,511 feet. There is also an old trail that starts westward above the Bessie G Mine, then swings south through a pass with Lewis Mountain. This offers an easier route than starting at the Notch. At the pass, turn right and climb back up the ridge north to the Snowstorm summit.

Still one more hike from your parking place is a short one worth exploring. At the west side of the parking area, this route follows an old road just to the right of the Taylor Lake route. It goes two-thirds mile around a low ridge to an old quarry. This opens up more northwesterly vistas, including Lizard Head and the San Miguels (including Mount Wilson, Wilson Peak, and El Diente— all Fourteeners).

❖ Bolam Pass and ❖ Hotel Draw

Starting elevation: 11,100 feet (Bolam Pass);
10,200 feet (Hotel Draw)
Rating: Easy to moderate, depending on distance
Maps: 7.5′ Hermosa Peak; 7.5′ Elk Creek; 7.5′
Orphan Butte; 7.5′ Engineer Mountain;
San Juan National Forest

Introduction

Bolam Pass and Hotel Draw are two separate locations on the Colorado Trail, but they are approached by the same road. As in the La Plata Canyon description preceding this one, there are multiple options, including a climb up Blackhawk Mountain (12,681 feet), whose summit is just three-tenths mile off of the Colorado Trail.

The Approach

From Thirty-Second Street and Main Avenue in Durango, take U.S. Highway 550 north twenty-five miles and turn left (west) into the main entrance for Durango Mountain Resort. At the north end of the parking area, pick up the gravel road (Forest Service Road 578) going north; it soon turns back to the west and climbs in several switchbacks up the ski hill, with some of the runs visible to the south. At the top, the road turns to the north; in a half mile, it turns left downhill (Relay Creek Road goes to the north). Follow Forest Service Road 578 west down into Hermosa Park, a nice, secluded, meadowed valley. In about five miles, past the turnoff to the upper end of the Hermosa Creek Trail, the road gets rougher. With good driving, you can make it up to Bolam Pass in any car, but it's much easier to have high clearance and low gearing.

One more potential tricky part for vehicles: The road swings to the northwest and in a little more than a mile fords Hermosa Creek. This is a wide crossing with a rocky bottom. After the spring snowmelt (the third week of June or later in some years), most cars can make this—don't lose momentum through the water.

About a mile beyond the ford there is a junction. Hotel Draw Road (Forest Service Road 550) goes to the left, and the Bolam Pass Road (Forest Service Road 578) goes to the right.

Take the Bolam Pass Road, which continues for several miles, staying near or above the creek and eventually climbing through several switchbacks to the ghost town of Graysill, which is located at the edge of a ledge. The last pitch before Graysill is quite steep. Weaker cars without a good low gear could have trouble here. Having to park below this grade, however, would not be disastrous, for it would add less than a mile of hiking up to the Colorado Trail.

The road goes on and quickly makes a swing around to the left, climbing to another flat spot where there is a little lake on the left. This is a mile below the top of Bolam Pass, and here the Colorado Trail crosses the road. Park somewhere near the lake (N 37 42.787, W 107 54.226). You can take the trail in either direction from here.

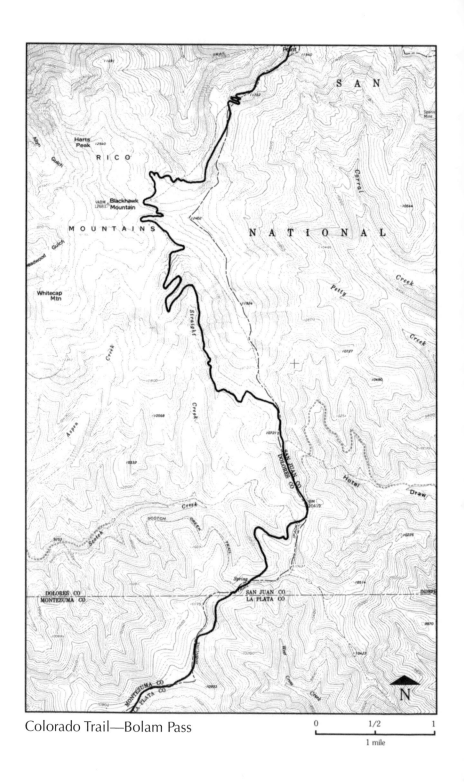

Colorado Trail—Bolam Pass

The Hike

The trail should be marked in both directions from the lake. If you take the trail northeast, it soon joins another road; in about a third of a mile, it swings to the right at a right angle over another old road that is now closed to vehicles. In a short distance it moves out of the forest and goes gradually uphill along a route marked by posts to a crossing of Sliderock Ridge, which descends from Grizzly Peak. Here the route follows the Highline Trail. On the other side of the ridge, the trail swings north and northeast. In another five miles, it descends to a crossing of Cascade Creek (N 37 44.795, W 107 50.894) below Grizzly Peak and then climbs up to Rolling Pass (N 37 44.959, W 107 49.007), directly south of Rolling Mountain and about three miles by trail from the South Mineral Creek access (see "South Mineral Creek—Cascade"). It crosses the Rico–Silverton Trail at the top of this pass and goes on around to Little Molas Lake in another eleven-plus miles— definitely a backpack distance. Rolling Pass is nine miles from the parking spot. Day hikers will want to turn around before this, probably at or before crossing Cascade Creek. There are no great objectives along this portion of the trail, but much of it is above timberline and affords many fine vistas.

Back at the parking place, you can take the southwesterly direction of the Colorado Trail along the side of the little lake. In a hundred yards it enters the trees. In the first mile, it climbs a couple of hundred feet and comes out into the flat meadow north of Hermosa Peak. It then joins a road coming southwest from the Bolam Pass Road (N 37 42.966, W 107 55.513). It follows this road for more than a mile, passing along the rocky side of Hermosa Peak.

311

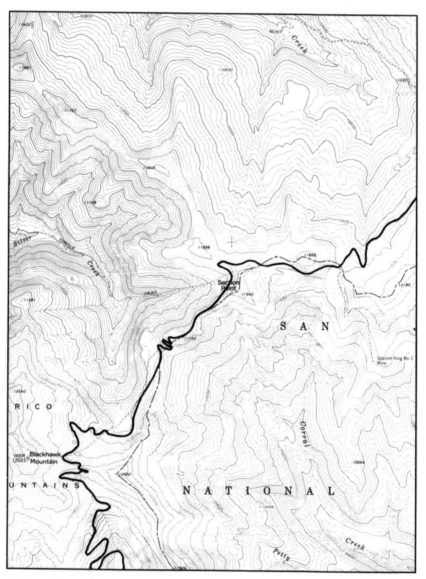

Colorado Trail—Bolam Pass and Hotel Draw

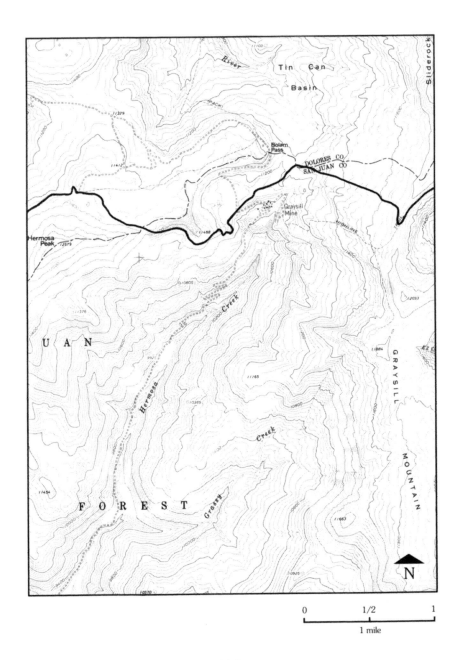

0   1/2   1
1 mile

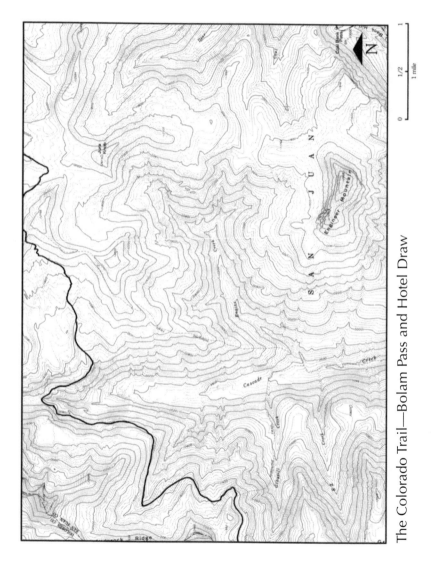

The Colorado Trail—Bolam Pass and Hotel Draw

The Colorado Trail as it crosses the saddle below, with Blackhawk Mountain beyond.

Where the road curves around to head straight to the south, the trail takes off to the right (west), climbing into the woods. In about three miles, after some up-and-down travel, the trail rises to a pass (N 37 41.068, W 107 58.816) at 12,000 feet between Blackhawk Mountain, less than a half mile west, and an unnamed sharp point a third of a mile east. Blackhawk Mountain, at 12,681 feet, is an easy climb up the ridge from the pass. The unnamed point is quite steep from here and is more easily climbed from its south-descending ridge. The pass east of Blackhawk is just short of seven miles from the parking spot.

There are other climbing opportunities you may want to consider in addition to Blackhawk Mountain. Behind it, from northwest to southwest, are Harts Peak (12,540 feet),

315

Dolores Mountain (12,112 feet), and Whitecap Mountain (12,376 feet). All or most of these can be done in one day, especially if you drive on over Bolam Pass and down the road to the barrier a short distance north of Hermosa Peak.

If you want to go on, you will reach the Hotel Draw road in 4.5 miles of almost all downhill travel.

Options

For the Hotel Draw trailhead, use the approach described above to the junction of Hotel Draw and Bolam Pass roads. Turn sharply left on the Hotel Draw Road (Forest Service Road 550). Follow it through a valley and to the top of the ridge. In 3.8 miles from the junction, you'll come to a Colorado Trail trailhead at 10,400 feet (N 37 38.976, W 107 57.416) that will take you up toward Blackhawk Mountain; this would be a quicker access to Blackhawk than Bolam Pass.

Instead, continue driving along the road, now going south along the ridge, to a split. Forest Service Road 550 goes to the right. The left side (now Forest Service Road 564) is what you want to take; follow it a little more than a hundred yards to the Colorado Trail. Park here (N 37 38.401, W 107 58.060). The Colorado Trail goes south along the ridge, most of the time at or near Forest Service Road 564, for about six miles. Where the road turns west, the trail goes straight on to the south toward Orphan Butte (a tree-covered point 200 feet high), just over a mile distant. For the entire distance from the top of Hotel Draw, the trail follows at or near the top of the ridge with a gradual net altitude rise of 1,919 feet. It continues on south along the ridge, now called Indian Trail Ridge, in eleven-plus miles to Taylor Lake, and in another mile east to the top of La Plata Canyon. The highest spot on this route is next to the last ridge point at 12,338 feet; it comes shortly before the descent to Taylor Lake, three-quarters mile away by the trail.

Scotch Creek Access

Back at the split of Forest Service Roads 550 and 564, the road to the right is the Scotch Creek Road (Forest Service Road 550), which descends in several miles to the Dolores River valley and Colorado State Highway 145, about three miles south of Rico. Access from the west to the Colorado Trail is possible from this route. This is a four-wheel-drive road that is quite good at the top but rough farther down; there are a lot of aspen at the upper levels.

Roaring Forks Access

From where it links with and follows along the Colorado Trail, Forest Service Road 564 ultimately joins the Roaring Forks Road (Forest Service Road 435) and descends into the Dolores River valley, joining Colorado Highway 145 about six miles southwest of Scotch Creek. Roaring Forks is a good gravel road and makes a good access from the west that is usable by most cars.

Bolam Pass from Barlow Creek

The Bolam Pass access can also be reached from the west out of the Dolores River valley via the Barlow Creek Road

(Forest Service Road 578). It turns east off of Colorado Highway 145 about halfway between Lizard Head Pass and the town of Rico, roughly five miles from both. At the turnoff, the road immediately crosses the river and then passes, on the left, the access to a nice forest service campground—a good overnight spot if you need it. The road then climbs about seven miles (the last two are quite rough, making four-wheel-drive highly advisable) to a flat opening in the forest; soon after this, the road splits. The right side swings to the east and then south to a barrier near Hermosa Peak. The Colorado Trail joins this road just beyond the barrier (N 37 42.963, W 107 55.511). The left side turns sharply over an arroyo and goes north over the top of Bolam Pass. It reaches the little lake where the trail is located about two miles from the split.

❖ Molas Pass ❖

Starting elevation: 10,900 feet
Rating: Easy to moderate, depending on distance
Maps: 7.5′ Snowdon Peak; 7.5′ Silverton; 7.5′ Ophir;
San Juan National Forest

Introduction

Within a mile in each direction, Molas Pass is the starting point for two hikes that use the Colorado Trail and were mentioned previously in the "Hikes Between Durango and Silverton" section: the Molas Trail hike, which drops down to the Animas River; and the Sultan–Grand Turk climbs.

318

Therefore, this description won't spend a lot of time repeating itself. If you want the full Colorado Trail experience from the top of Molas Pass to the Animas River, park where suggested below on "The Approach," hike along the highway a couple of hundred yards to the Colorado Trail crossing, and take the Colorado Trail to the east. The Colorado Trail descends in a series of switchbacks to where it connects with the Molas Trail. This adds a mile and about 300 feet of altitude to the Molas Trail hike.

This description will spend its time detailing the way west, which splits from the Sultan–Grand Turk climbs in a couple of miles from the start. For a high-altitude hike with great views, it's hard to beat this one. You'll get a great panorama of the San Juans.

The Approach

The Colorado Trail crosses U.S. Highway 550 a couple of hundred yards north of the top of Molas Pass, which is located 7.5 miles south of Silverton, about forty miles north of Durango. There is a good rest stop at the top of the pass that has a nice overlook to the north (Silverton area) and east (Grenadiers). A paved parking area and restrooms are also available.

The Hike

Cross the highway carefully, go north, and find the Colorado Trail climbing west off of the highway. After climbing some, you tend back downhill and around the south end of Little Molas Lake, then start north around to the west side of the lake. Here the trail crosses a gravel

319

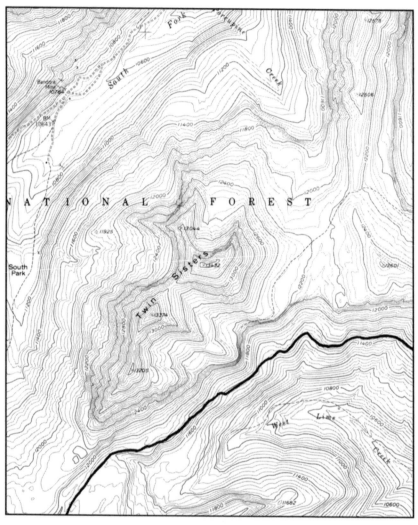

Colorado Trail—Molas Pass

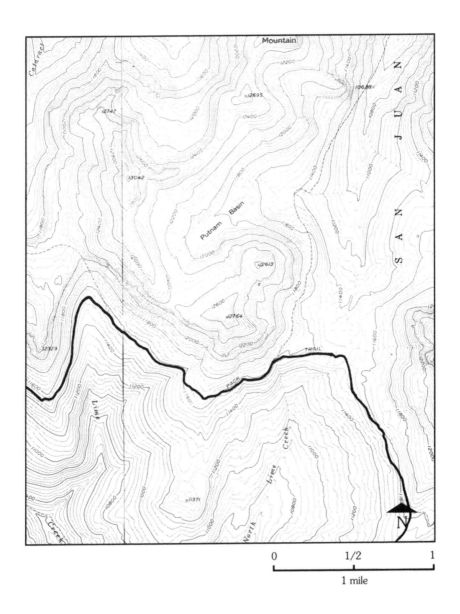

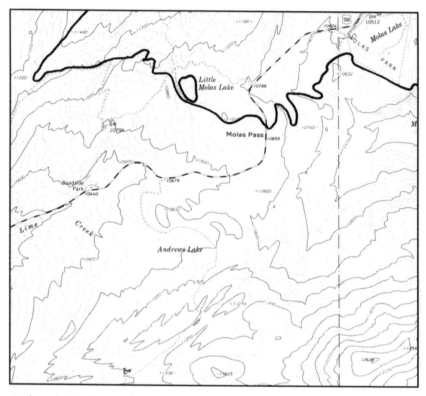

Colorado Trail—Molas Pass

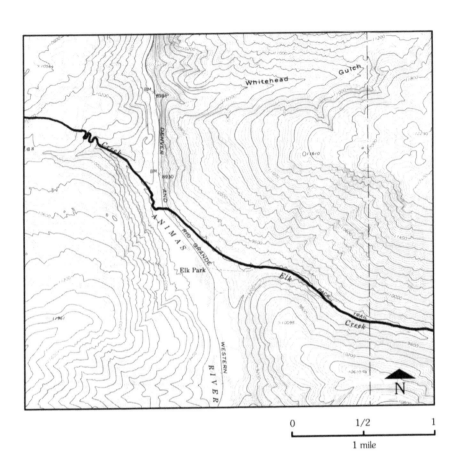

The remains of a once-prosperous mill, with the ghost town of Tomboy in the distance behind, located at timberline between Ouray and Telluride.

Oil boilers at the mill.

road (there should be signs showing the way, N 37 44.694, W 107 42.611) and starts a steady climb to the west.

The trail zigzags upward, then swings south and then back north, climbing gradually all the while. It follows a ridgeline north-northeast with great views until it veers left at a three-way junction (N 37 45.144, W 107 43.138). At about three miles from the lake, it swings west along a saddle (N 37 45.969, W 107 43.631), at 11,600 feet, that separates the Bear Creek drainage to the north and North Lime Creek to the south. Shortly before the saddle, it passes under a high, unnamed point that is part of the massif that becomes Grand Turk and Sultan Mountain farther north. After leaving the saddle, the trail dips and climbs but doesn't gain much overall altitude as it passes under some more high, unnamed points. It eventually passes under Twin Sisters and, later, Grizzly Peak on its way to Bolam Pass, about twenty miles from Little Molas, a good two- or three-day backpack.

Use your own good judgment, but the Twin Sisters are approximately eight miles from the lake and are a good place to turn around on a day hike—if not before. Much of this trail is above timberline, affording good views to the south, southeast, and southwest.

Option

Because the first mile from the highway is a relatively uninteresting hike, consider driving to where the trail crosses the dirt road near Little Molas Lake. There is good parking away from the busy pass. To do so, drive north from the pass four-tenths mile to a left turn on a gravel road. This winds around about a mile before coming to the trail on the west side of Little Molas Lake. There is adequate parking here, in addition to good camping and fishing administered by the forest service. It should be easy to find signs to the trailhead.

A well-preserved tower for tram cables once used to carry ore across difficult terrain.

Appendix:
Tread Lightly

Most of the hikes described in this book are on U.S. National Forest land, some are on land administered by the U.S. Bureau of Land Management (BLM), a tiny bit is on private land. In any land use, responsible-usage ethics are essential. The forest service and BLM have cooperated in promoting such an ethic under the title "Tread Lightly." Most of the problems of land deterioration due to human traffic have arisen in connection with vehicles: four-wheel-drives, all-terrain vehicles (ATVs), mountain bicycles, dirt motorcycles, and snowmobiles. These are all great recreational vehicles that can be used for fun and profit in the backcountry, but they cause much damage to the land and general environment if proper precautions are not observed—so much so that damaged spots have to be closed to them at times. Hikers are much less trouble, but they can cause some damage, especially in high-use areas. Also, hikers often use some of these vehicles to get to trailheads; thus, they need to be aware of and observe good environmental ethics, too.

The pledge developed for this program follows:

I Pledge to TREAD LIGHTLY by:

Traveling only where motorized vehicles are permitted.
Respecting the rights of hikers, skiers, campers, and others to enjoy their activities undisturbed.
Educating myself by obtaining travel maps and regulations from

public agencies, complying with signs and barriers, and asking owners' permission to cross private land.

Avoiding streams, lakeshores, meadows, muddy roads and trails, steep hillsides, wildlife, and livestock.

Driving responsibly to protect the environment and preserve opportunities to enjoy my vehicle on wild lands.

The pledge is for vehicle use. Hikers need to observe other responsible-use practices as well; for instance, carrying out all trash; avoiding walking in eroded areas; taking care not to damage tender, sensitive plants; and avoiding the disturbance of wildlife.

The forest service and BLM offices carry additional materials about this program. There are informational brochures, bumper stickers, shoulder patches, and individual logos for each separate type of transportation in the backcountry, including hiking and skiing.

The San Juan National Forest has an auxiliary volunteer support organization—the San Juan Mountains Association (SJMA)—which you may be interested in getting information from, or even joining. It states its purpose thus: "The SJMA is a nonprofit organization which helps the U.S. Forest Service promote public education, conservation, and interpretation of natural and cultural resources. Our goal is to instill in the public a land ethic . . . a sense of pride and stewardship toward our public lands." Among other things, the association currently publishes relevant books, pamphlets, video and audio tapes, and maps. It helps in the forest with trails, campsites, and archeological projects, and it sponsors workshops, seminars, and research projects.

For further information, contact the San Juan Mountains Association. Contact information is listed in the "Resources" section.

Trails 2000

Trails 2000 organized in 1990 to promote public interest in trails and trail building and to advocate for new trails and trail connections. Bill Manning, who led this group until leaving to become director of the Colorado Trail Foundation in 2006, and the Trails 2000 board have done an outstanding job in seeing numerous projects to fruition. Thanks to Bill, the board, and all the volunteers who moved dirt. The group's own description of what it does:

"Trails 2000 is a trails advocacy group in Southwest Colorado. It is headquartered in Durango and coordinates with all land management agencies, the business community, and the public. The purpose is to fix and link trails, sign and map systems, and educate users. Founded in 1990, its volunteers accomplish most of the work, with organization provided by the group director.

Trails 2000 saved an existing network of trails from development on the west side of town. It facilitated a land purchase for the public and raised money to establish these trails, located in what is now called the Durango Mountain Park. The group fostered the Telegraph Trail System on the east side of town. It worked with a generous private landowner and brokered another deal to bring ten miles of trail into public ownership. Trails gifted to the public link with others into a system of more than twenty miles of pathways right next to Durango. Other accomplishments include helping the forest service establish the Dry Fork Loop and Log Chutes trails. Energetic volunteers have also contributed thousands of hours of trail maintenance every year to keep trails in good shape."

RESOURCES

The following organizations may provide help if you have
questions about trail use.

San Juan Public Lands Center
(San Juan National Forest and
  Bureau of Land Management)
15 Burnett Court
Durango, CO 81301
970-247-4874; (fax) 970-385-1243
Web: www.fs.fed.us/r2/sanjuan

San Juan Mountains Association
P.O. Box 2261
Durango, CO 81302
970-385-1210; (fax) 970-385-1224
Web: www.sjma.org
Visit the SJMA bookstore at the San Juan Public Lands
  Center, 15 Burnett Court, in the Durango Tech Center,
  just west of town.

Trails 2000
P.O. Box 3868
Durango, CO 81302
970-259-4682; (fax) 970-259-6699
Web: www.trails2000.org

Colorado Division of Wildlife
151 E. 16th Street
Durango, CO 81301
970-247-0855; (fax) 970-382-6677
Web: http://wildlife.state.co.us

City of Durango Parks and Recreation
2700 Main Avenue
Durango, CO 81301
970-375-7300
Web: www.ci.durango.co.us

Colorado Trail Foundation
710 Tenth Street, Suite 210
Golden, CO 80401-5843
303-384-3729
Web: www.coloradotrail.org

The Fourteeners Initiative
710 Tenth Street, Suite 220
Golden, CO 80401
303-278-7525
Web: www.14ers.org

INDEX